The Campus History Series

UNIVERSITY OF MASSACHUSETTS AMHERST

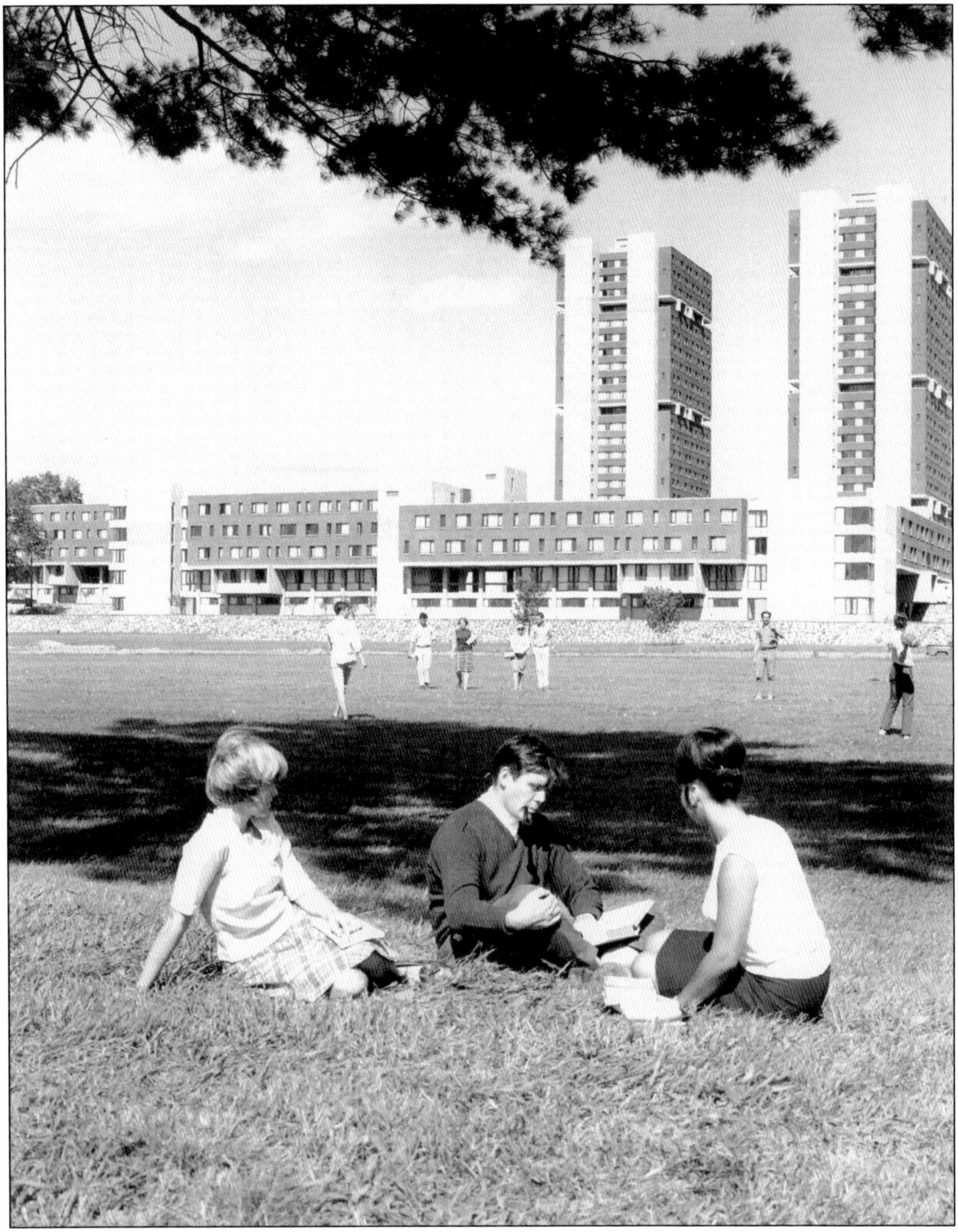

Students enjoy the open fields in Southwest *c.* 1966. (Photograph courtesy of the Special Collections and Archives, W.E.B. Du Bois Library, University of Massachusetts Amherst.)

The Campus History Series

UNIVERSITY OF MASSACHUSETTS AMHERST

STEVEN R. SULLIVAN

ARCADIA PUBLISHING

ISBN 978-0-7385-3530-2

Published by Arcadia Publishing
Charleston, South Carolina

Printed in the United States of America

Library of Congress Catalog Card Number: 2003116545

For all general information contact Arcadia Publishing at:
Telephone 843-853-2070
Fax 843-853-0044
E-mail sales@arcadiapublishing.com
For customer service and orders:
Toll-Free 1-888-313-2665

Visit us on the Internet at www.arcadiapublishing.com

To my son Alec and my daughter Eliza,
who were born on January 20, 2004.

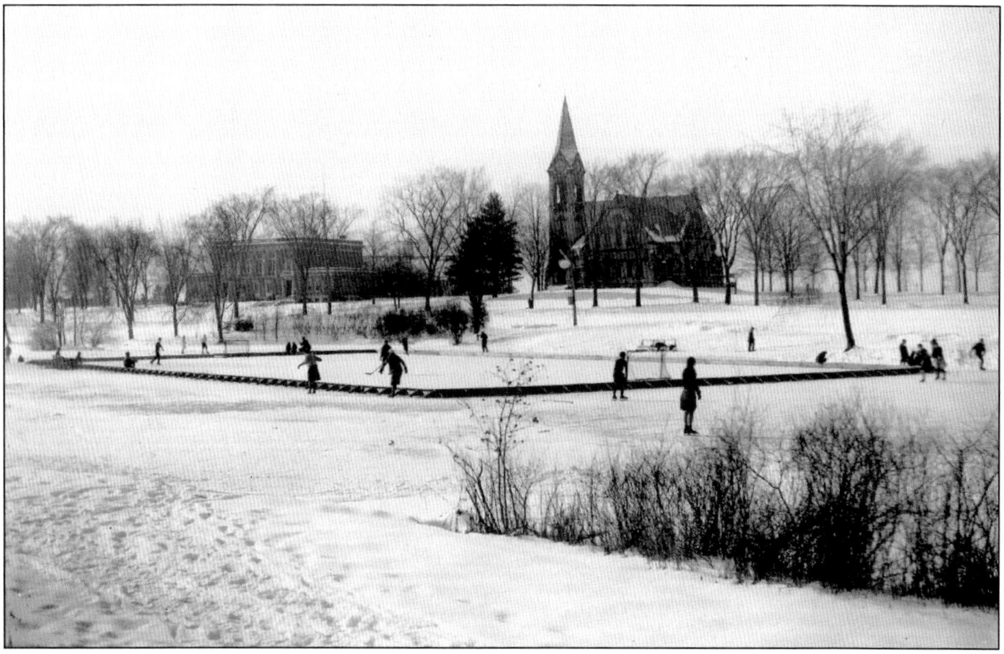

The MAC Pond is shown during the winter in this postcard from 1920. Some students are enjoying a pickup hockey game on the rink, while others skate around the perimeter on the campus pond. (Photograph courtesy of the Special Collections and Archives, W.E.B. Du Bois Library, University of Massachusetts Amherst.)

Contents

FOREWORD

What do you remember most fondly about your UMass Amherst experience? Standing in line to register for classes? Walking through campus during a snowstorm? Talking with a favorite professor? Living in the residence halls? Cheering the basketball team to victory?

Since its founding in 1874, the UMass Amherst Alumni Association has been a vibrant part of the campus community and has strived to keep alumni in touch, informed, involved, and invested in their alma mater.

With more than 187,000 alumni worldwide, the alumni association sponsors a wide variety of programs to serve and support alumni and engage them in the life of the university. The alumni association provides networking and professional development through 40 alumni clubs, leadership and volunteer opportunities in student recruitment and legislative advocacy, and social activities for rekindling friendships and fostering new ones.

The alumni association invites graduates back to campus during the year for special celebrations, lifelong learning opportunities, and just plain fun through events such as homecoming, reunions, and football huddles. The alumni association keeps alumni connected to UMass Amherst and to each other through @UMass, UMass Magazine, and www.UMassAlumni.com. The alumni association adds to the vitality of the university by annually presenting 91 student scholarships and awards, by bringing outstanding alumni back to campus as Eleanor Bateman Distinguished Scholars in Residence, and by honoring outstanding alumni and faculty with the Distinguished Alumni Award.

As president of the UMass Amherst Alumni Association, I urge you to get involved in the life of your university; come back to campus for an alumni event, join an alumni club, help us recruit students, send us a class note. Above all, become a member of the alumni association. Your membership helps foster programs that make UMass Amherst the kind of place you are proud to call your alma mater.

I hope this wonderful pictorial history will keep you connected to UMass Amherst and to the UMass Amherst Alumni Association.

—Jess Kane '70

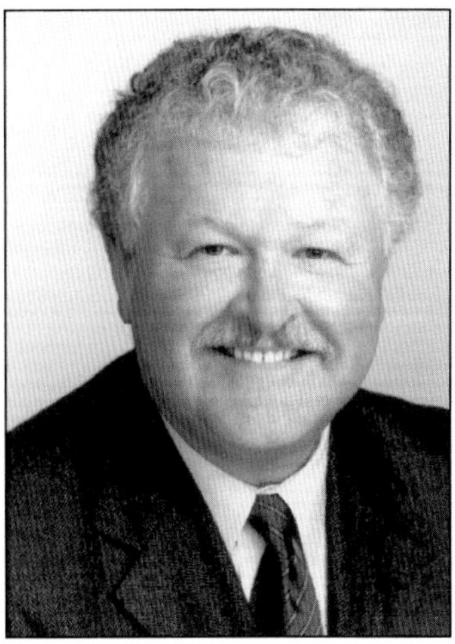

Dr. Jess Kane is the president of the UMass Amherst Alumni Association.

A Message from the Chancellor

As it opened its doors on October 2, 1867, the University of Massachusetts Amherst began its mission of educating the students and building the research capacity of the Commonwealth of Massachusetts. As tradition has it, the campus's first president, William Smith Clark, commented to Prof. Henry Hill Goodell as they made their way to the opening day of the newly constructed Massachusetts Agricultural College, "I do not know of a single man that is coming today, but I believe the heart of the old Bay State will beat true to the opportunity presented it."

When Clark and Goodell found 27 young men awaiting the opening, their joy knew no bounds. By the end of the first semester, the college counted 47 admitted students. In the 137 years since President Clark and Professor Goodell welcomed the first students to the Amherst campus, our institution has achieved many triumphs and overcome many obstacles to become one of America's top research universities.

This pictorial history introduces a university that, like many of this nation's premier land-grant institutions, has transformed itself from a small agricultural college to a dynamic, world-renowned university. This book reminds us of the exceptional people whose commitment and dedication achieved this remarkable result. In the transformation of American higher education during the decades after the Second World War, this campus grew to its current size and academic distinction. In part, this growth relied on the investment of the citizens of our commonwealth, but in ever-increasing proportion it relies today on the commitment of alumni and friends, the investment of students and their families, and the research preeminence of its faculty.

This book displays the traditions that define the mission of this campus and renews our commitment to sustaining and enhancing the quality and performance that underlie all that makes us proud of the University of Massachusetts Amherst.

—Chancellor John V. Lombardi

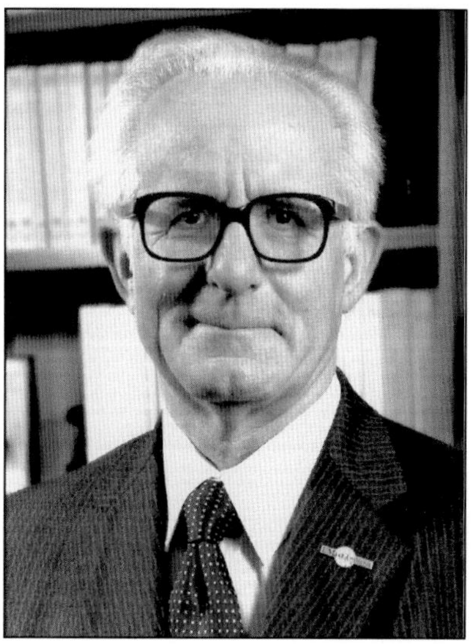

John V. Lombardi is chancellor and professor of history at the University of Massachusetts Amherst. He also serves as coeditor of the center's Top American Research Universities project on measuring university performance. Lombardi served as dean of international programs and dean of arts and sciences at Indiana University, as provost at the Johns Hopkins University, and as president of the University of Florida. He is a specialist in Latin America with a focus in Venezuelan history, and is the author of a variety of books and articles, one of which is coauthored by his wife, Cathryn. He received his doctorate and master's from Columbia University and his bachelor's degree from Pomona College.

INTRODUCTION

On July 2, 1862, Pres. Abraham Lincoln signed into law what is generally referred to as the Land Grant Act. The new piece of legislation, introduced by Rep. Justin Smith Morrill of Vermont, granted to each state 30,000 acres of public land for each senator and representative under apportionment based on the 1860 census. Proceeds from the sale of these lands were to be invested in a perpetual endowment fund, which provided support for colleges of agriculture and mechanical arts in each of the states.

Due to the 1862 Morrill Land Grant Act, Massachusetts Agricultural College was born with very humble beginnings in 1863. The campus opened the doors to its first class of students in 1867 on a 310-acre campus in Amherst, Massachusetts. Massachusetts Agricultural College opened with four wooden buildings, 56 students, and 4 faculty members. In 1867, tuition was $36 per semester; it was not raised until 1884, when it ascended to $84 a semester. The Phi Sigma Kappa fraternity was founded at Massachusetts Agricultural College in 1873. In 1892, the first women enrolled.

By 1916, there were 668 students, 72 instructors, a total staff of 175, and 275 courses of study. Massachusetts Agricultural College (MAC) was the only college in the country concerned exclusively with agriculture. Also in 1916, as the country entered World War I, 1,304 Aggie students, alumni, and faculty members donned uniforms. A student army training corps was formed on campus. Some of the buildings were converted into barracks.

On March 26, 1931, as the economy became less and less reliant on farming and agriculture, Massachusetts Agricultural College became Massachusetts State College. Then on May 6, 1947, Massachusetts State College became the University of Massachusetts.

Today, UMass Amherst is a world-renowned research institution with a sprawling physical plant of 350 buildings, which host 24,000 students and over 300 faculty members. UMass Amherst has evolved into a highly sought-after place of higher education for college students from all over the world. UMass Amherst has been the college choice for many of Massachusetts's sons and daughters for the past 140 years. The 1,450-acre modern-day campus is one of the most beautiful in all of New England. The campus has a wonderful mix of both new and old buildings, which are used to their fullest capability. UMass has graduated many notable alumni, such as John "Jack" Welch '57, chief executive officer of General Electric; John "Jack" Smith '60, chief executive officer of General Motors; Natalie Cole '72, entertainer; and Gary DiSarcina '88, professional baseball player.

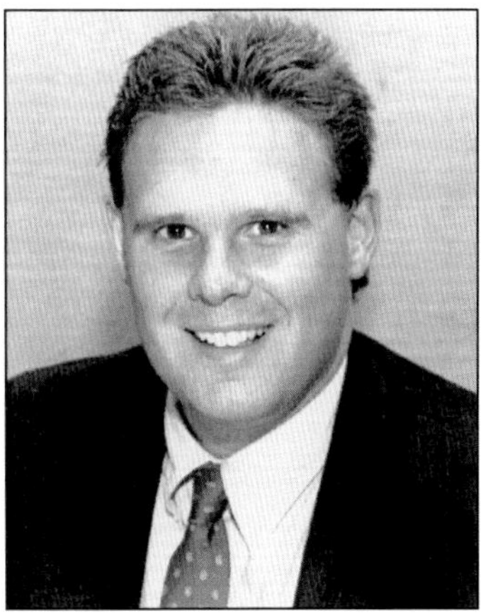

Steven R. Sullivan, Secretary of the UMass Hockey Pond Club

One

In the Beginning

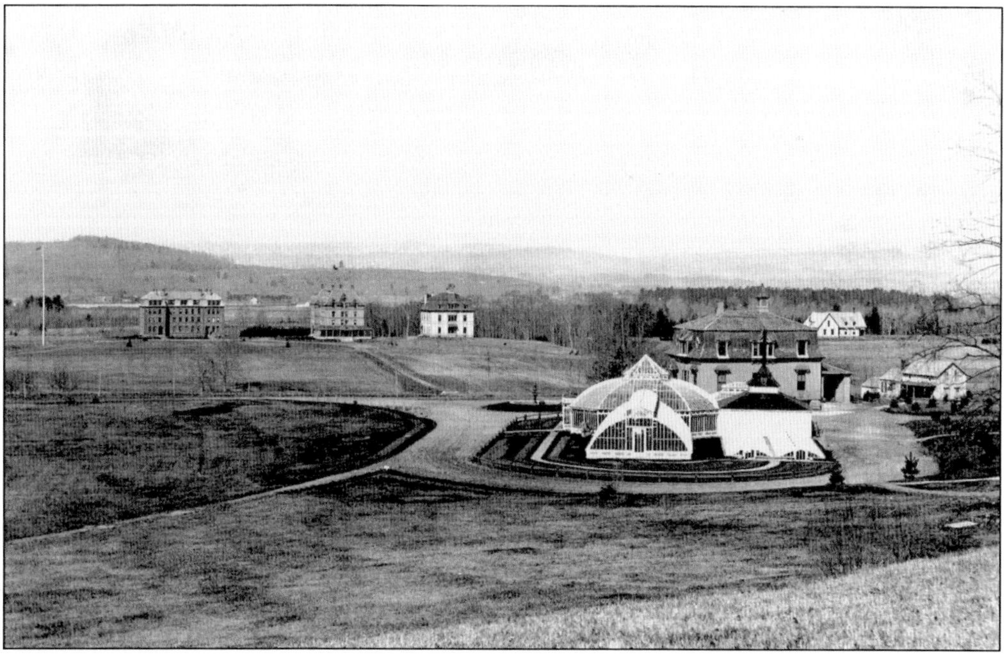

This photograph depicts the campus before the campus pond was built. In the background are, from left to right, South College, North College, College Hall, and the Farm House. In the front of the image, at the right, is the Durfee Plant House and the Botanic Museum. (Photograph courtesy of the Special Collections and Archives, W.E.B. Du Bois Library, University of Massachusetts Amherst.)

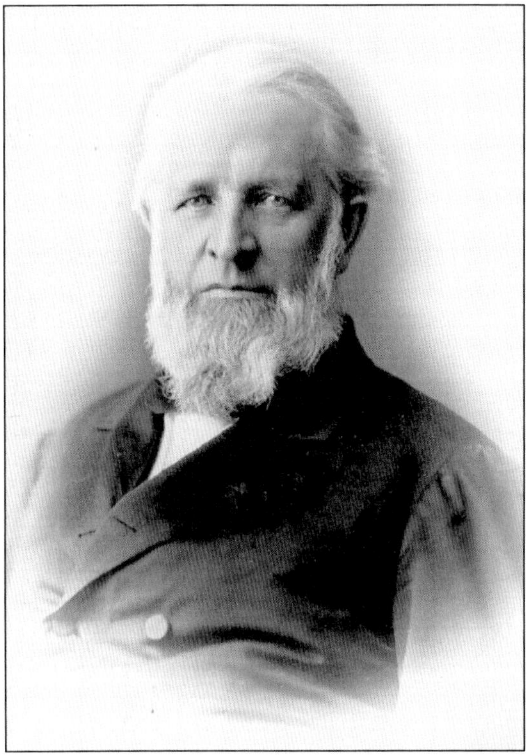

Henry Flagg French was the first president of the college, presiding from 1864 to 1866. He was the father of the renowned sculptor of the Lincoln Memorial and Lexington Minuteman, Daniel Chester French, who he considered to be the first student at Massachusetts Agricultural College. Daniel Chester French lived with his father on campus before the students arrived in 1867. (Photograph courtesy of the Special Collections and Archives, W.E.B. Du Bois Library, University of Massachusetts Amherst.)

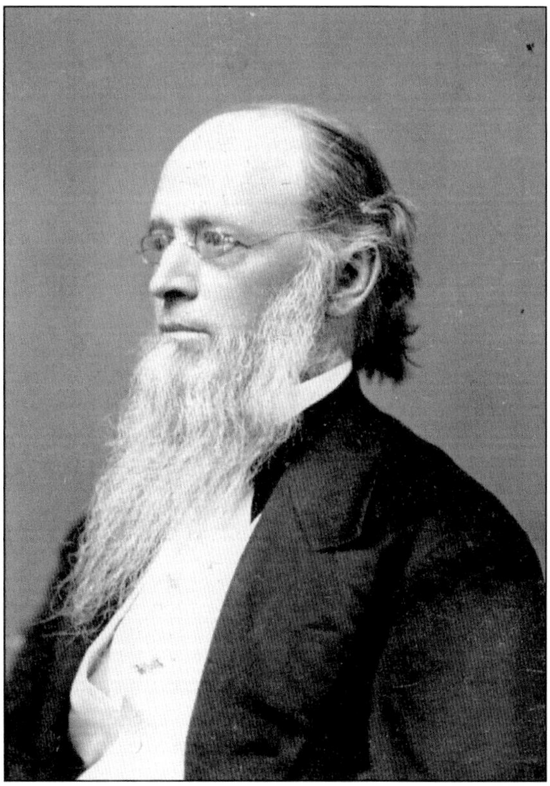

Paul Ansel Chadbourne served as the president of the college on two different occasions, once from 1866 to 1867 and then again from 1882 to 1883. A graduate of Williams College, he was appointed to the esteemed state board of agriculture, where he met many of the founders of the college. Along with Henry Flagg French, Chadbourne served as president before the students arrived on campus in 1867. (Photograph courtesy of the Special Collections and Archives, W.E.B. Du Bois Library, University of Massachusetts Amherst.)

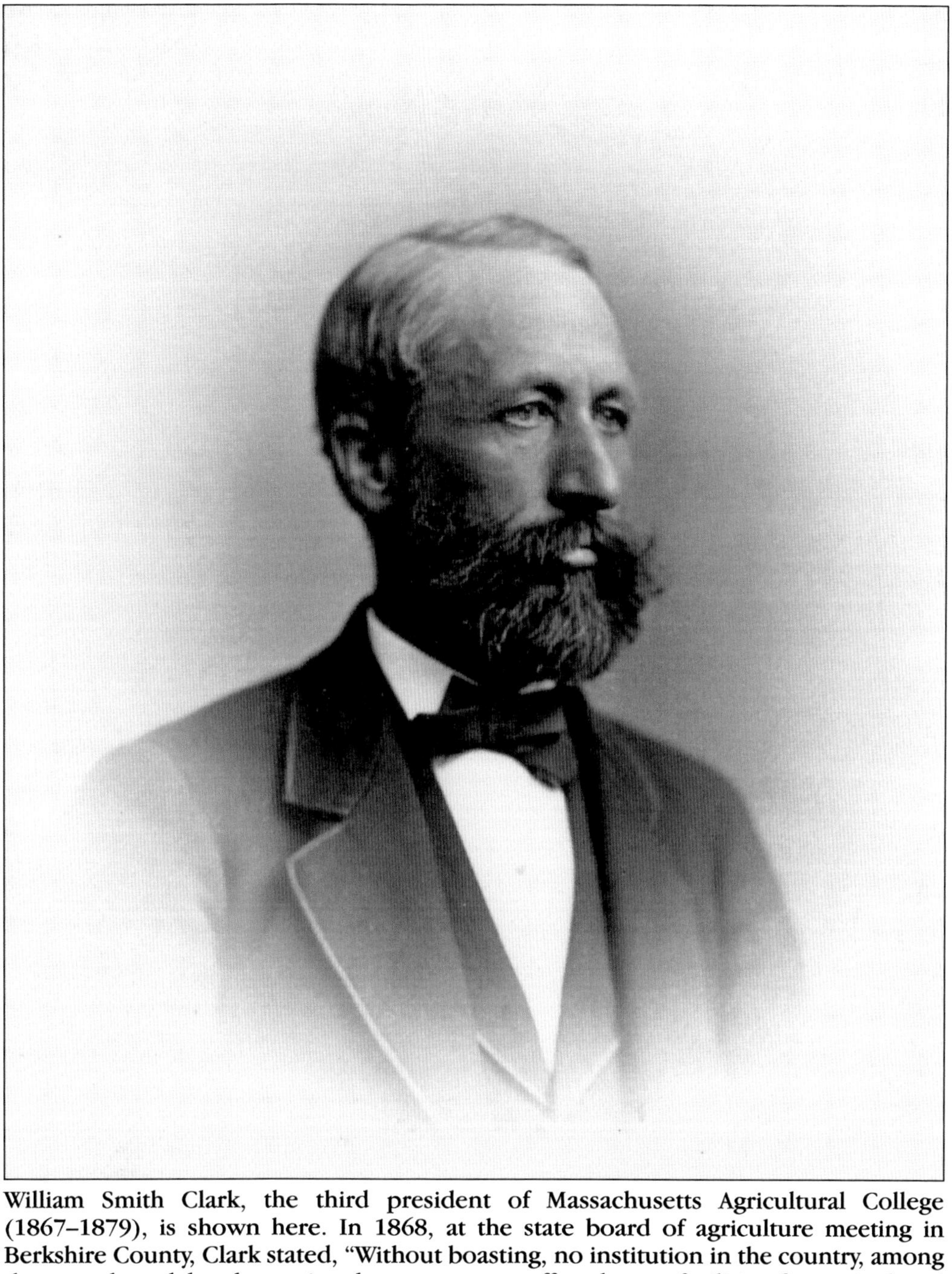

William Smith Clark, the third president of Massachusetts Agricultural College (1867–1879), is shown here. In 1868, at the state board of agriculture meeting in Berkshire County, Clark stated, "Without boasting, no institution in the country, among those endowed by the national government, offers better facilities for agricultural education than the Farmers College of Amherst." An Amherst College graduate and resident of Amherst, he was a strong advocate for locating the Massachusetts Agricultural College in Amherst. During the 1876–1877 school year, he traveled to Japan, where he was invited to establish and organize the Imperial College of Agriculture at Sapporo. (Photograph courtesy of the Special Collections and Archives, W.E.B. Du Bois Library, University of Massachusetts Amherst.)

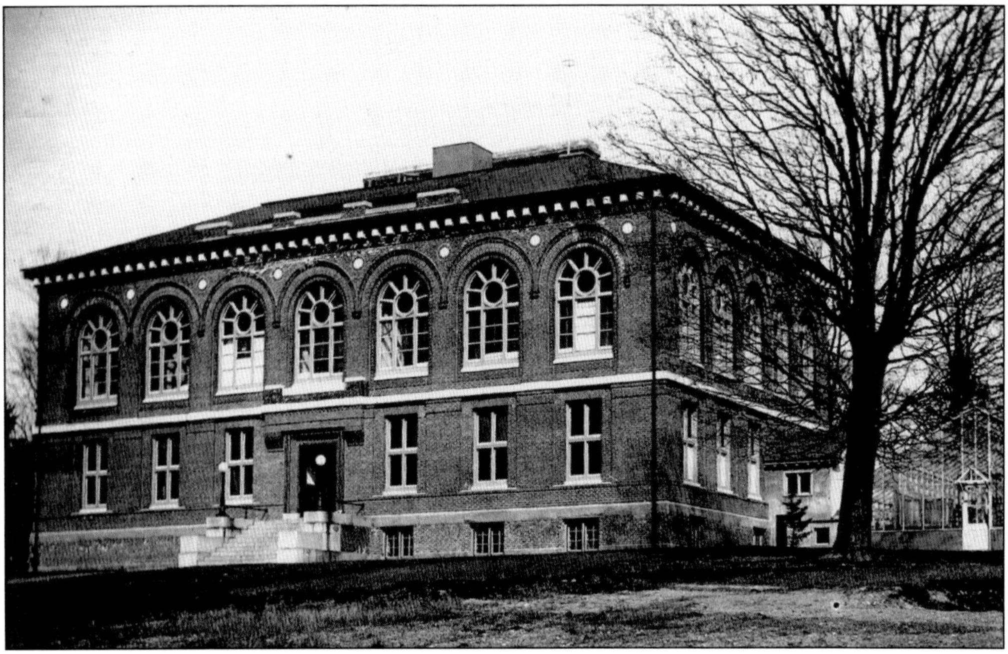

Clark Hall was built in 1907 for scientific research and the teaching of botany. The hall was named after the college's third president, William Smith Clark. Clark served as MAC president from 1867 to 1879. He also served as a member of the prestigious state board of agriculture and of the Massachusetts House of Representatives. Clark was one of the leaders in the effort to obtain the Massachusetts Agricultural College charter. He was a very distinguished professor of chemistry, botany, and zoology.

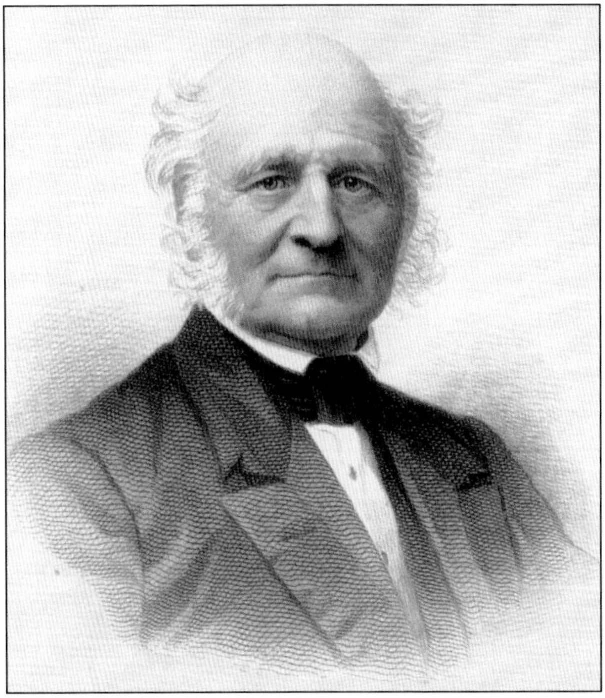

Marshall Pickney Wilder was a founder of the New England Horticultural Society. He helped establish the Massachusetts Academy of Agriculture, and as president of the Massachusetts State Senate in 1850, he introduced a bill authorizing the governor to establish a board of 10 commissioners who would have the power to establish an agricultural school or college. Some call him the grandfather of Massachusetts Agricultural College. (Photograph courtesy of the Special Collections and Archives, W.E.B. Du Bois Library, University of Massachusetts Amherst.)

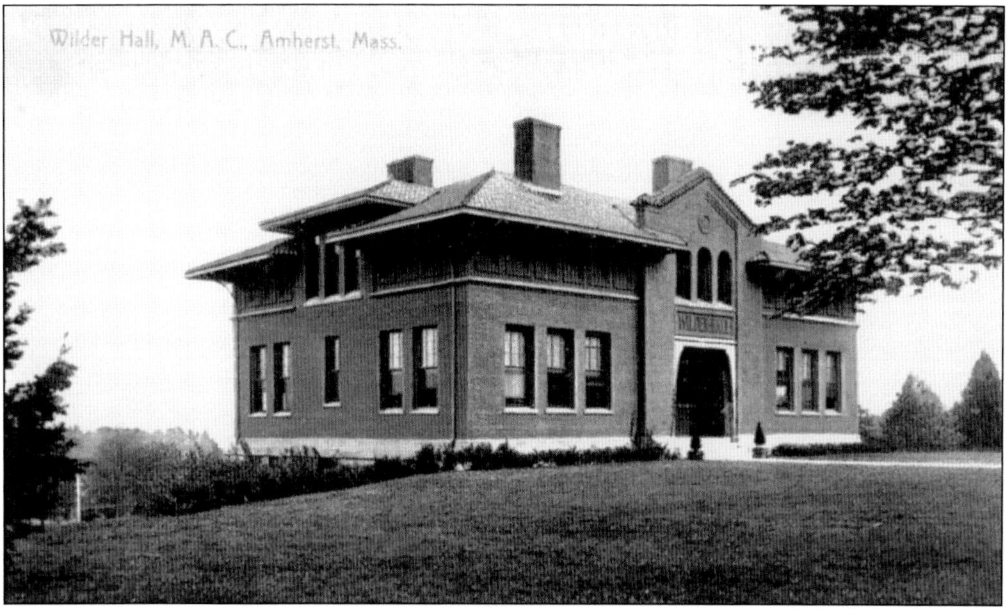

Created for the study of gardening, floriculture, greenhouse management, and landscape gardening, Wilder Hall, pictured here in 1906, was named after Marshall Pickney Wilder.

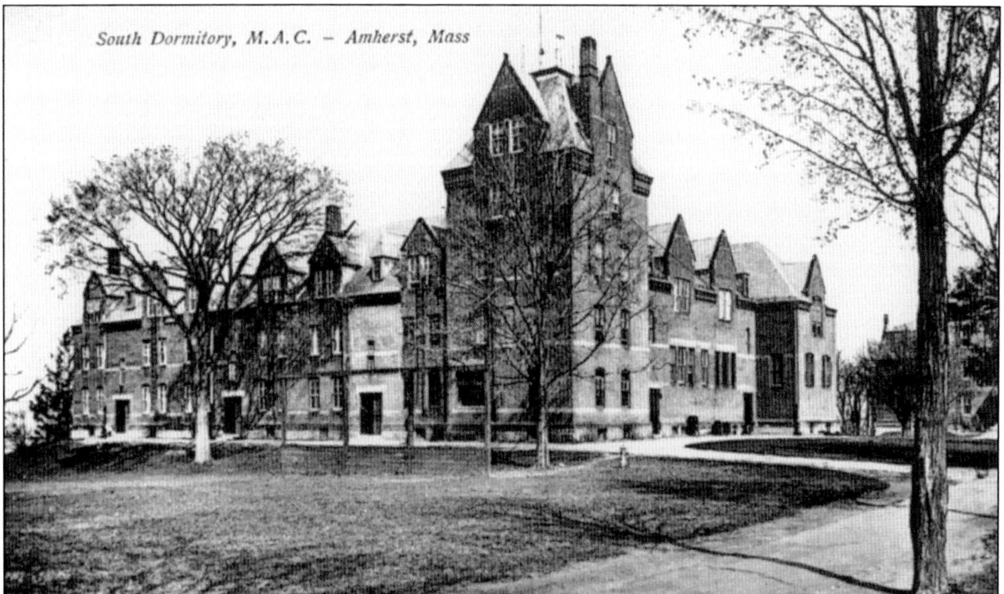

In February 1885, South Dormitory, built in 1867, was gutted by a fire caused by the explosion of a kerosene burner in an egg incubator. A new building was completed in October 1885. The quickness of the construction was due to the fact that the contractors were able to use some of the walls from the original structure. This building still plays an active role on campus. South Dormitory served as the college's administration building before the construction of the Whitmore Administration Building in 1967.

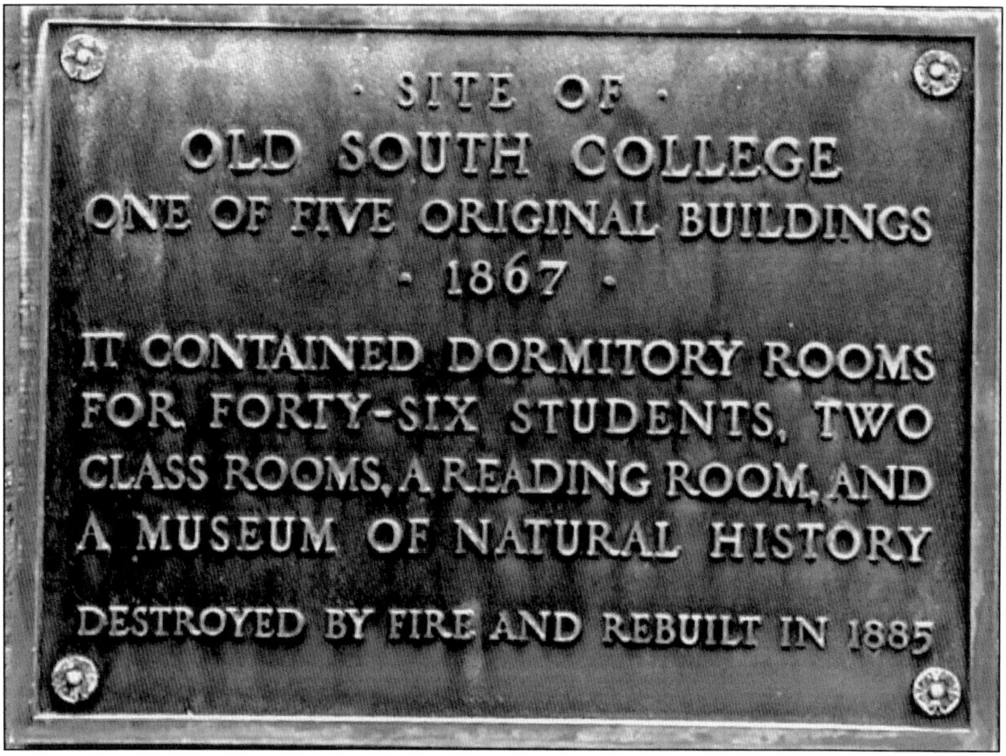

This plaque can be found on the side of Old South College.

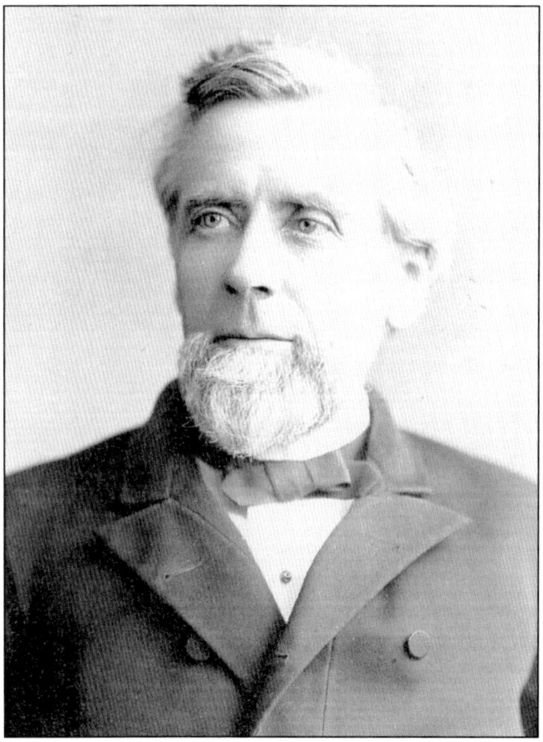
James Carruthers Greenough was the eighth president of Mass. Aggie, serving from 1885 to 1886. Greenough oversaw the construction of the Old Chapel, South College, and the West Experiment Station. In 1946, Massachusetts State College welcomed the Greenough Dormitory in the central part of the campus. (Photograph courtesy of the Special Collections and Archives, W.E.B. Du Bois Library, University of Massachusetts Amherst.)

Henry Hill Goodell was one of the first professors at the new Massachusetts Agricultural College in 1867. Goodell was also the college's first librarian, and he was credited for drastically expanding the library collection. In 1886, Goodell was chosen to lead the college as president, serving until 1905. In 1934, the newly constructed library was named after Henry Hill Goodell. (Photograph courtesy of the Special Collections and Archives, W.E.B. Du Bois Library, University of Massachusetts Amherst.)

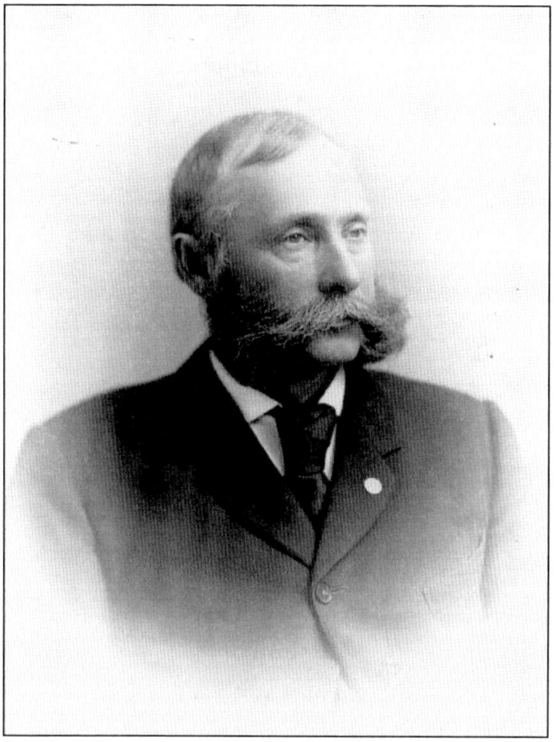

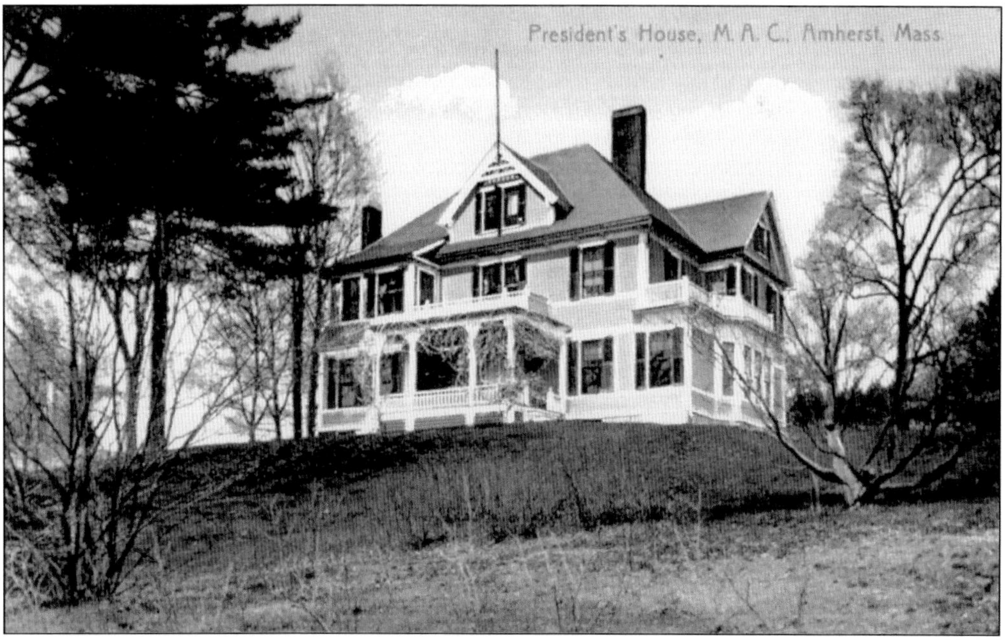

Referred to as Hillside, the president's house was built in 1884 for president Greenough for a cost of $11,500. On the land surrounding Hillside, the horticultural department used to experiment with growing small fruits and berries. John and Cathryn Lombardi, the chancellor and first lady of the campus, currently occupy the house.

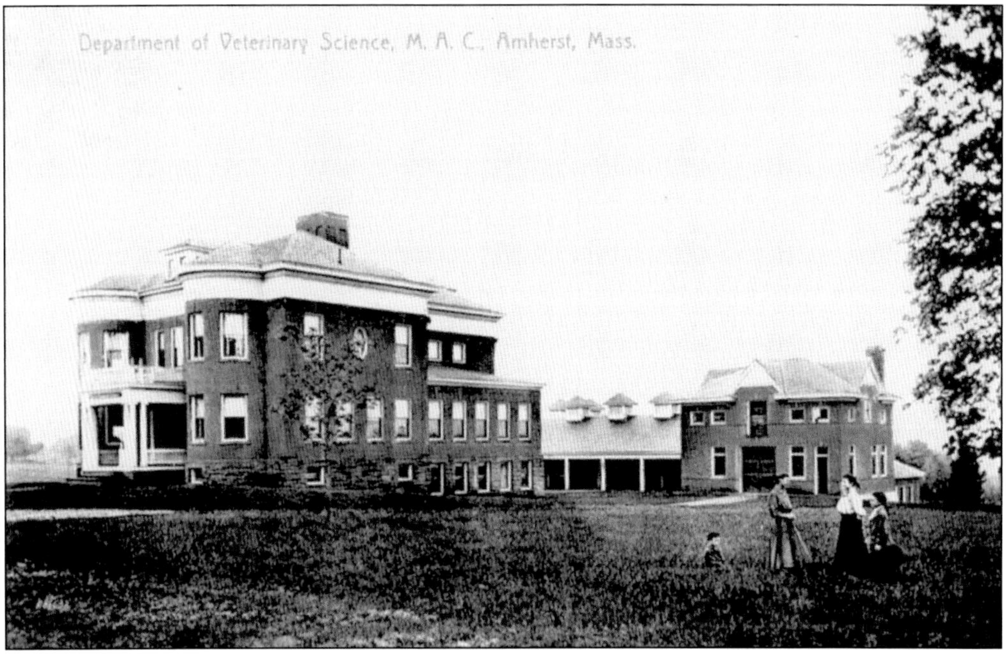

Munson Hall, built in 1898, was originally named Paige Laboratory after Dr. James B. Paige, a respected member of the faculty. Before the existence of Paige Laboratory, Dr. Paige used to keep animals and laboratory supplies in his home basement. In 1951, Paige Laboratory was renamed after Willard A. Munson, the powerful fullback on the 1904 MAC football team. Munson was director of the University Extension Service from 1926 to 1950. In 2004, Munson Hall houses the university's communication and marketing division.

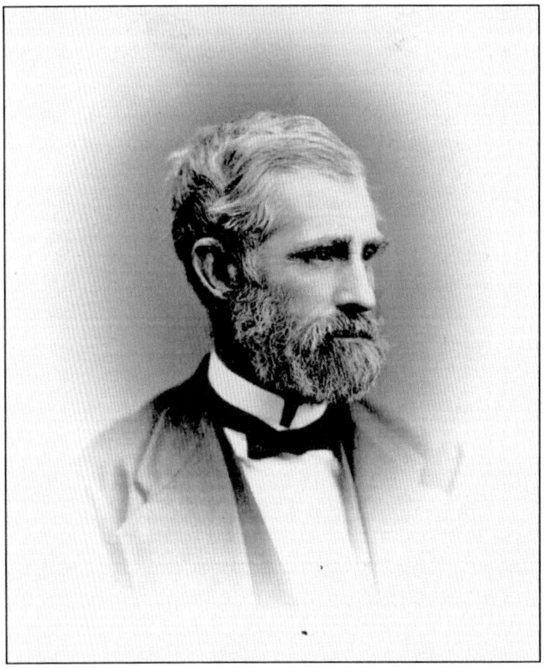

Levi Stockbridge was born in Hadley in 1820. Stockbridge was called to a professorship at the newly established Massachusetts Agricultural College in Amherst in 1867. He was one of the first four professors at MAC. Stockbridge devised and prosecuted a series of experiments concerning the effect of moisture on plants and trees, using an apparatus that he invented. He was the fourth president of MAC, and the university's Stockbridge School of Agriculture was named after him. (Photograph courtesy of the Special Collections and Archives, W.E.B. Du Bois Library, University of Massachusetts Amherst.)

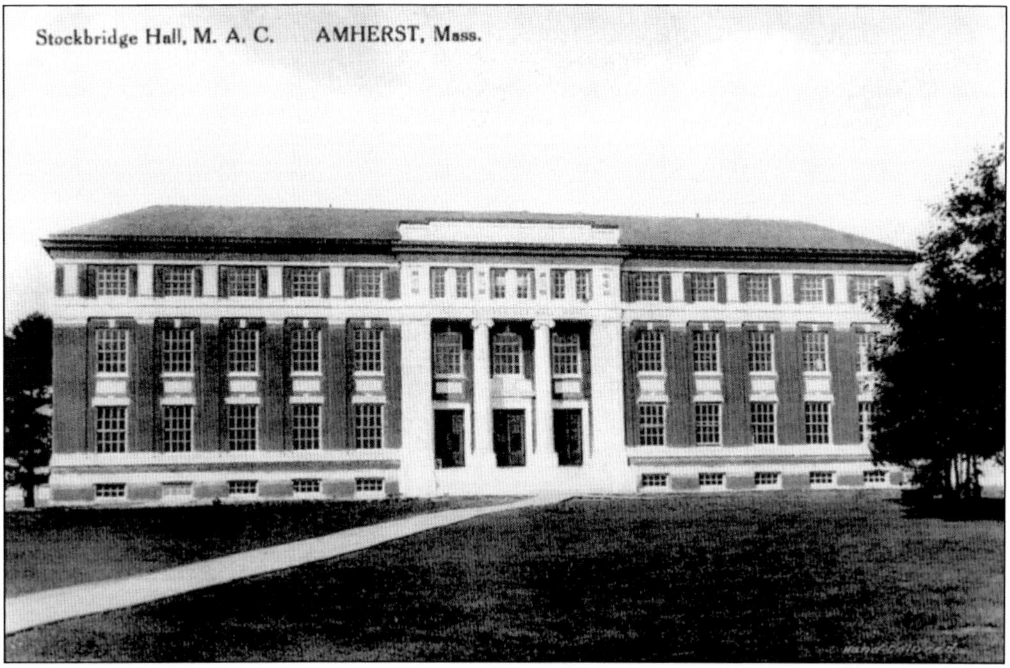

Stockbridge Hall was built in 1914. It is named after Levi Stockbridge, the university's first professor of agriculture and fourth president. It houses the Bowker Auditorium.

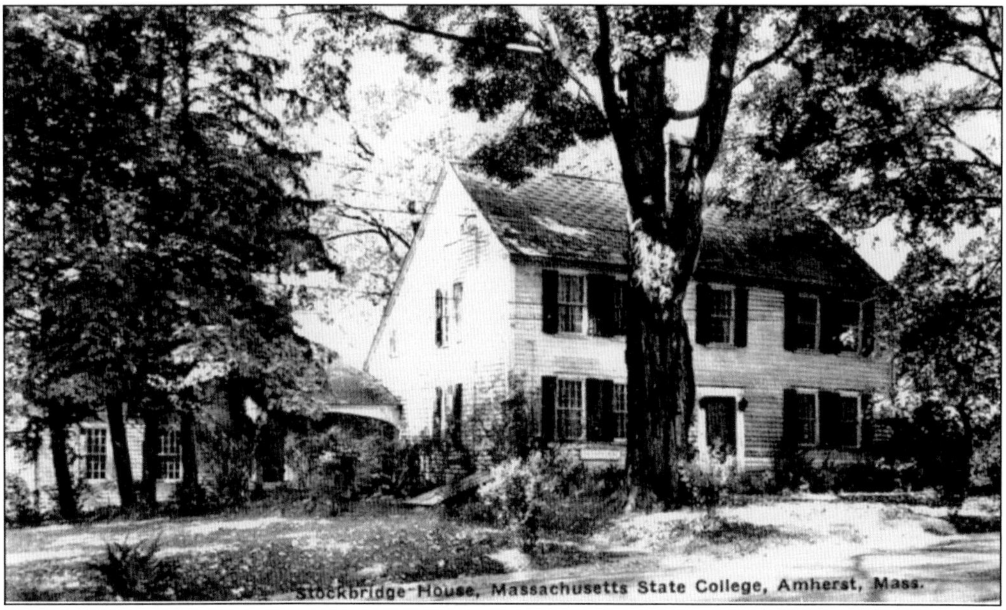

The Boltwood-Stockbridge House, built in 1728, is the oldest house in Amherst. It is named after the Boltwood family, who in 1864 sold their 111 acres along North Pleasant Street (then Sunderland Road) to the Commonwealth of Massachusetts for the new Massachusetts Agricultural College. Henry Flagg French, the first president of the college, lived and had his office in the house in 1865. In 1934, the house was moved from its original location to a new site across campus. Today, the house serves as the Faculty Club.

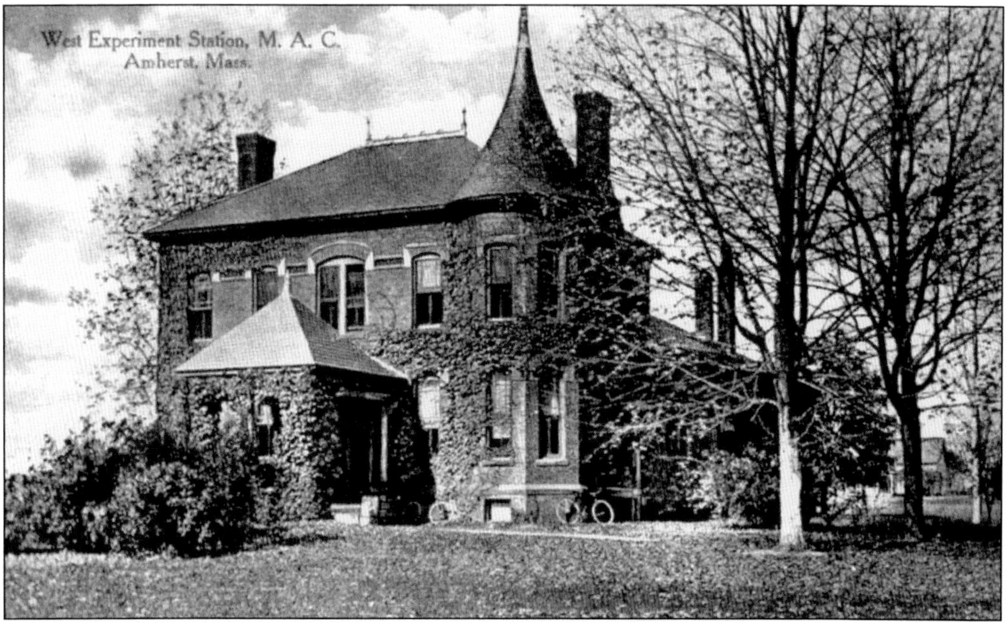

Built in 1886, the West Experiment Station is one of the most beautiful pieces of architecture on campus. It was the first experiment station in the United States that was directly connected to a state college. The West Experiment Station was devoted to the chemical analysis of crops, fruits, and fertilizers. The building was designed by Holyoke architect Emory A. Ellsworth.

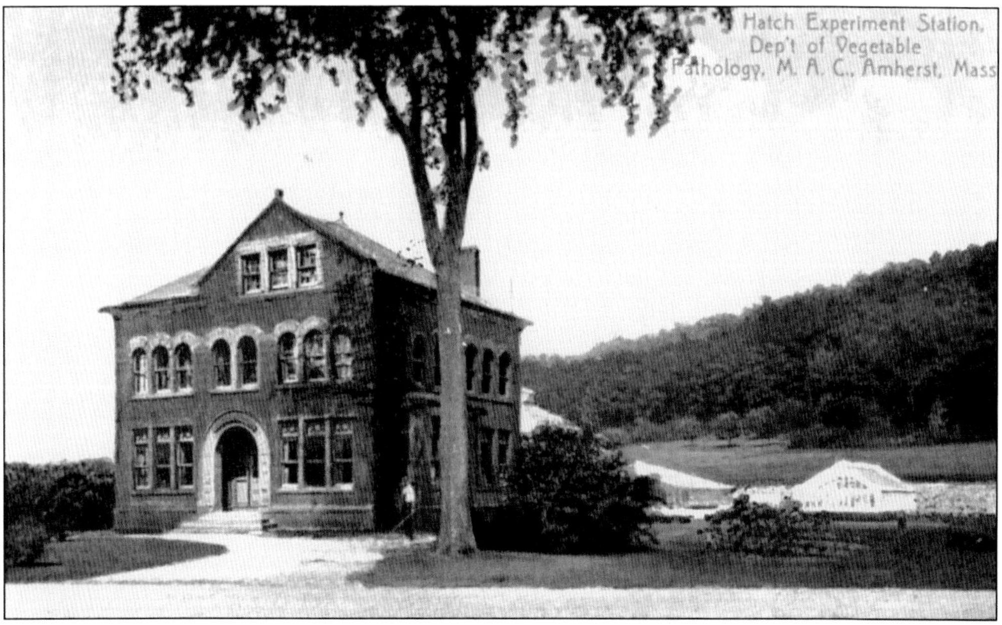

In place since 1889, the Hatch Experiment Station was originally devoted to plant pathology and insect control. The original building had a large protruding greenhouse and shed, which has since been removed. In 2004, it remains an active building on campus.

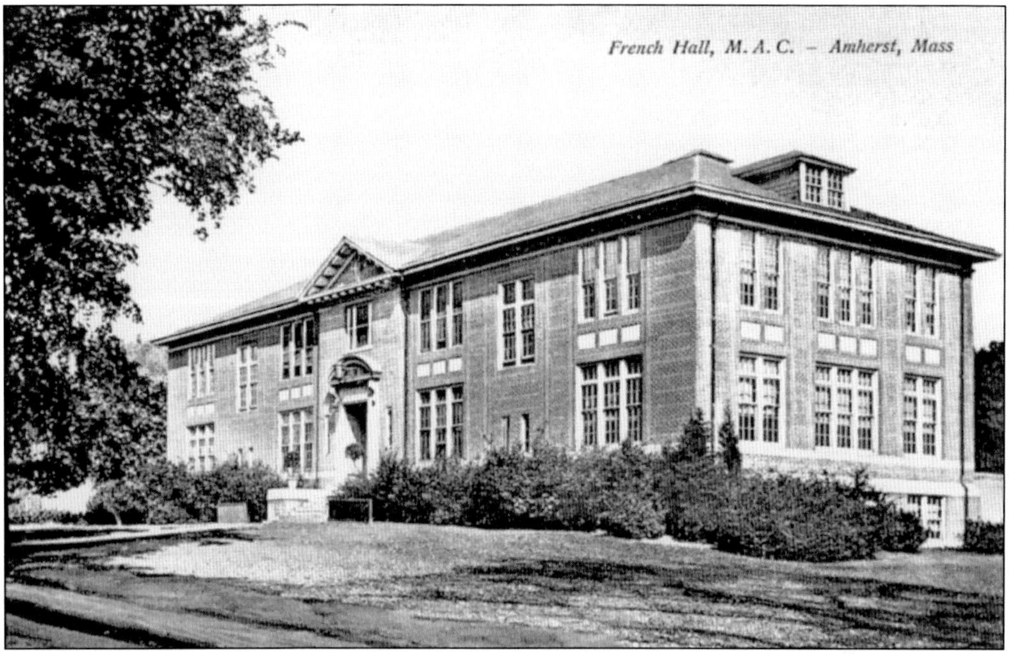

French Hall was named after Henry Flagg French, the first president of the new Massachusetts Agricultural College; he presided from 1864 to 1866. French, a graduate of Dartmouth College and Harvard Law School, was an avid farmer. French Hall was built to provide the additional space needed for instruction in floriculture and gardening. During World War II, it became a barracks for the Student Army Training Corps at MAC.

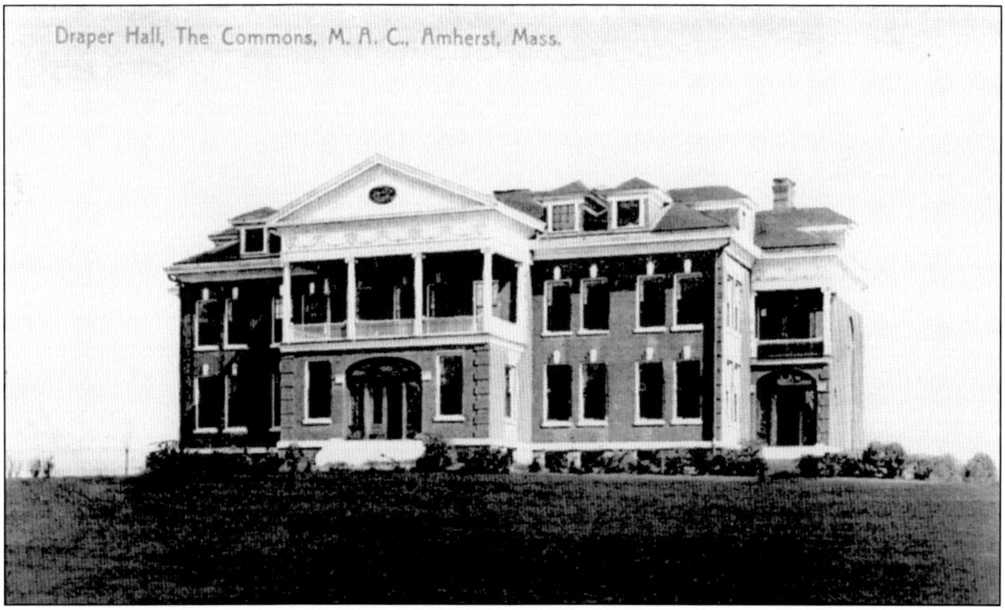

More attractive than most campus buildings of the same vintage, Draper Hall was built in 1903 as a dormitory for women and as a dining common. It was dedicated to James Draper of Worcester, trustee of the college from 1898 to 1910.

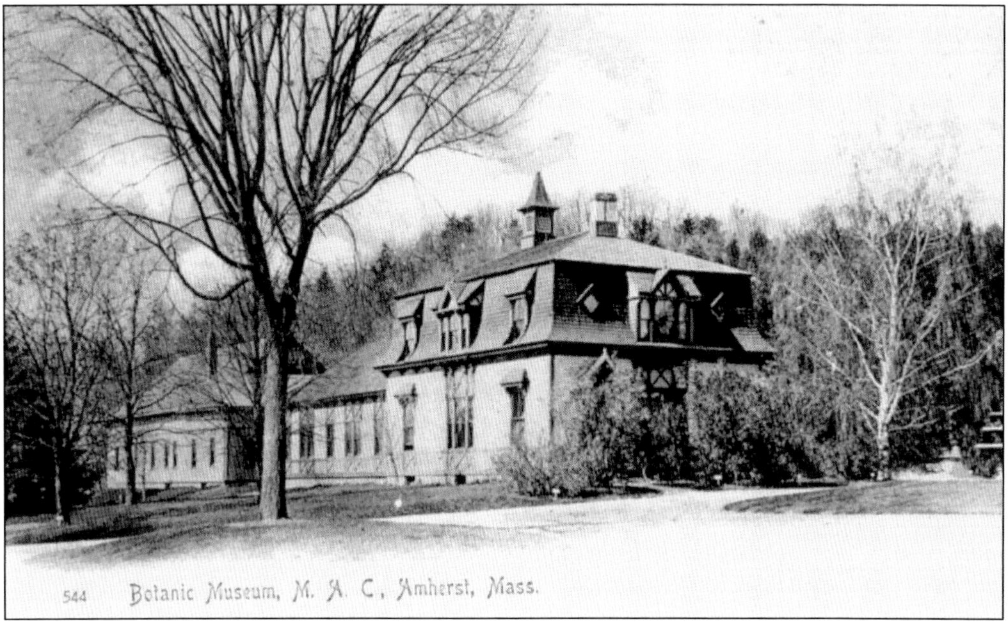

The Botanic Museum was built in 1867 at a cost of $5,180. The two-story square structure measured 43 feet by 45 feet and was one of the four original buildings on the new Massachusetts Agricultural College campus. The first floor had a laboratory and recitation room. The second floor housed 15,000 species of plants, a collection that was one of the largest in the country. The building was destroyed by fire in 1967.

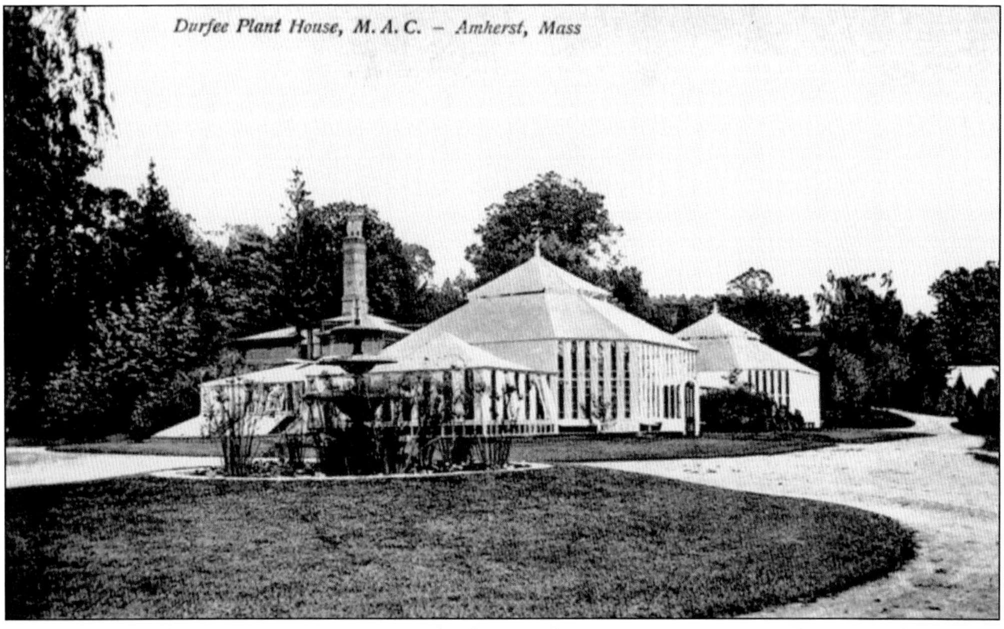

The Durfee Plant House was named after college trustee Dr. Nathan Durfee, who generously gave $10,000 for the construction costs. This significant engineering feat was the first great all-glass house within hundreds of miles of Amherst. It was the site of the growth of the first 5,000-pound pumpkin.

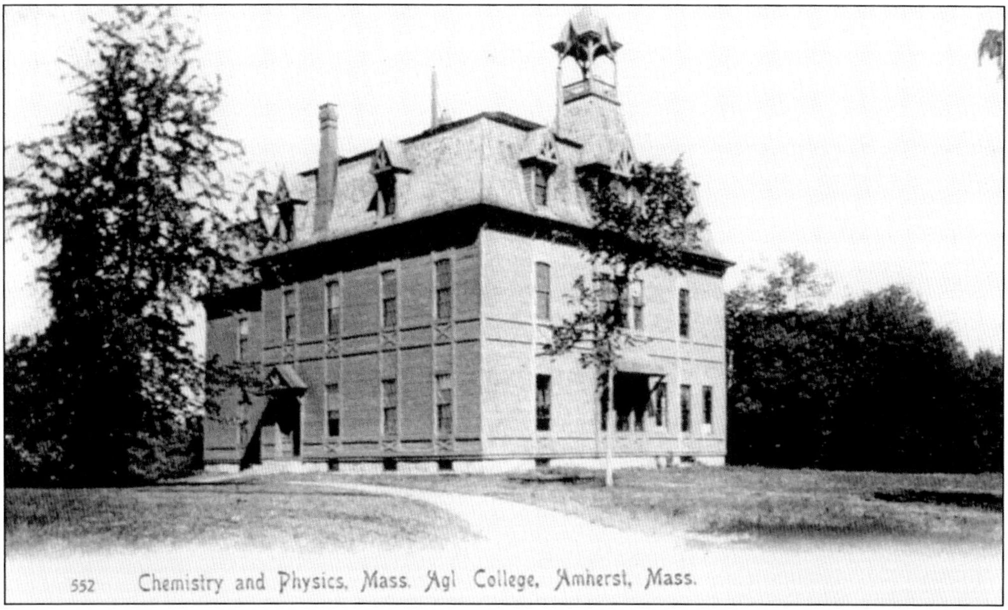

Old Chemistry Building, or College Hall, erected in 1867, was one of the college's first buildings. Originally a two-story building, College Hall received a third story with a mansard roof in 1869. The building contained a chapel used for morning prayers, the laboratory of the zoological department, and a part of the chemical department. Until 1939, all students were required to take at least two courses in chemistry.

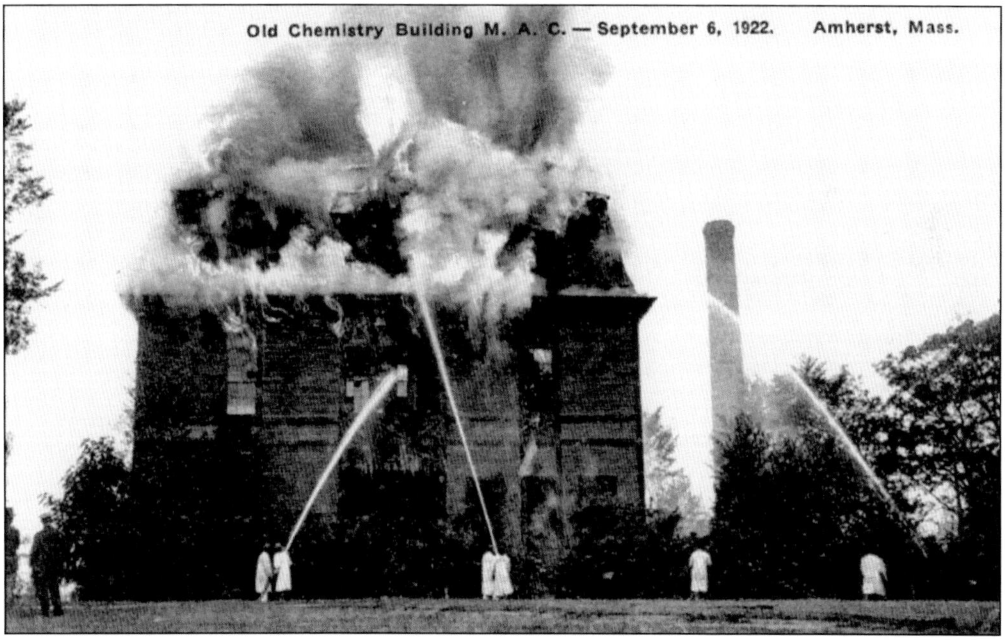

On September 6, 1922, Amherst firefighters had to physically stop Prof. Charles A. Peters and Prof. Joseph S. Chamberlain from returning to the burning building to retrieve their precious belongings. Both had been running in and out, ignoring the warnings of fire officials. Peters went as far as securing a ladder and climbing into his office to salvage his papers, books, and lab equipment.

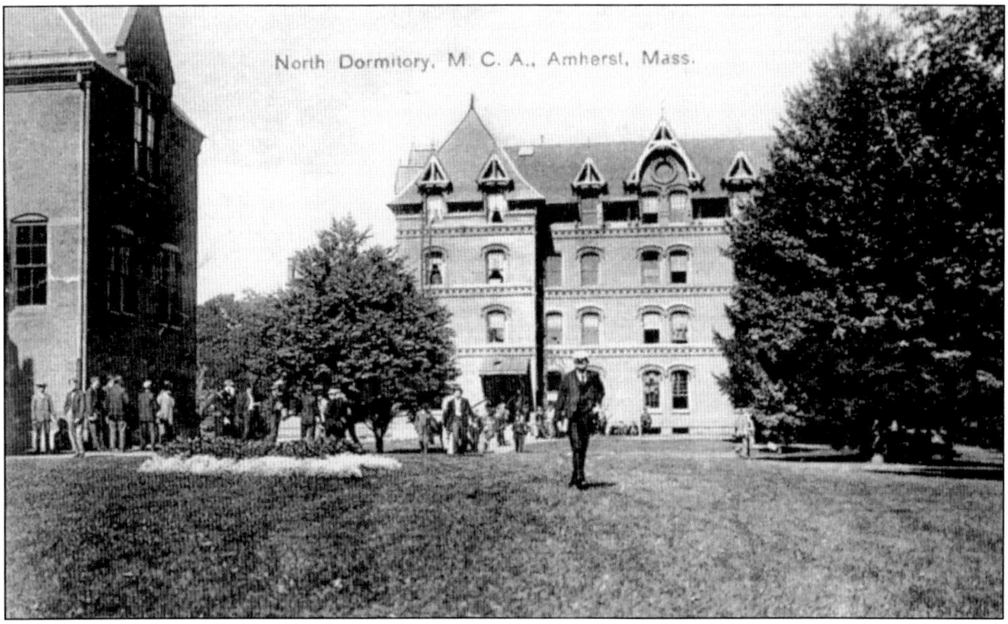

This antique postcard displays life on campus in 1910. It shows students leaving class between South College (on the left) and North College (in the center). The student in the immediate foreground is about to walk onto what was then the football gridiron.

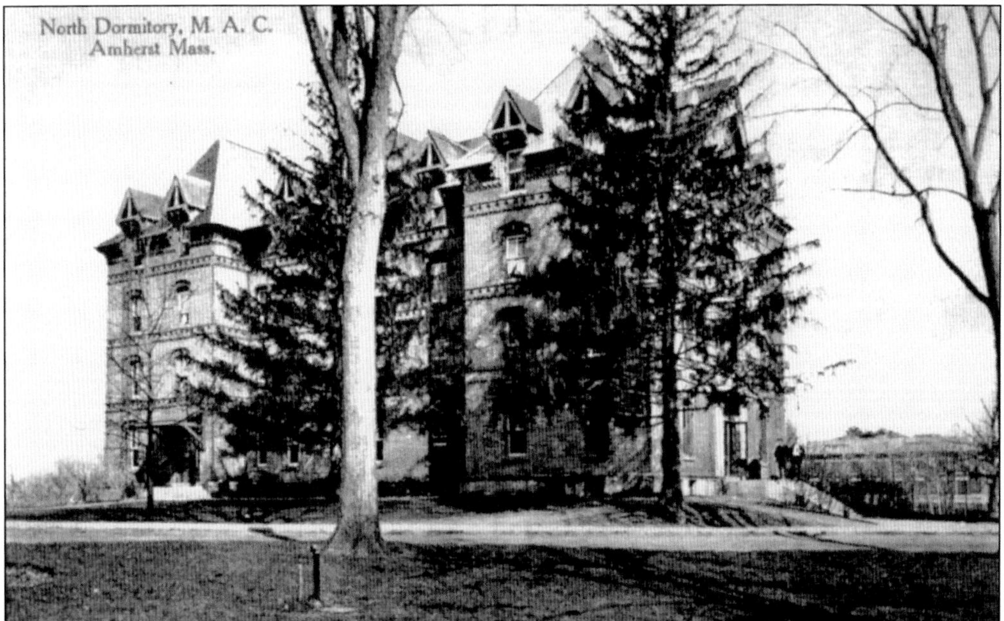

Completed in the fall of 1868, North Dormitory was one of the original buildings at Massachusetts Agricultural College. It cost $36,000 to build and housed up to 64 students. It was razed in 1955 to make room for William L. Machmer Hall.

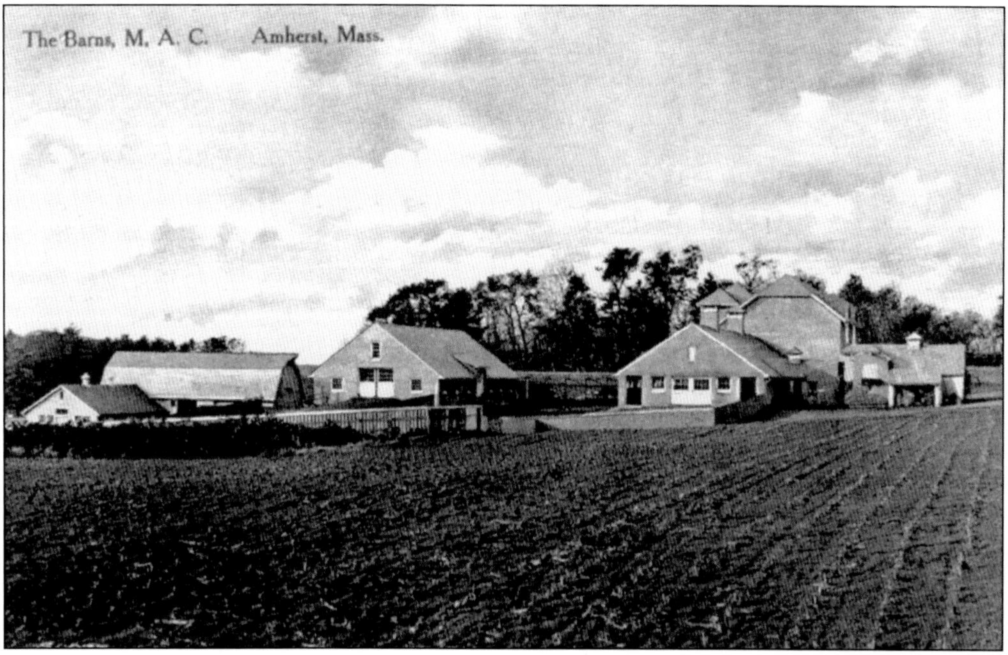

In the early years of MAC, there were countless barns strewn all over the campus. There were dairy barns for milking the cows, livestock barns for the veterinary science program, and barns for the horses that worked on campus. Today, many of the early campus barns are still in use.

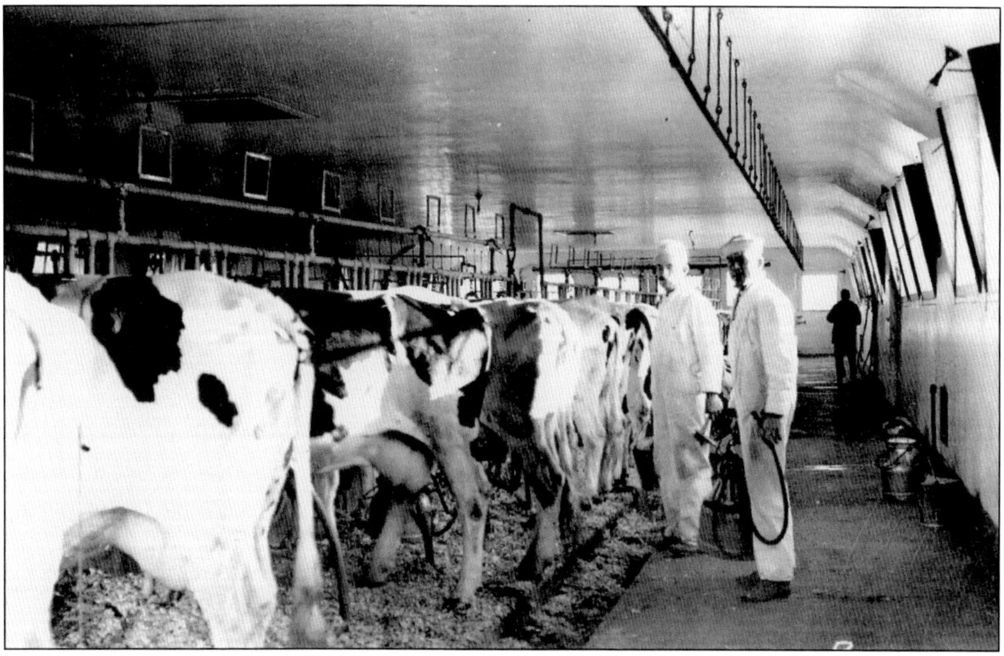

These students are getting ready to milk the cows.

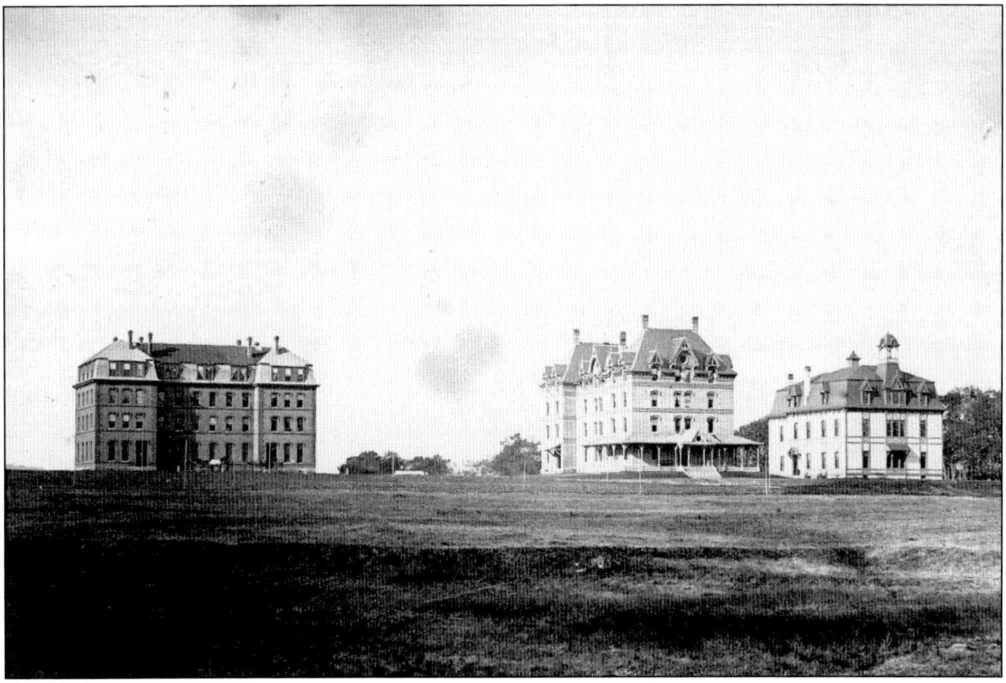

This photograph, taken before the creation of the campus pond, shows three of the first five buildings on the new Massachusetts Agricultural College campus. Shown in this image are, from left to right, South College, North College, and the chapel and chemistry building. Forty-seven students paid $15 per year to board in South College.

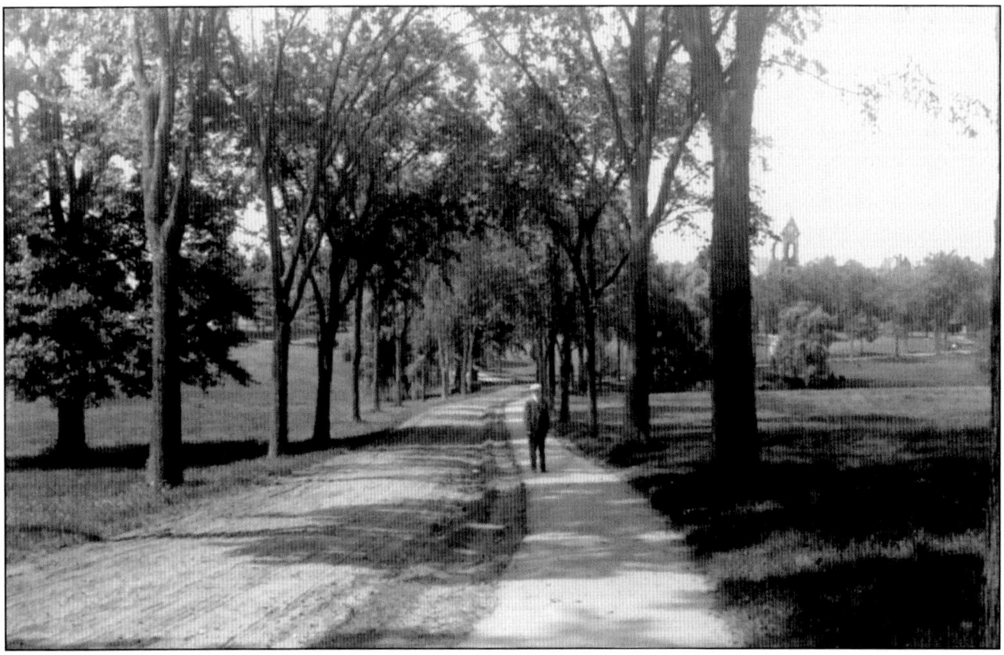

The Avenue was considered the main entrance to the campus in the early days. Perpendicular to North Pleasant Street, the Avenue ran through what is now the University Fine Arts Center.

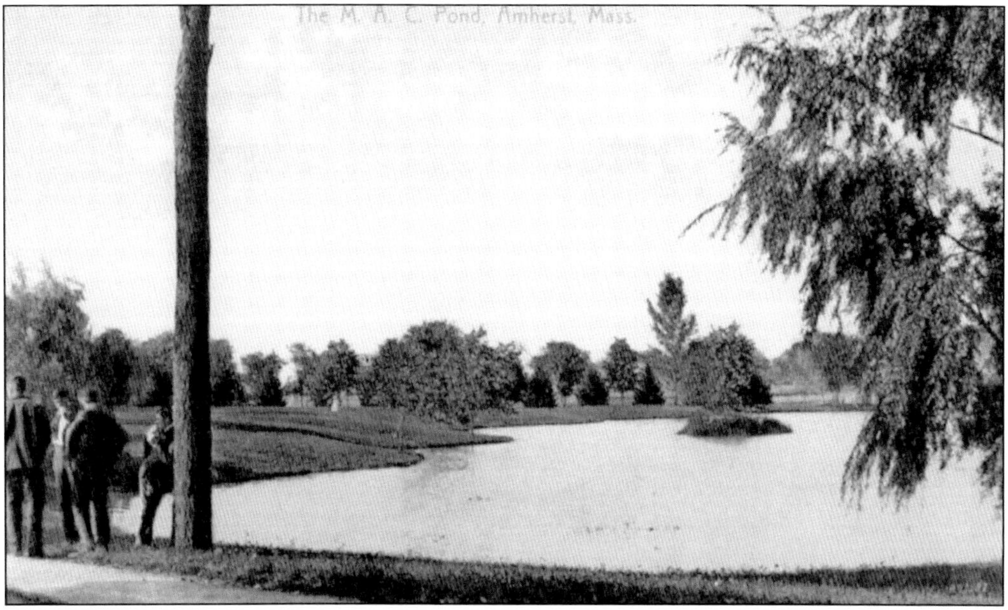

UMass students have enjoyed the campus pond since its creation in 1892. The man-made pond sits prominently in the middle of the campus, in front of the Old Chapel and Memorial Hall. Although made for scientific and experimental reasons, it served the practical purpose of supplying ice for the students and faculty to refrigerate food in the winter. In 1908, the Massachusetts Agricultural College men's hockey team played its first game on the pond. The fund-raising arm of the current UMass men's ice hockey team calls itself the Pond Club.

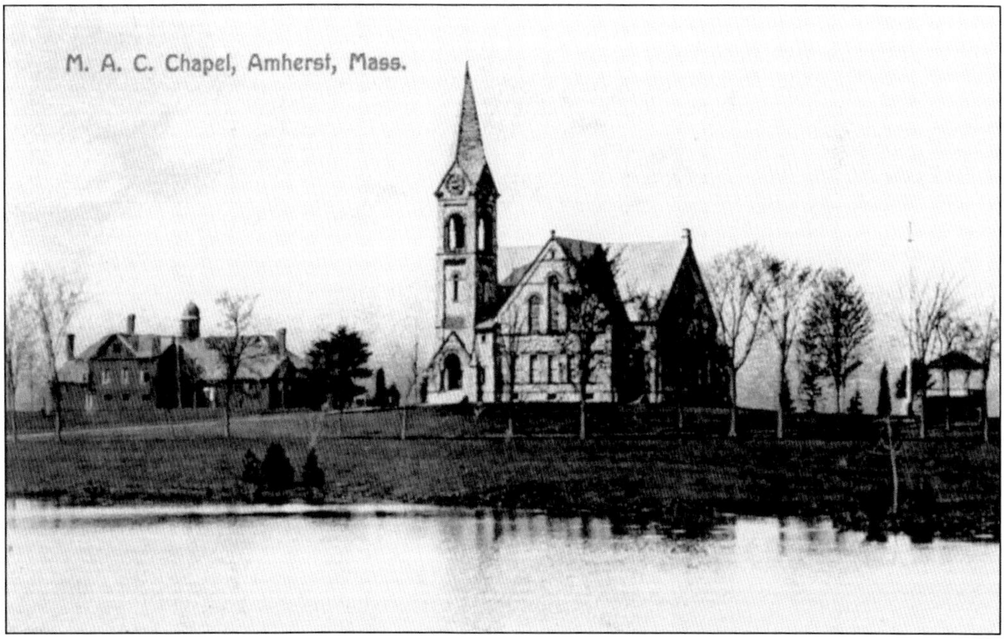

This photograph shows the early campus, with the concert bandstand next to the Old Chapel. The bandstand was set on fire as a college prank in 1912.

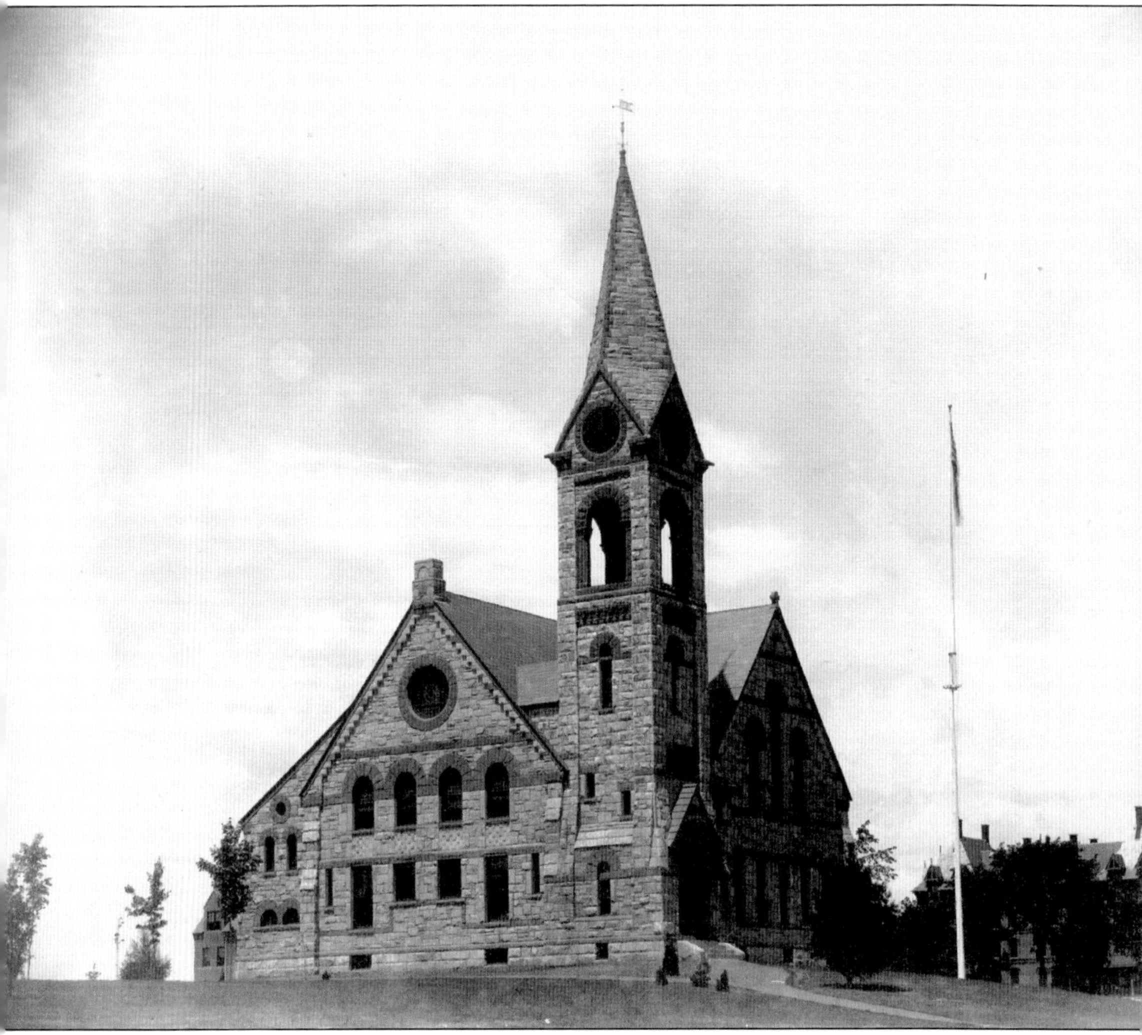

Clearly the most prominent building on campus, Old Chapel sits in the middle of campus among many newer buildings. The brownstone and Pelham-granite chapel and library building was built to replace the wooden chapel in 1884. The college library, with 1,200 volumes, occupied the first floor of the building. The president's office also was situated on the first floor. The second floor had enough room to seat 400 people. Sunday services and commencement were conducted on the second floor of the chapel. Today, the Old Chapel is vacant. (Photograph courtesy of the Special Collections and Archives, W.E.B. Du Bois Library, University of Massachusetts Amherst.)

Two

Faculty, Staff, and Administration

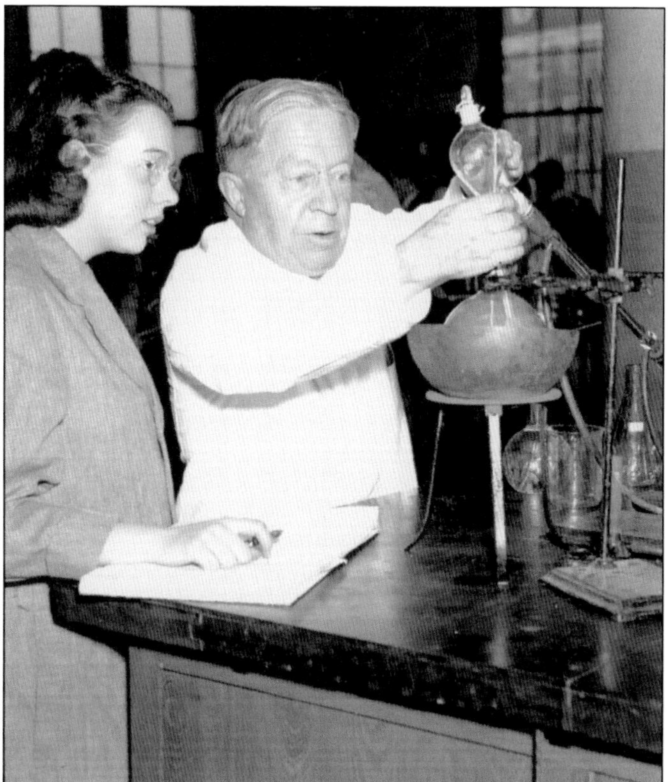

Prof. Joseph Chamberlain demonstrates an experiment to a student. Chamberlain came to the university in 1909 as an agricultural chemist and a highly regarded scientist. He completed his training, research, and teaching experience at Iowa State College of Agriculture, Johns Hopkins University, and in the U.S. Department of Agriculture. (Photograph courtesy of the Special Collections and Archives, W.E.B. Du Bois Library, University of Massachusetts Amherst.)

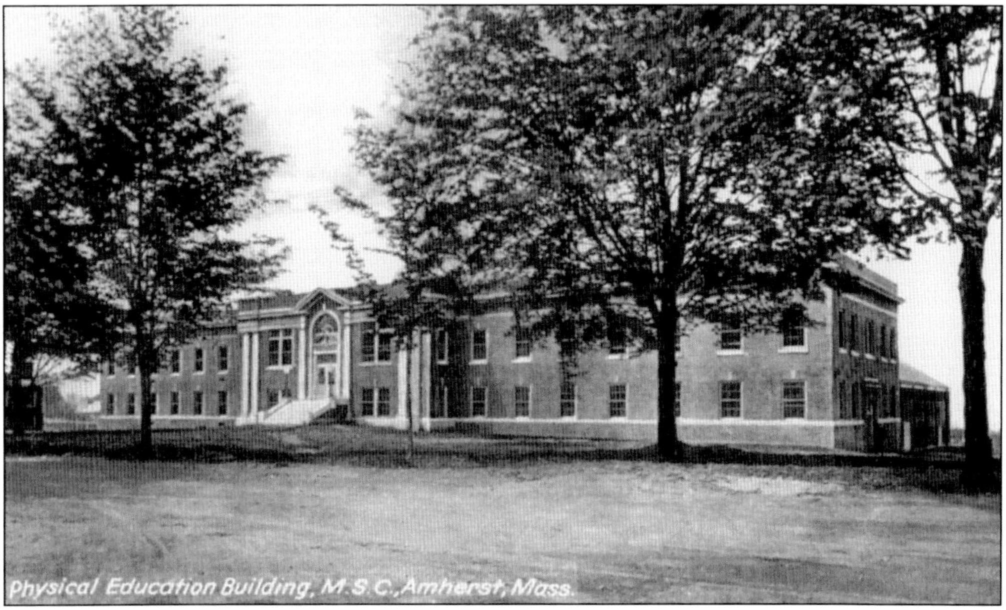

This building was dedicated as the Physical Education Building on June 13, 1931. Physical education was first established on campus in 1909. Professor Curry Starr Hicks arrived at the college to take charge of the department in 1911. Before the construction of the cage, the Drill Hall was made available for use in carrying out the physical education program.

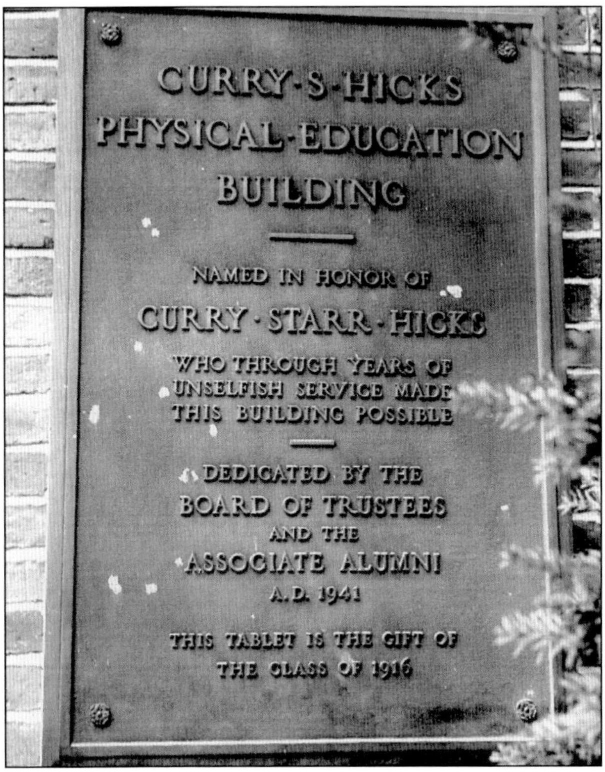

This plaque hangs on the Curry Hicks Cage. It was a gift from the MAC class of 1916. (Photograph courtesy of the Special Collections and Archives, W.E.B. Du Bois Library, University of Massachusetts Amherst.)

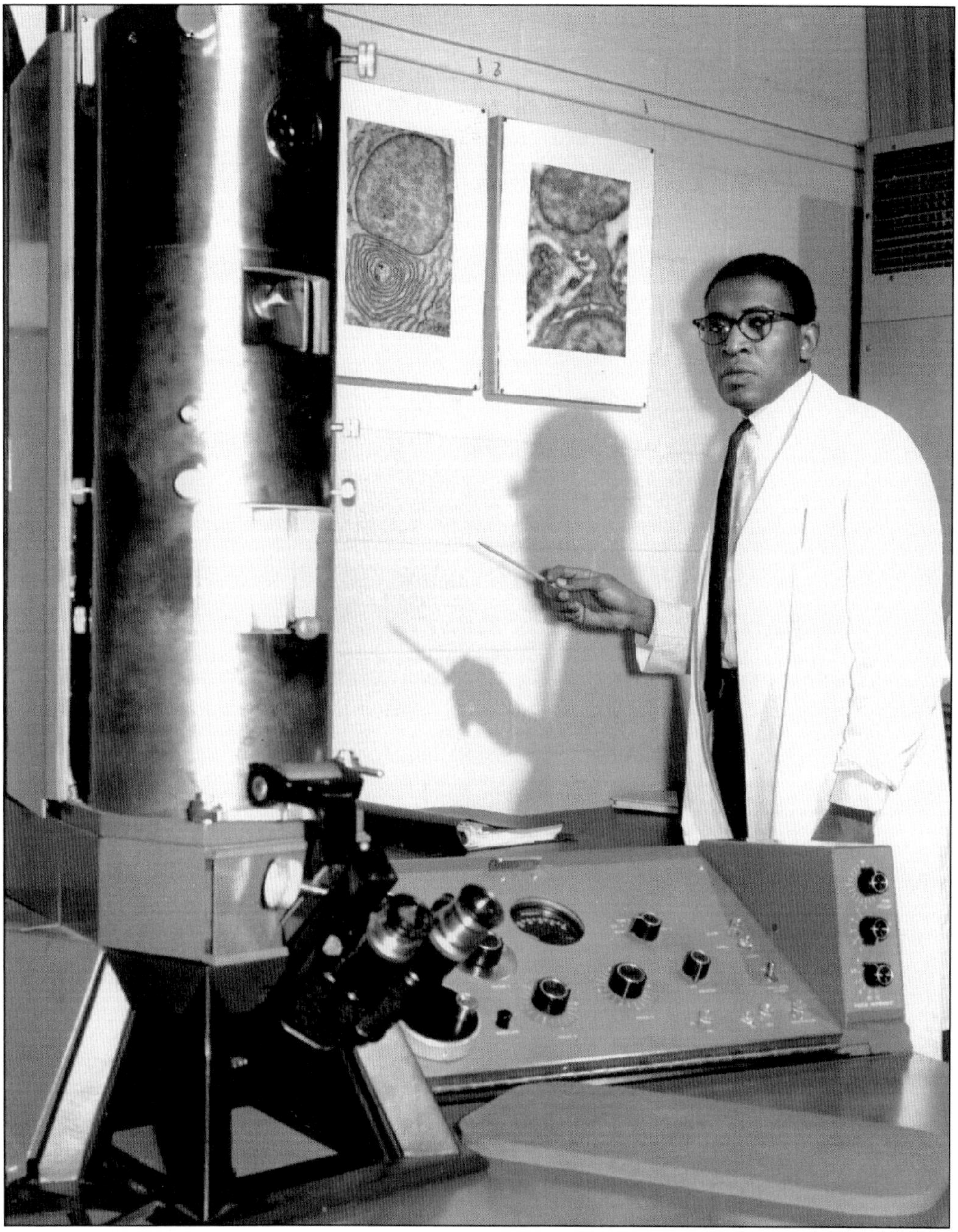

In 1962, university zoologist Dr. Everett Anderson received an $82,000 grant from the U.S. Public Health Service for a three-year study of the world of living cells. Anderson used the electron microscope shown on the left to get a closer look at the inner composition of parts of cells from different kinds of animals. (Photograph courtesy of the Special Collections and Archives, W.E.B. Du Bois Library, University of Massachusetts Amherst.)

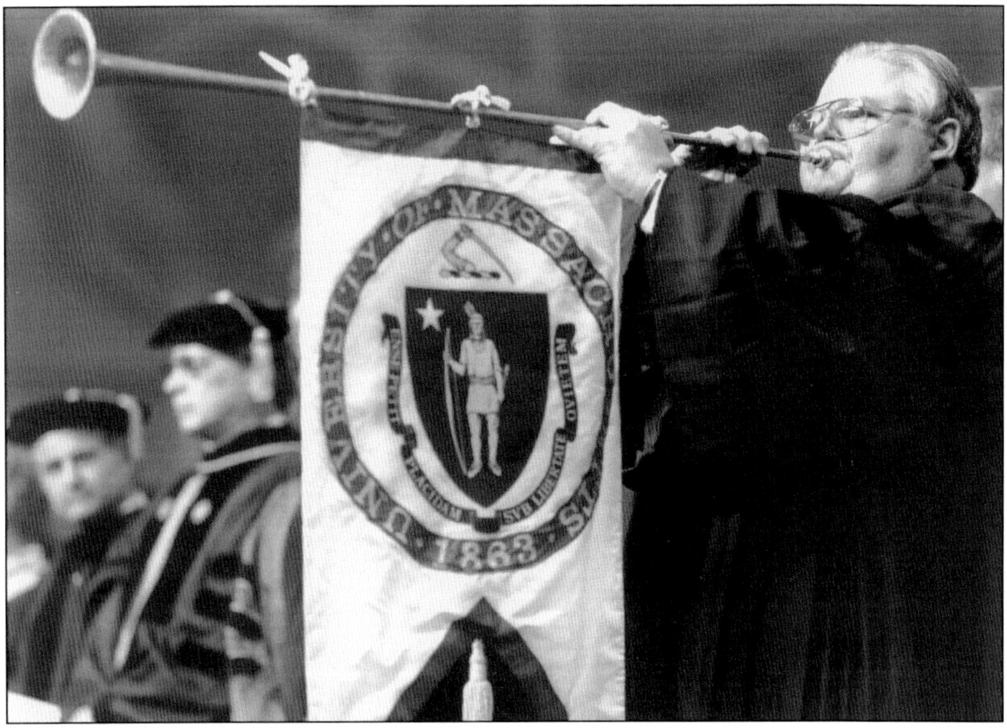

Walter Chesnut has blown his bugle at graduation for almost 30 years. Chesnut works for the university in the music department. (Photograph courtesy of the Special Collections and Archives, W.E.B. Du Bois Library, University of Massachusetts Amherst.)

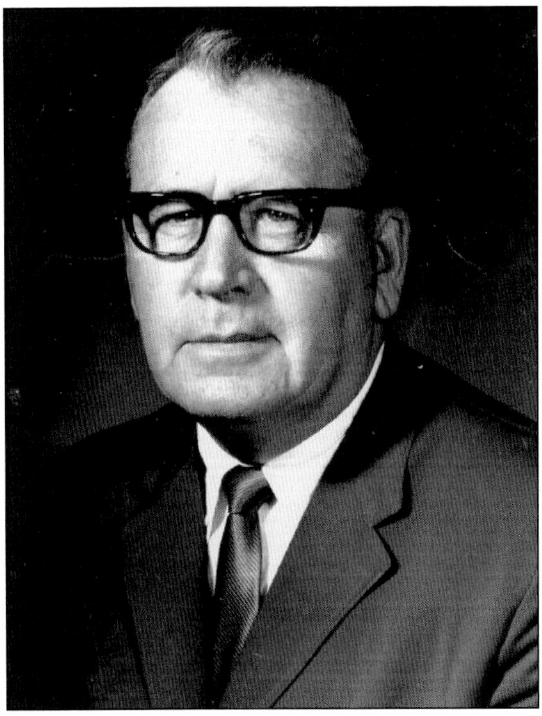

Warren Pierce McGuirk served as the dean of the school of physical education and as director of athletics for over three decades. McGuirk was instrumental in securing the funding of the Women's Physical Education Building in 1958, the Boyden Gym in 1963, and the football stadium in 1965; the stadium is named after him. It was under McGuirk that women's sports began to flourish. (Photograph courtesy of the Special Collections and Archives, W.E.B. Du Bois Library, University of Massachusetts Amherst.)

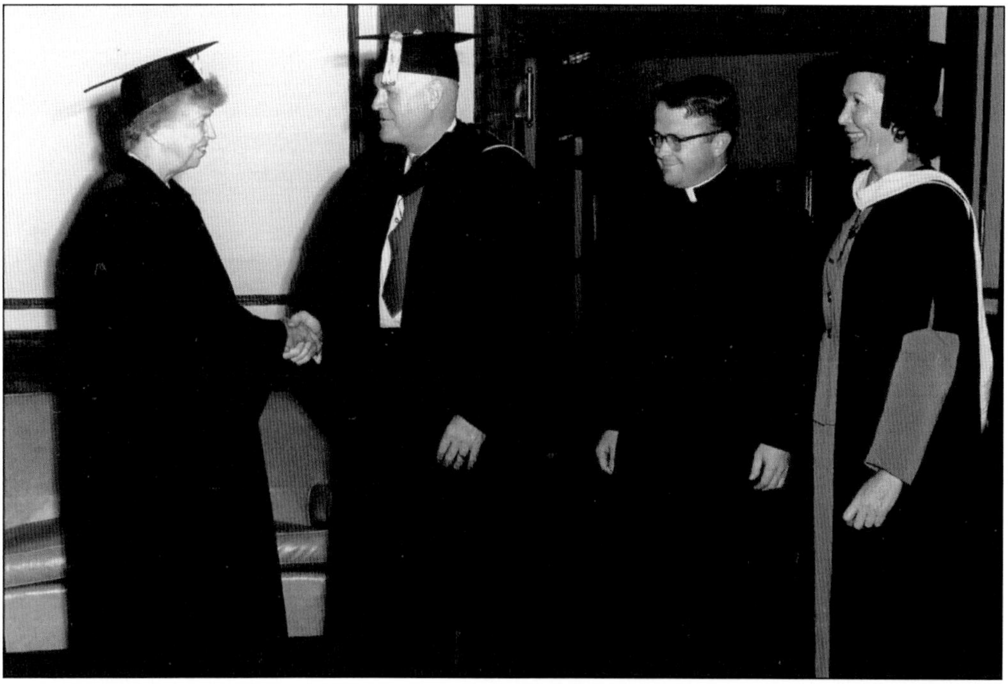

Eleanor Roosevelt is greeted by Pres. Ralph Van Meter at convocation on September 25, 1952, as Fr. David Power and Dean of Women Helen Cole Curtis look on. (Photograph courtesy of the Special Collections and Archives, W.E.B. Du Bois Library, University of Massachusetts Amherst.)

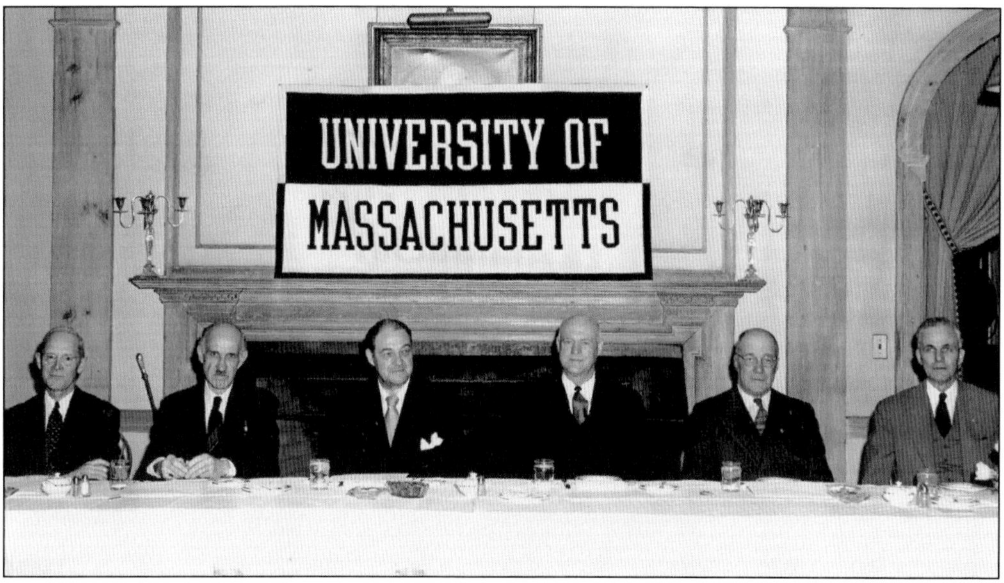

Sitting under the University of Massachusetts banner, from left to right, are the following: Horace Jones, Clark Thayer, LeRoy Talcott, Pres. Ralph Van Meter, Willard Munson, and Myron Peabody. The event was the Ford Motors dinner and *Lord Jeffrey Waves of Green* premier, held on May 22, 1950. (Photograph courtesy of the Special Collections and Archives, W.E.B. Du Bois Library, University of Massachusetts Amherst.)

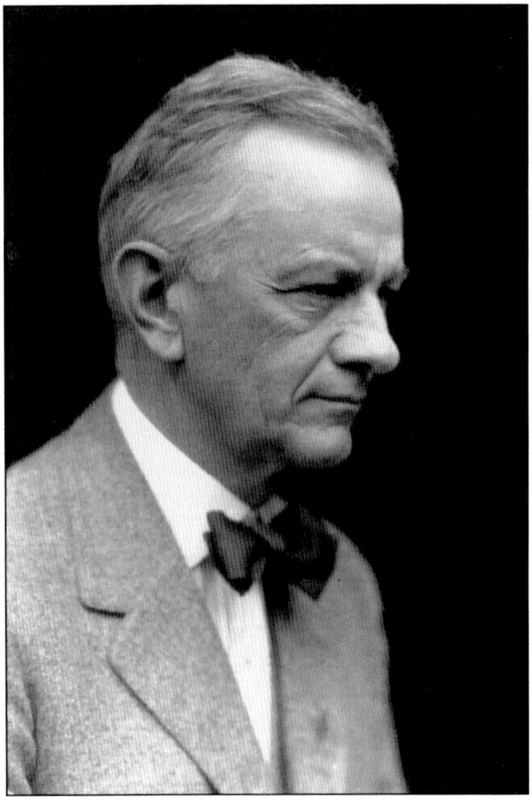

Kenyon Leech Butterfield was the ninth president of Massachusetts Agricultural College, presiding from 1906 to 1924. Butterfield, a son of the state of Michigan, was a major contributor to the growth of MAC. During his tenure as president, he made many changes to the campus, doubling the size of the faculty and recruiting faculty from all over the country. His college budget increased from $150,000 to $700,000 between 1906 and 1916. During his 18 years as president, 12 new buildings were constructed on campus. Butterfield was a strong advocate for the integration of women's curriculum at MAC. (Photograph courtesy of the Special Collections and Archives, W.E.B. Du Bois Library, University of Massachusetts Amherst.)

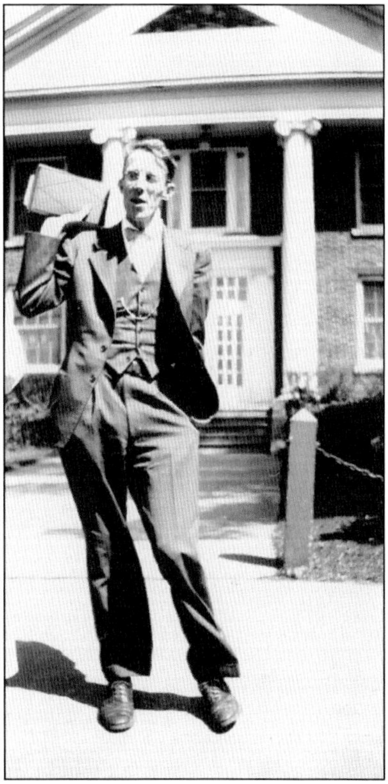

Here, Ellsworth "Dutchy" Barnard '28 looks like the archetypical English professor. Barnard landed his first teaching position at Massachusetts Agricultural College in 1930. He taught in the English Department from 1930 until 1933. His last teaching position brought him back to the university from 1968 to 1973. (Photograph courtesy of Mary Taylor Barnard '34.)

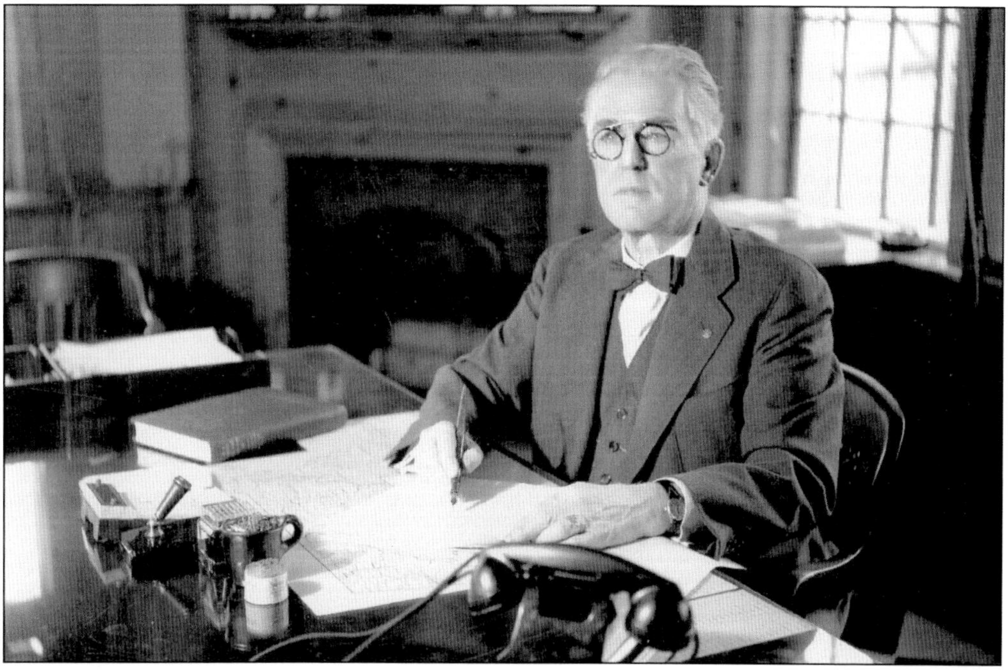

Hugh Baker served as president of Massachusetts State College (MSC) for all but two years of its existence. Baker became president in 1933, two years after the college changed its name from Massachusetts Agricultural College. He served as president of Massachusetts State College from 1933 until 1947. Baker was educated at Yale, Michigan State, and the University of Munich. Before joining Massachusetts State College, Baker taught at Syracuse University, Iowa State College, and Pennsylvania State. (Photograph courtesy of the Special Collections and Archives, W.E.B. Du Bois Library, University of Massachusetts Amherst.)

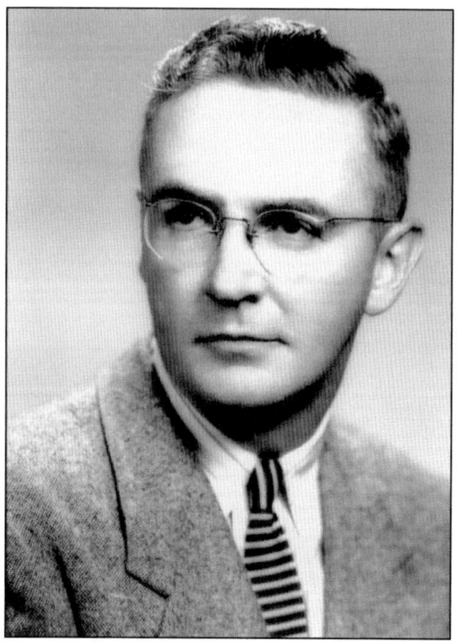

John Paul Mather was the youngest president in his era to lead a land-grant university. He joined the University of Massachusetts in 1953 as provost, and in 1954, at the age of 39, was appointed president. Mather advocated fiscal autonomy for the university and struggled with state officials to raise salaries for the faculty. In 1956, he gained authority from the state to appoint faculty without state approval. His work is credited with building a foundation for the academic strength of the university. Several important campus buildings were completed under his leadership, including the Morrill Science Center, the Student Union, Bartlett Hall, and Machmer Hall. (Photograph courtesy of the Special Collections and Archives, W.E.B. Du Bois Library, University of Massachusetts Amherst.)

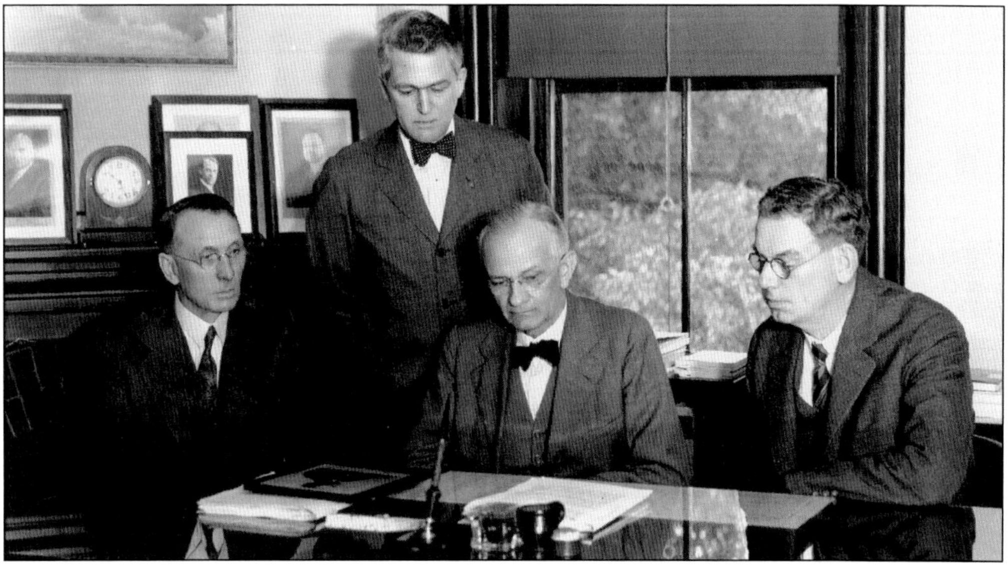

Shown in this photograph are, from left to right, Edward M. Lewis, Hugh P. Baker, Kenyon L. Butterfield, and Roscoe W. Thatcher. This image displays years of institutional wisdom; all four men were at one time the president of UMass. (Photograph courtesy of the Special Collections and Archives, W.E.B. Du Bois Library, University of Massachusetts Amherst.)

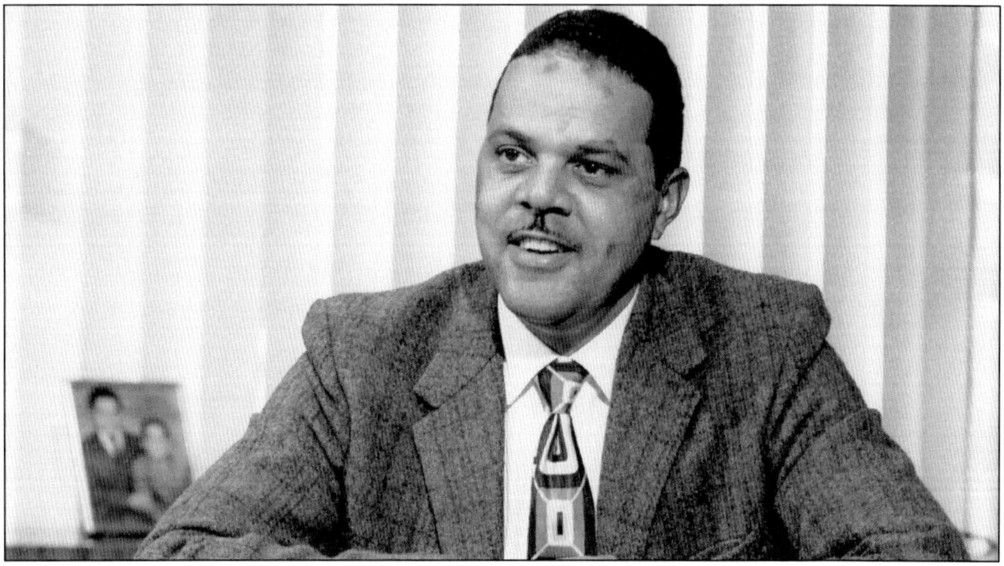

Randolph Bromery guided the campus through most of the difficult 1970s. Prior to his appointment as chancellor in 1971, Bromery served as a vice chancellor for student affairs and as a faculty member in the geosciences. He enjoyed a successful career as a research scientist before coming to the university, and was noted for designing instruments for aeromagnetic surveying. The university became a more diverse institution under Bromery's leadership. The ratio of undergraduate men to women shifted from 60:40 to 50:50, and the number of faculty of color increased. (Photograph courtesy of the Special Collections and Archives, W.E.B. Du Bois Library, University of Massachusetts Amherst.)

William M. Bulger assumed office as president of the UMass system in January 1996 and served until September 2003. On Bulger's watch, SAT scores among accepted students went up a system-wide average of 36 points, with the most dramatic results coming from Boston, Lowell, and Dartmouth. At those three campuses, which draw less-affluent, commuter-oriented students, SAT scores rose by between 43 and 50 points. At the Amherst flagship campus, combined SAT scores for the fall of 2003 entering class were up 19 points to 1,139. The goal of enrolling at least 3,700 students in the class of 2007 will most likely be exceeded by several hundred. These days, the number of accepted students who plan to enroll is up from 28 percent to 33 percent. During Bulger's tenure, annual private support grew by more than $79 million to reach $113.5 million. The university's endowment grew by $100 million to reach $146.4 million. And the number of endowed professorships rose from 4 to 46. Funding for research and the revenue generated by licensing UMass research increased from $754,000 in 1996 to $14.9 million in 2002, and grew to $20.2 million in 2003.

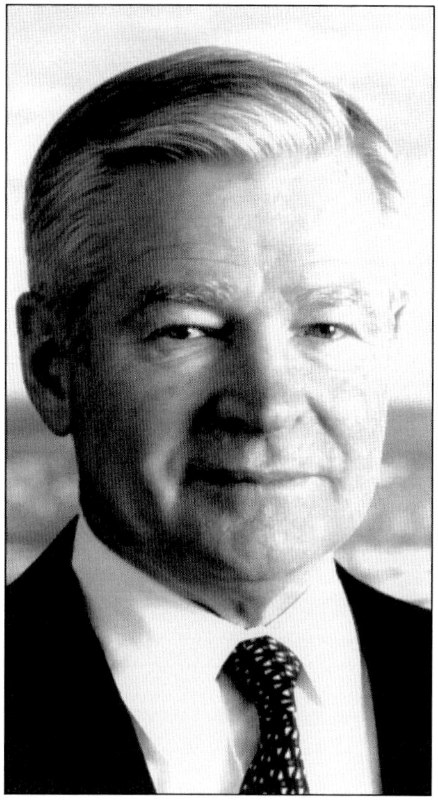

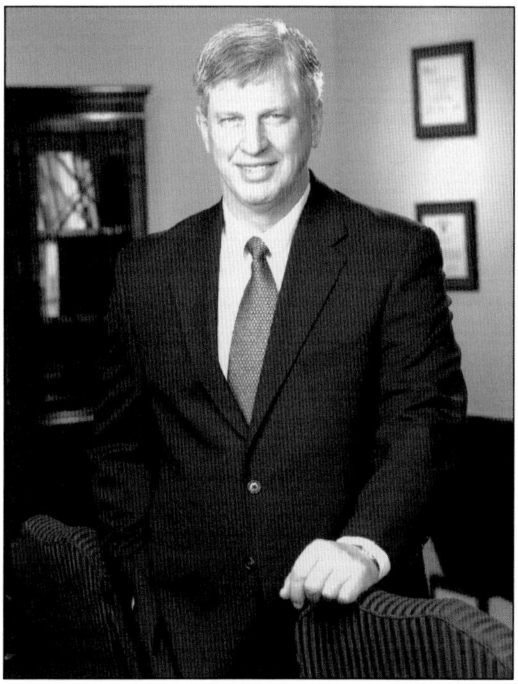

Dr. Jack Wilson was named president of the five-campus, 60,000-student University of Massachusetts on March 24, 2004. He had served as interim president since September 2003. Previously, he had served UMass as the vice president for academic affairs and as the founding chief executive officer of UMass Online. He is also a tenured professor of management at UMass Amherst. As the chief executive officer of UMass Online, he helped to build the system-wide initiative into one of the largest externally directed online programs in the United States, with 39 graduate and undergraduate degree and certificate programs serving 14,000 enrollees.

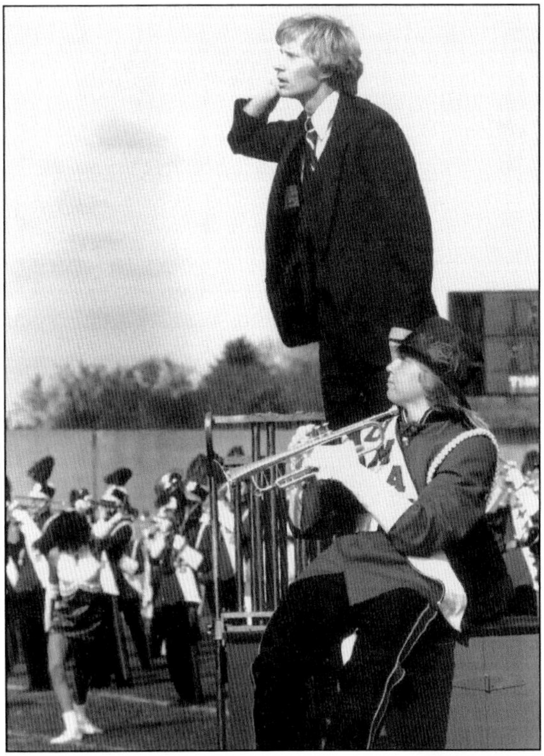

George Parks is shown here directing the UMass Minuteman Marching Band in 1986; Heidi Sarver is at his side. Parks is credited with building the band into a national presence. (Photograph courtesy of the Special Collections and Archives, W.E.B. Du Bois Library, University of Massachusetts Amherst.)

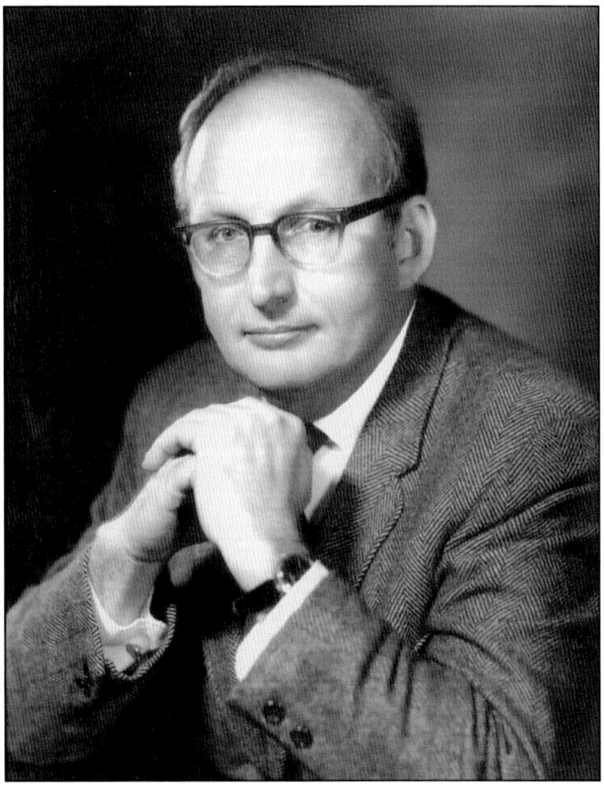

In 1970, Robert Wood became the first president of the new UMass system of campuses in Amherst, Boston, and Worcester. (Photograph courtesy of the Special Collections and Archives, W.E.B. Du Bois Library, University of Massachusetts Amherst.)

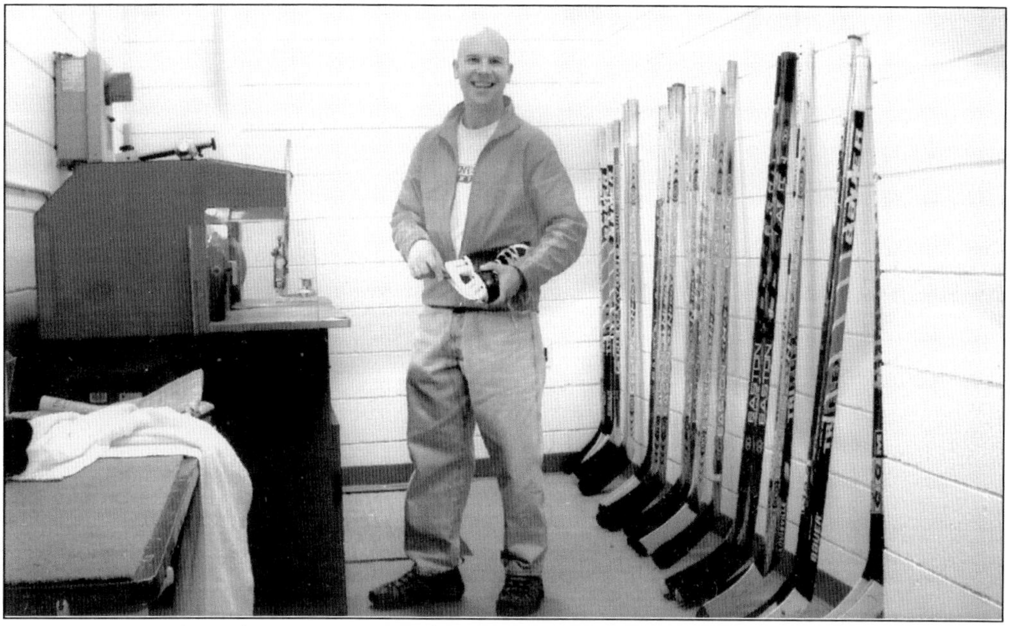

Pete "Stoney" Stoneham serves as the equipment manager for the UMass men's ice hockey team. He and many other staff members on the university payroll are the unsung heroes of the campus.

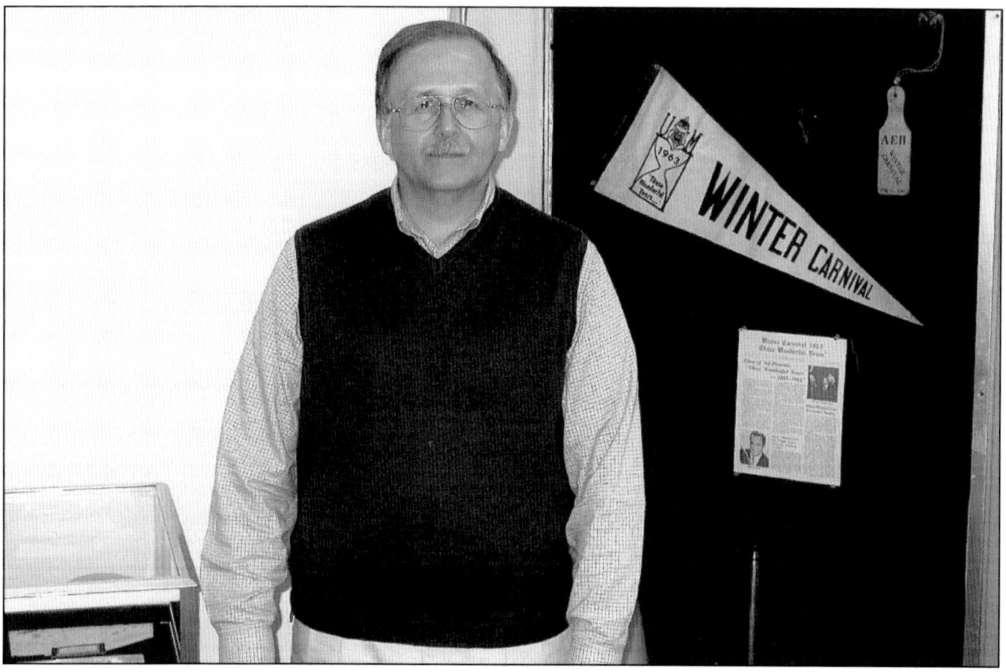

Mike Milewski '77, senior archives assistant, works in the Special Collections and Archives Department of the W.E.B. Du Bois Library. Mike is the campus guru when it comes to questions about the rich history of the campus. Mike has over 10,000 digitized images and many campus publications and records at his fingertips in this department. Those interested in UMass history should visit Mike on campus.

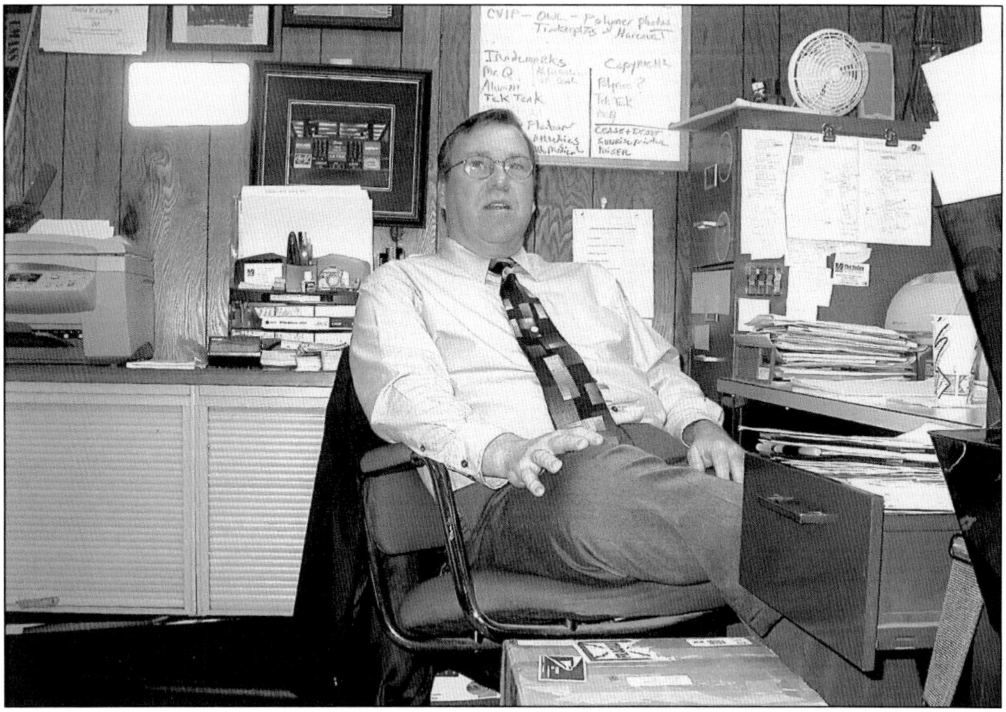

Dave Curley serves the university with distinction as the licensing director. Dave, a 20-year employee of UMass Amherst, works to license UMass clothing and paraphernalia.

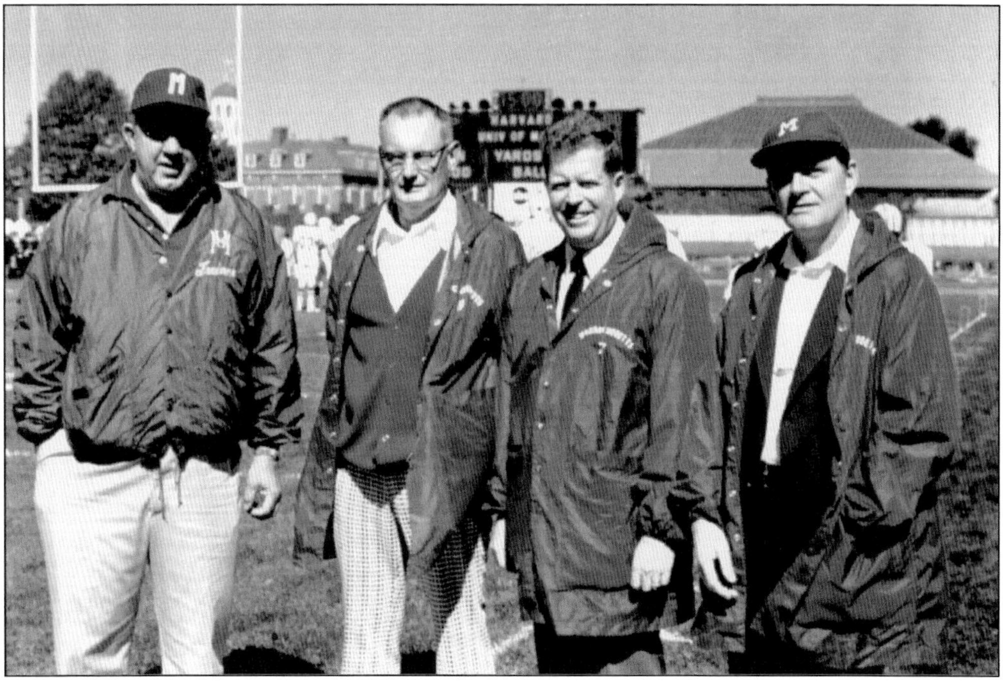

Posing before a football game in 1976 are, from left to right, trainer Vic Keedy, orthopedic surgeon George Snook, team physician Dr. James R. Ralph, and team physician James C. Contanche.

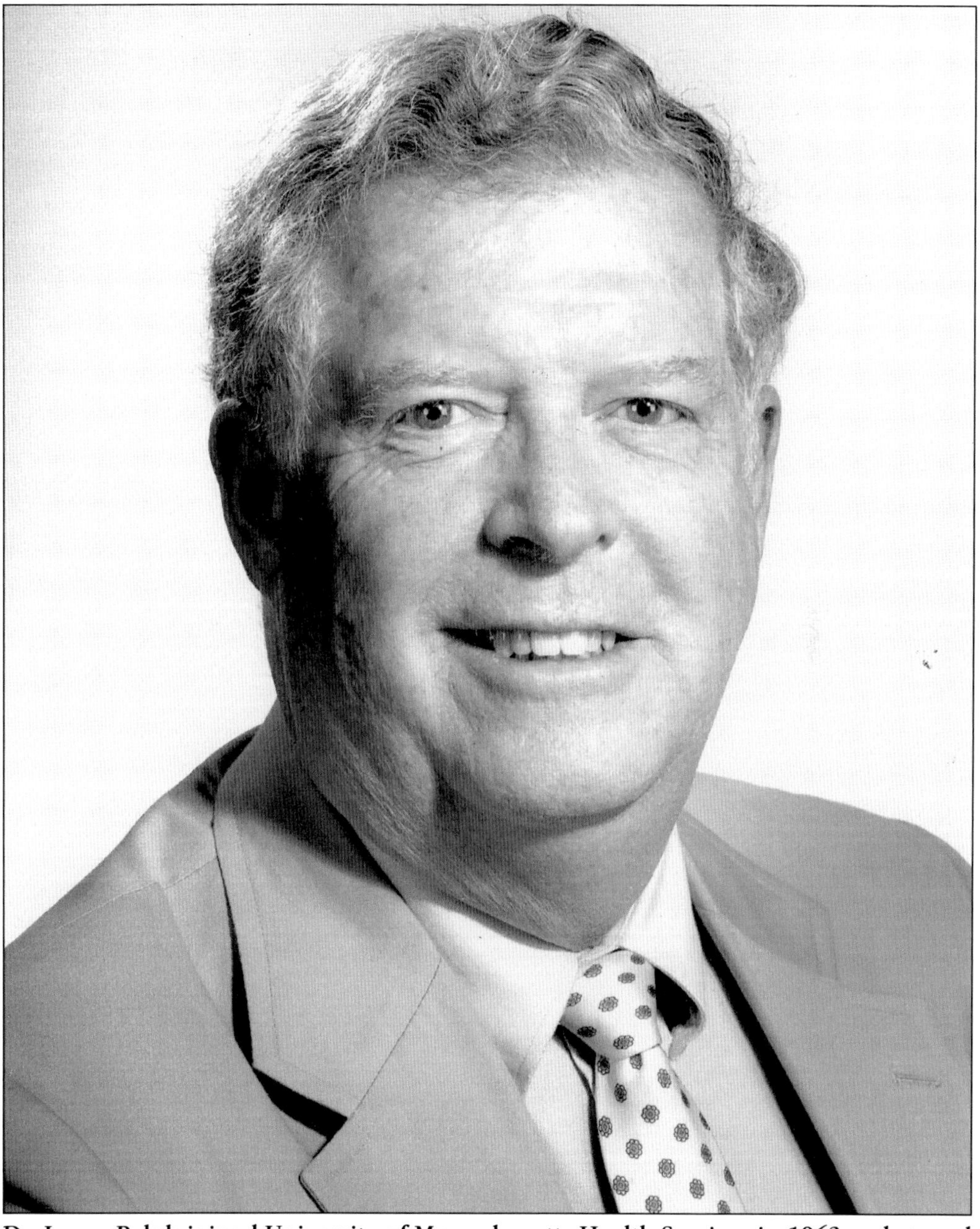

Dr. James Ralph joined University of Massachusetts Health Services in 1963 and started his 33-year career as team physician in 1964. As team physician, he worked primarily with the football and men's basketball teams, but also worked closely with other sports, including women's basketball and men's and women's gymnastics. Dr. Ralph was presented with the UMass Chancellor's Citation Award in 1991. He was also given a special award by the football captains in 1986 for his service to football, and was presented with a Final Four ring by the basketball team in 1996 for his outstanding service to men's basketball. A native of Bennington, Vermont, Ralph retired from service to the university in 1997. He resides in Amherst with his wife, Edie. He was inducted into the UMass Sports Hall of Fame in 1999.

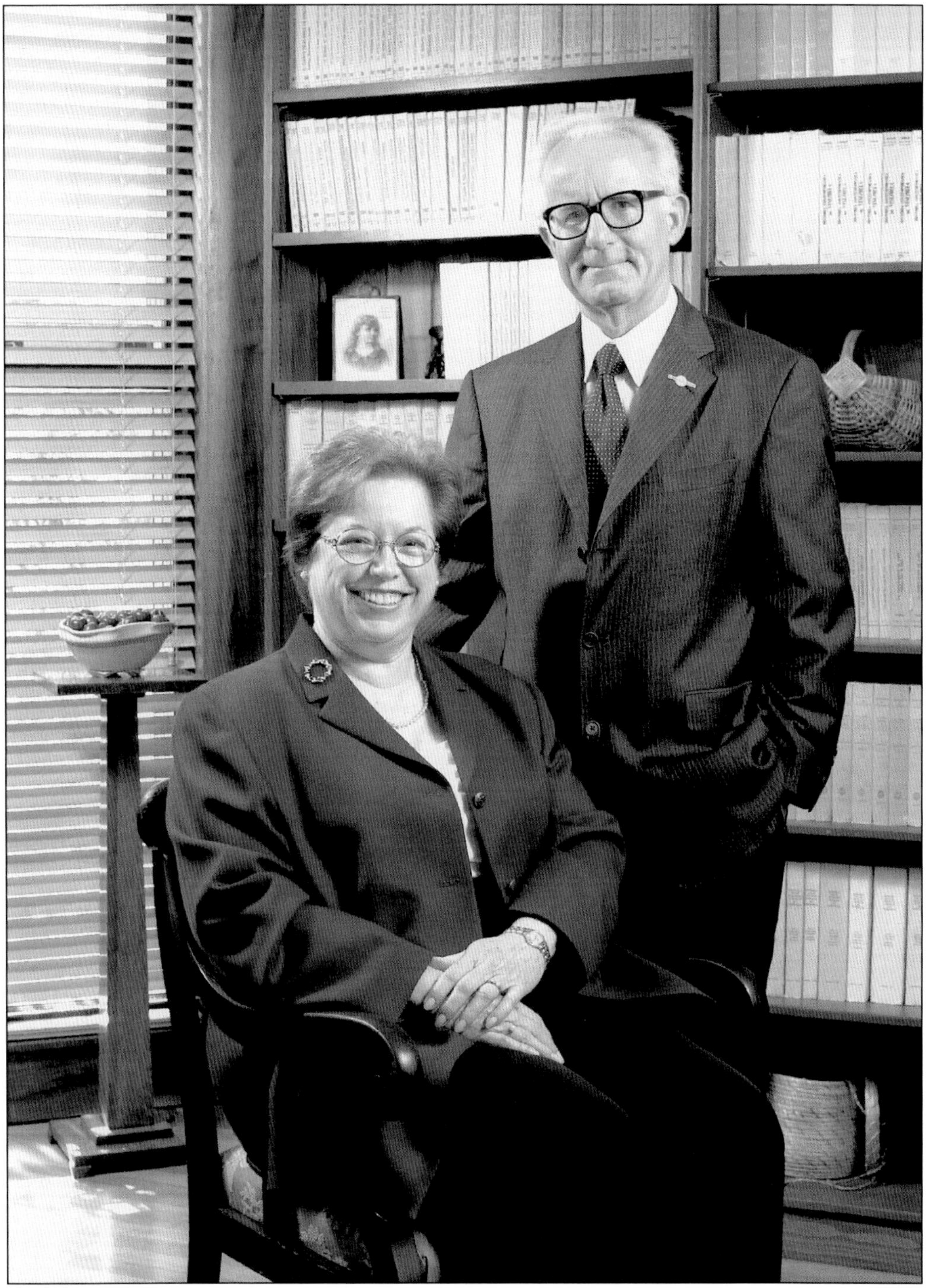

The chancellor and first lady of the campus, John Lombardi and his wife, Cathryn, arrived on campus on July 1, 2002. The former president of the University of Florida, John Lombardi became the 26th person to lead the Amherst campus. John V. Lombardi was born in Los Angeles in 1942. He received his bachelor's degree from Pomona College in 1963, a master's in 1964, and a doctorate in 1968 from Colombia University.

Three

Growth

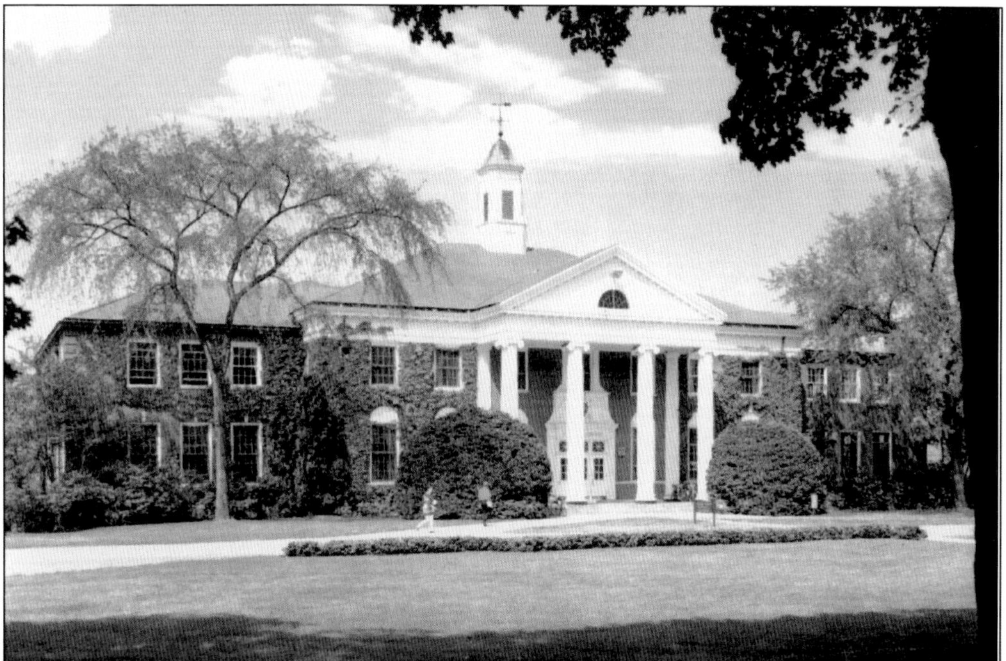

Goodell Library was built in 1934 and is named after Henry Hill Goodell, the ninth president of Massachusetts Agricultural College, who served from 1886 to 1905.

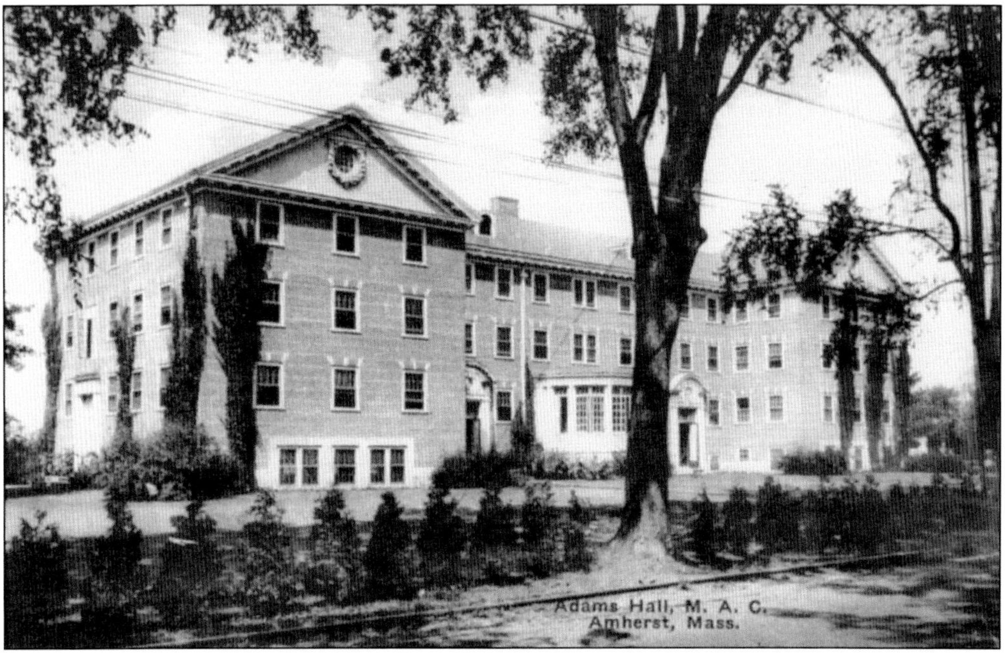

Called the Abbey, the Abigail Adams House, built in 1920, was the first all-female dorm on the Massachusetts Agricultural College campus. While many men were off to war, more women started to attend the college.

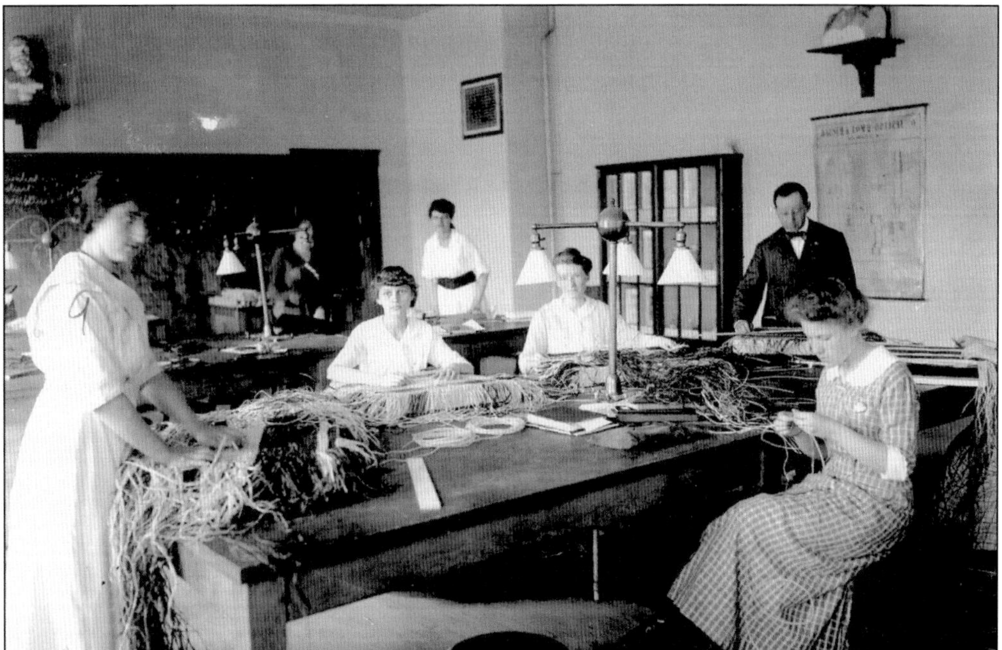

Women at Massachusetts Agricultural College were mandated to take courses in home economics. This photograph shows female students diligently weaving mats. (Photograph courtesy of the Special Collections and Archives, W.E.B. Du Bois Library, University of Massachusetts Amherst.)

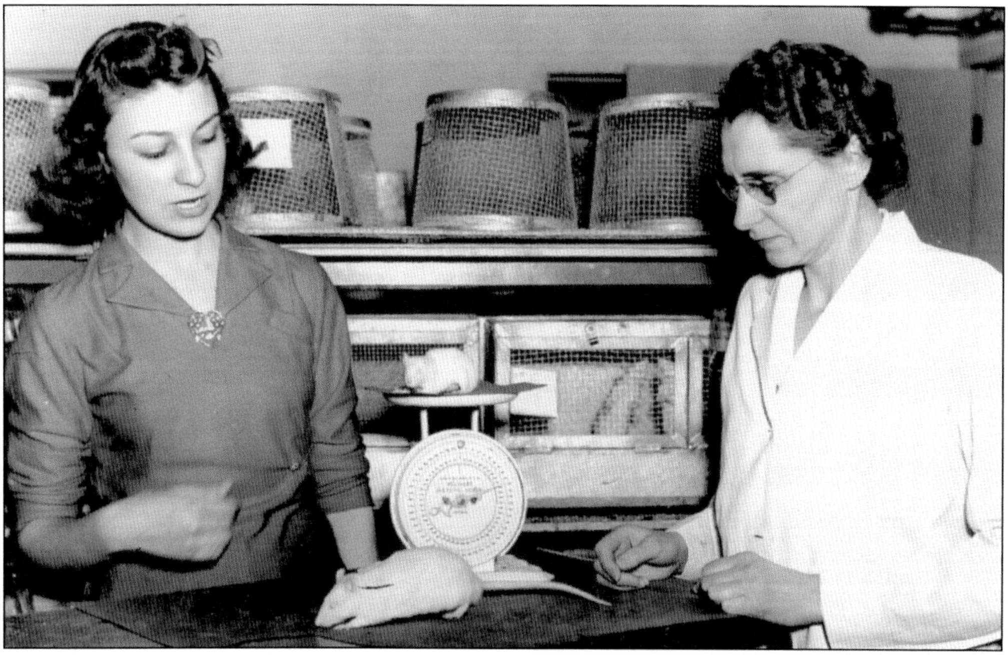

Two female students are shown here reluctantly weighing rats in a science class. In 1919, new courses were instituted for women, who were becoming a more and more significant part of the campus population. Most of the initial courses offered to women were in the fields of home economics and nursing. (Photograph courtesy of the Special Collections and Archives, W.E.B. Du Bois Library, University of Massachusetts Amherst.)

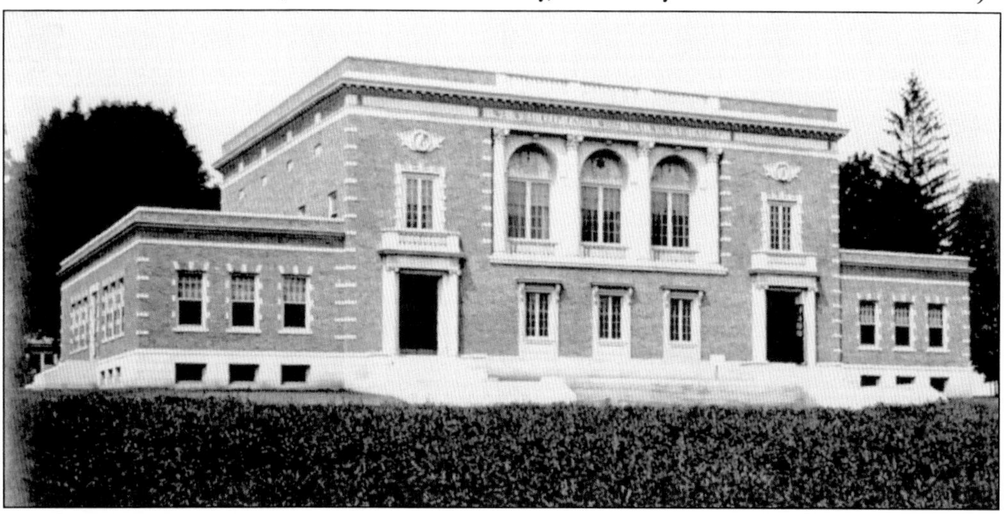

"We will keep faith with you while you sleep" are the words mounted on Memorial Hall. Memorial Hall is the commemorative building that honors the 51 alumni, students, and faculty who died in World War I. The North Room on the second floor has remained a memorial room since the building opened in 1921. Until the opening of the Student Union Building, Memorial Hall housed most of the student organizations as well as a bowling alley and an art gallery. During the anti-war movement in the 1960s, students protested the Vietnam War on and around the building. Today, Memorial Hall hosts the alumni association and the development office.

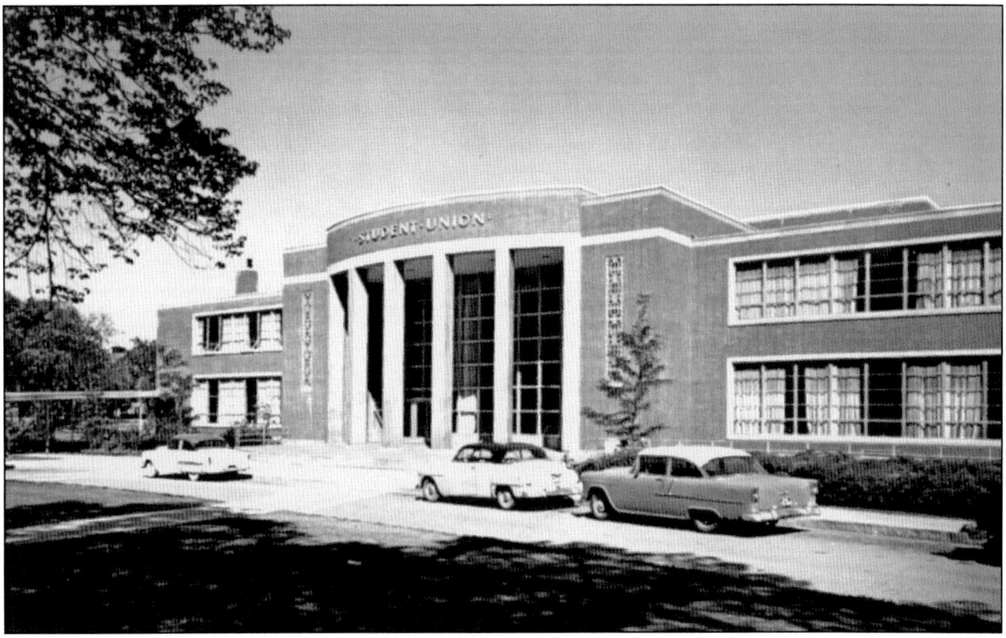

The Student Union Building opened its doors in February 1957. It was a welcome addition to the modern campus and serves as an artery for students passing through campus. The Student Union Building houses most of the RSOs (Registered Student Organizations), a barber shop, the Hatch cafeteria, a bowling alley, a video arcade, and a ballroom-auditorium.

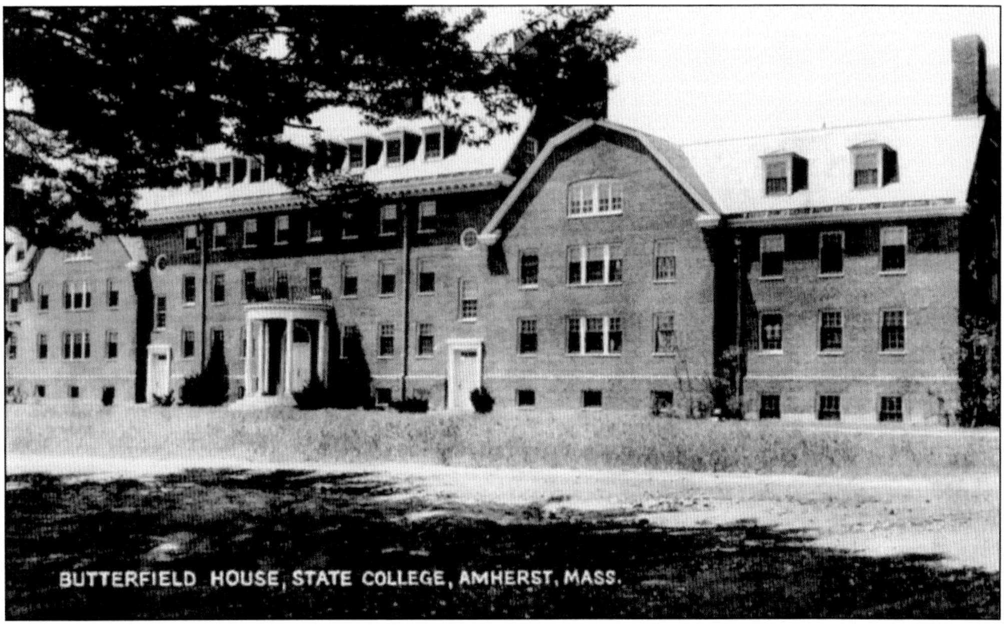

Built in 1940 and named after Kenyon L. Butterfield, the Butterfield House housed one of the campus cafeterias and continues to serve as a dorm in the central part of the campus for students in the Commonwealth College program.

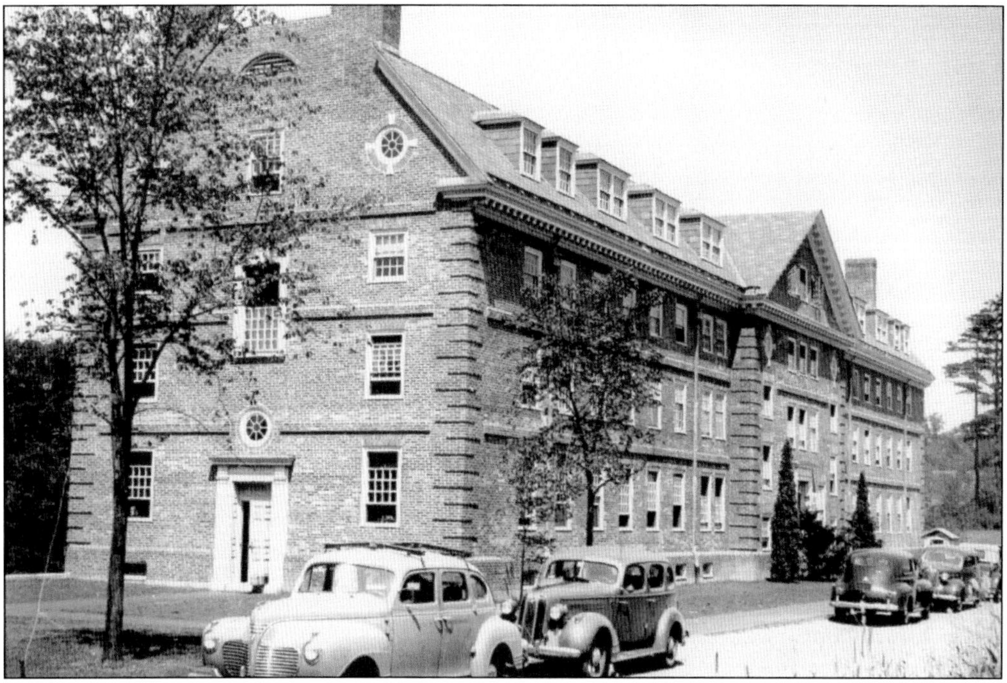

Named after James Carruthers Greenough, the sixth president of Massachusetts Agricultural College, this dormitory was built in 1946 to accommodate the post–World War II applicants to UMass. (Photograph courtesy of the Special Collections and Archives, W.E.B. Du Bois Library, University of Massachusetts Amherst.)

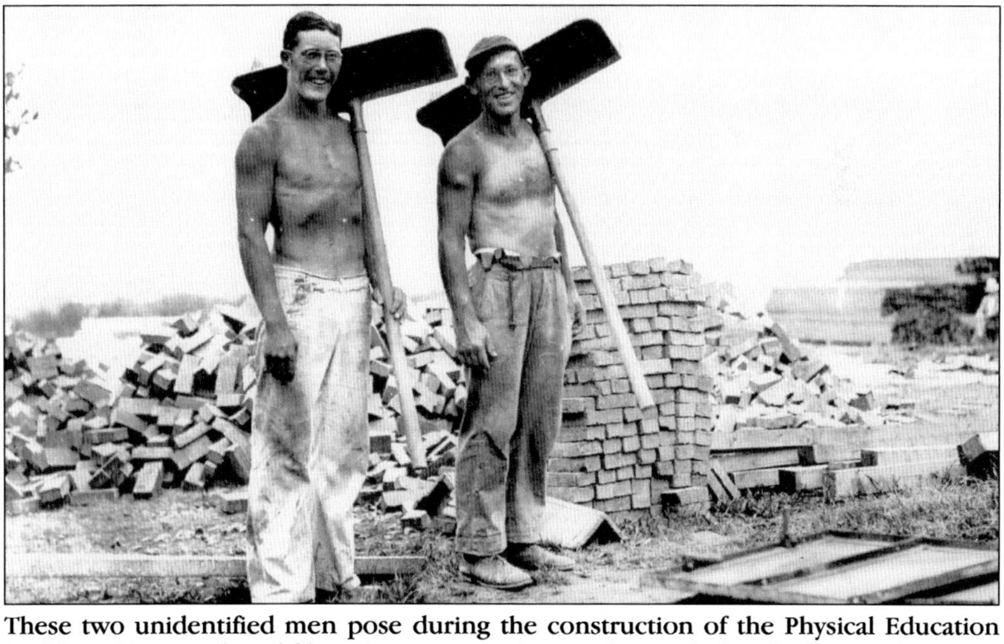

These two unidentified men pose during the construction of the Physical Education Building. Many rank-and-file union construction workers toiled in the heat and snow to build the UMass campus. (Photograph courtesy of the Special Collections and Archives, W.E.B. Du Bois Library, University of Massachusetts Amherst.)

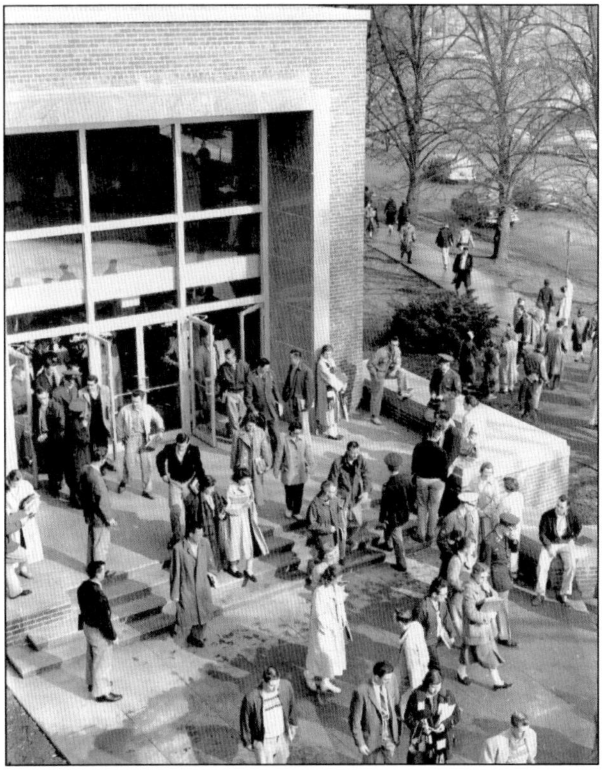

Machmer Hall, built in 1957, is named after William L. Machmer, professor of mathematics. Machmer Hall stands on the site of old North College. Students are seen here congregating between classes in 1960. (Photograph courtesy of the Special Collections and Archives, W.E.B. Du Bois Library, University of Massachusetts Amherst.)

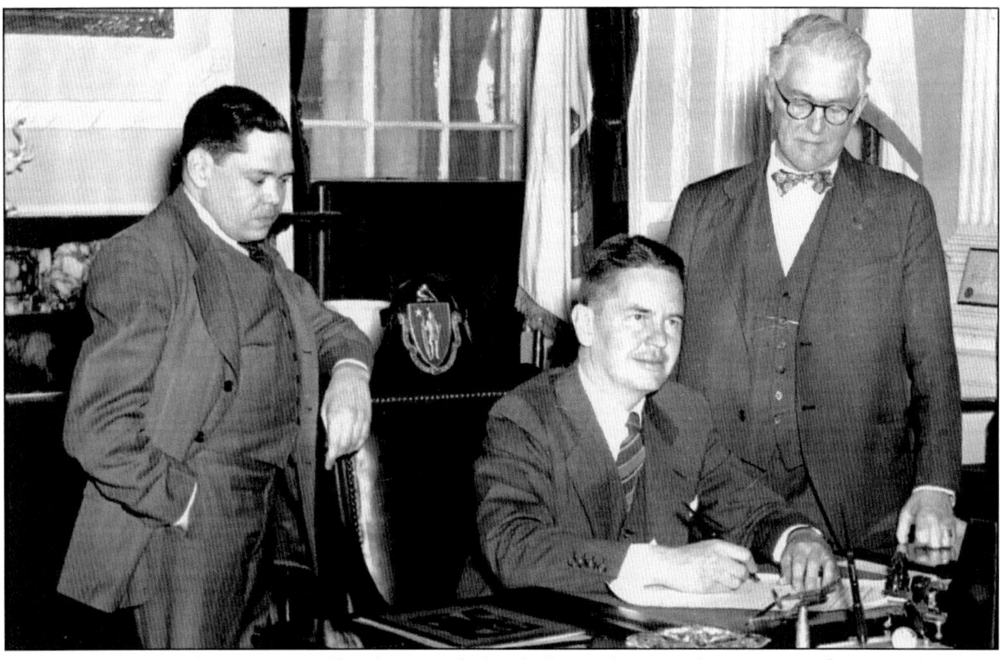

In 1947, Gov. Robert F. Bradford signed the bill to change the name of Massachusetts State College to the University of Massachusetts. Sen. Ralph Mahar and Pres. Hugh Baker witnessed the historic legislation. (Photograph courtesy of the Special Collections and Archives, W.E.B. Du Bois Library, University of Massachusetts Amherst.)

The Massachusetts State College campus sign next to Clark Hall is seen here *c.* 1935. (Photograph courtesy of the Special Collections and Archives, W.E.B. Du Bois Library, University of Massachusetts Amherst.)

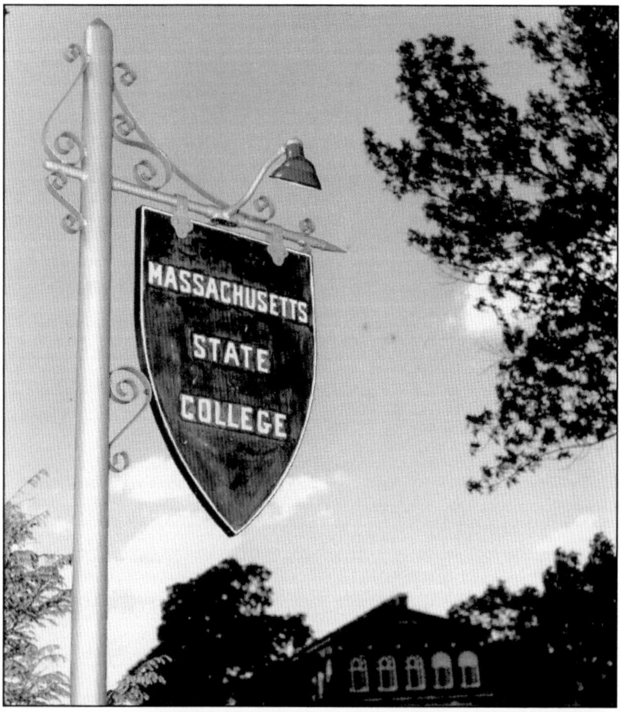

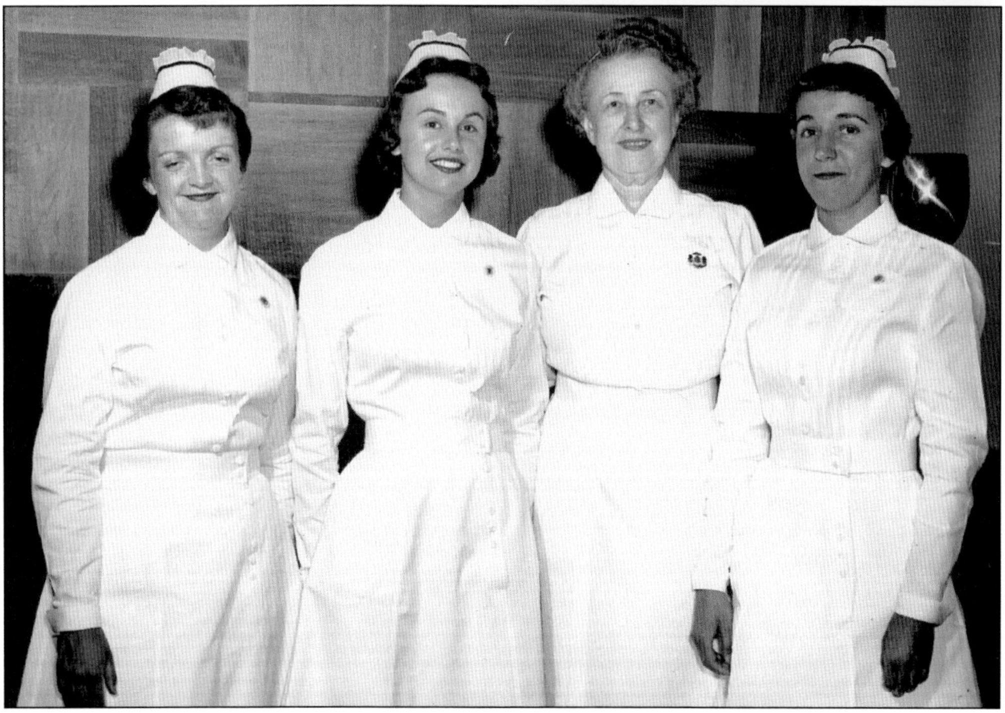

Shown here are, from left to right, Elizabeth Brown, Doris Kiesling, Mary Jean Maher, and Cynthia Sowydia, all nursing students of the class of 1959. (Photograph courtesy of the Special Collections and Archives, W.E.B. Du Bois Library, University of Massachusetts Amherst.)

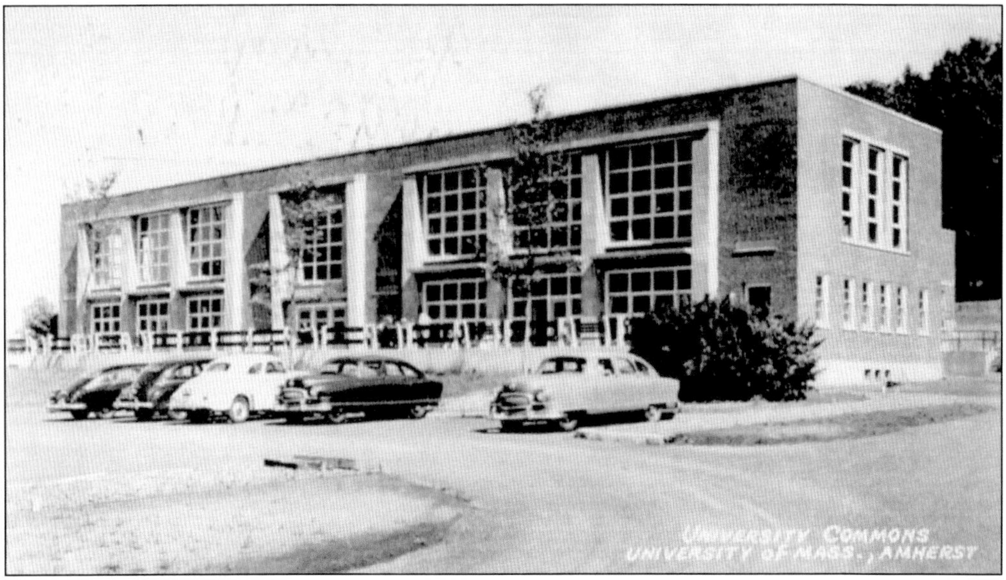

Set in the Northeast residential section of the campus, Worcester Dining Hall was built to offset the large number of students who enrolled after World War II. Until Worcester Dining Hall came along, Draper Hall was the only dining hall on campus. In 2004, the current dining halls on campus are all named after the western counties of Massachusetts: Worcester, Franklin, Hampden, and Berkshire.

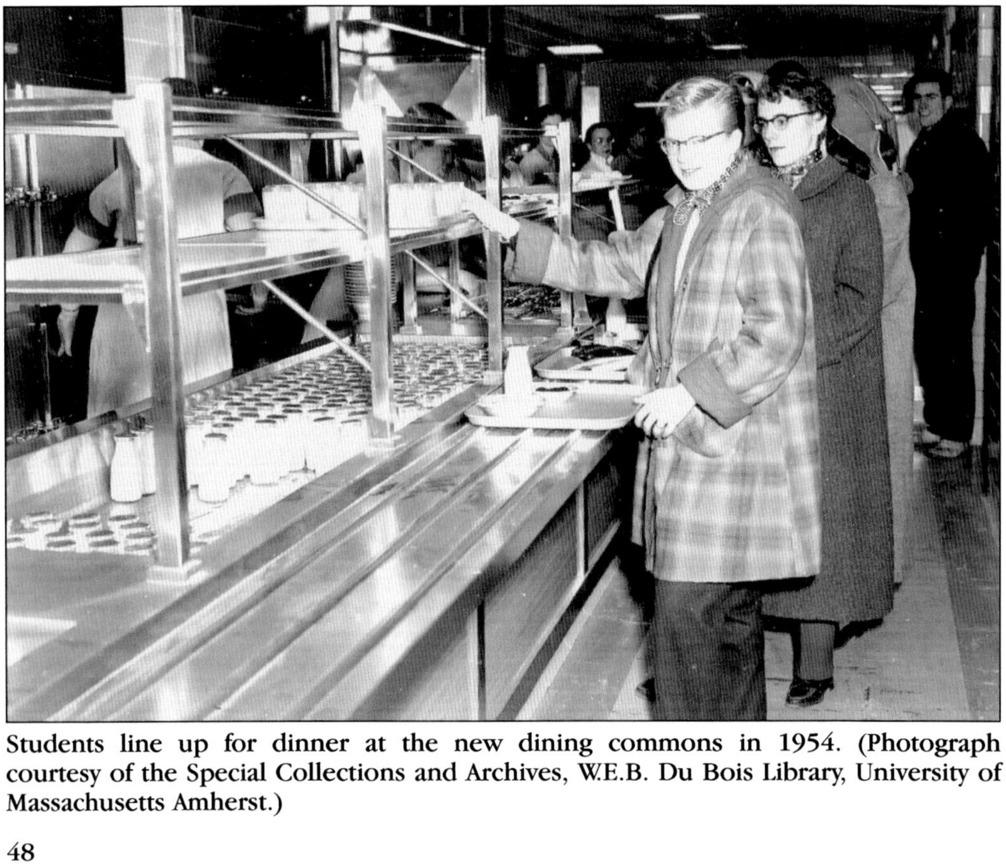

Students line up for dinner at the new dining commons in 1954. (Photograph courtesy of the Special Collections and Archives, W.E.B. Du Bois Library, University of Massachusetts Amherst.)

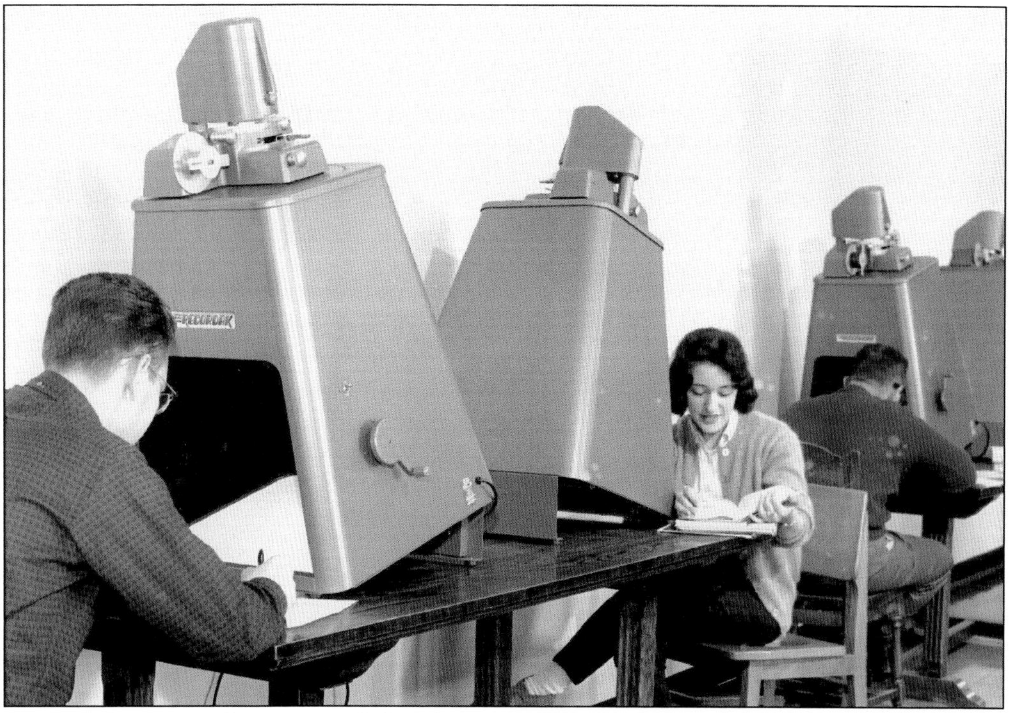

Two students study in Goodell Library using the then state-of-the-art microfilm machines. (Photograph courtesy of the Special Collections and Archives, W.E.B. Du Bois Library, University of Massachusetts Amherst.)

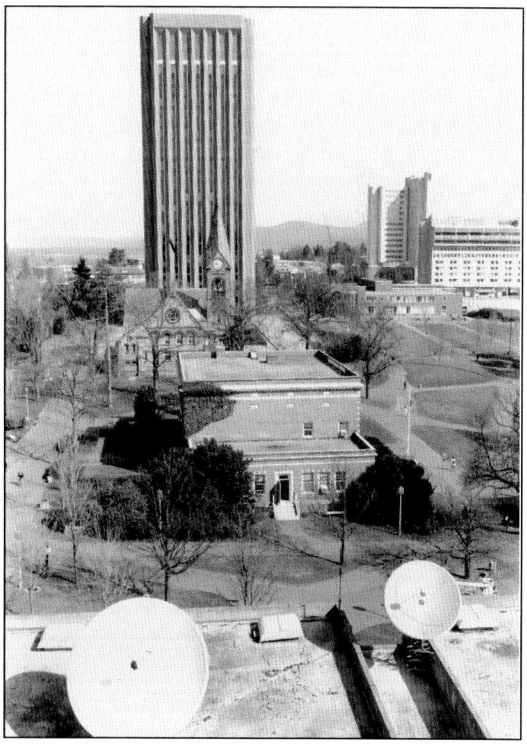

This view from Herter Hall depicts the current campus, with both old and new buildings mixed together. (Photograph courtesy of the Special Collections and Archives, W.E.B. Du Bois Library, University of Massachusetts Amherst.)

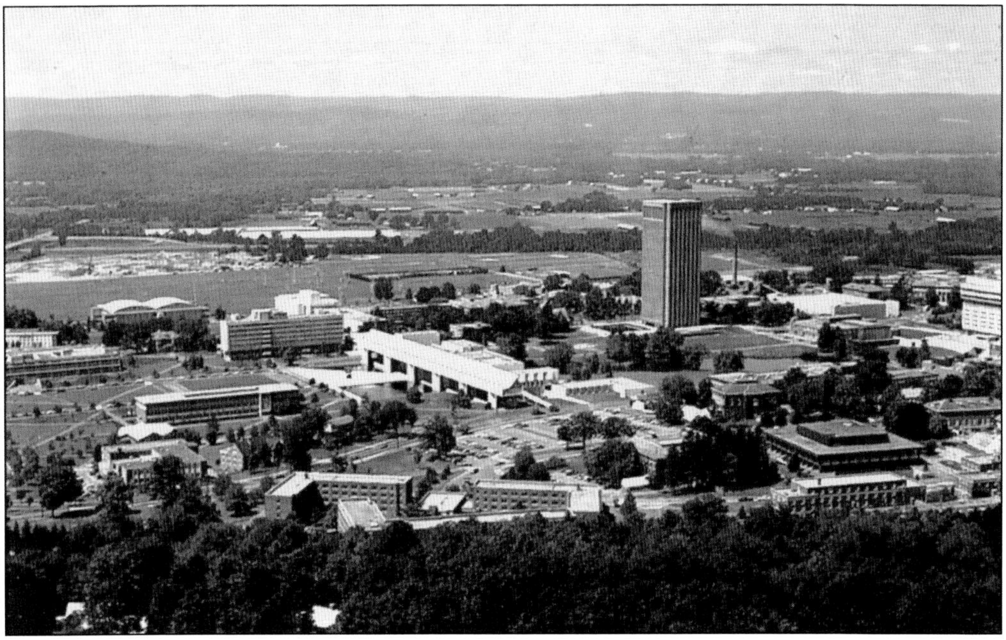

This photograph depicts the massive physical plant of the University of Massachusetts Amherst. The modern-day campus has come a long way from the original 4 buildings that existed in 1867; there are 350 buildings in 2004. There are 585 classrooms on campus, 24 teaching auditoriums, 412 acres of lawns, 94 acres of parking lots, 45.5 acres of roofs, 16 miles of campus roads, 30 miles of water lines, 350 miles of electrical conductor lines, and 58 miles of paved sidewalks. (Photograph by Frank L. Forward.)

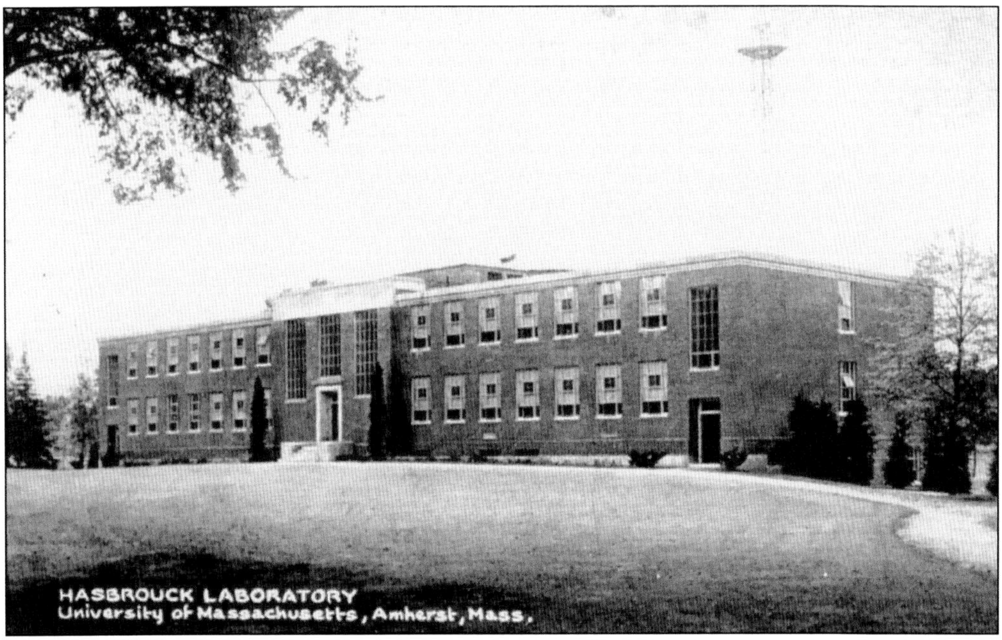

Hasbrouck Laboratory was built in 1949 and named after popular professor of mathematics Philip "Billy" Hasbrouck.

Four

THE JOHN W. LEDERLE YEARS: 1960–1970

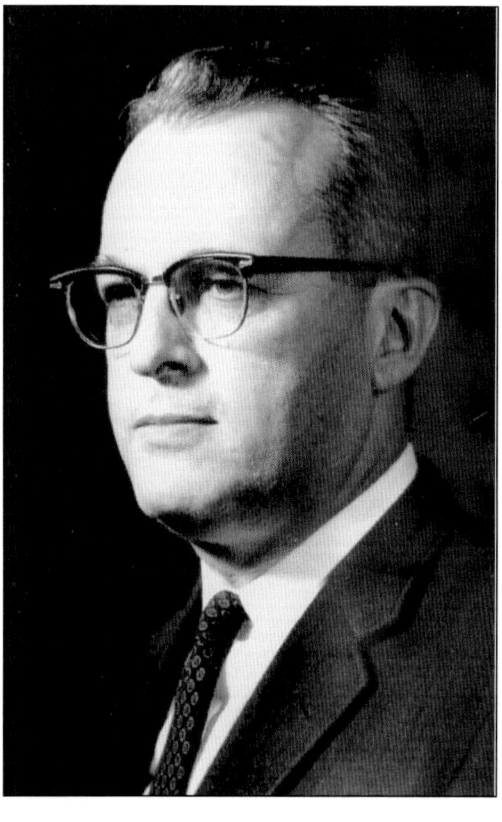

John Lederle was the 15th president of the University of Massachusetts. Born in Royal Oak, Michigan, he was a product of the Michigan public education system. Lederle took his bachelor's, master's, doctor of law, and doctor of philosophy degrees from the University of Michigan. Lederle is arguably the most effective and respected president in the long history of the University of Massachusetts. Under Lederle's tutelage, UMass tripled its enrollment, 70 new buildings were built, two new campuses were added (Boston and Worcester), and the budget went from $13,065,845 to $107,883,774. Professors' salaries rose from $9,942 to $21,126. (Photograph courtesy of the Special Collections and Archives, W.E.B. Du Bois Library, University of Massachusetts Amherst.)

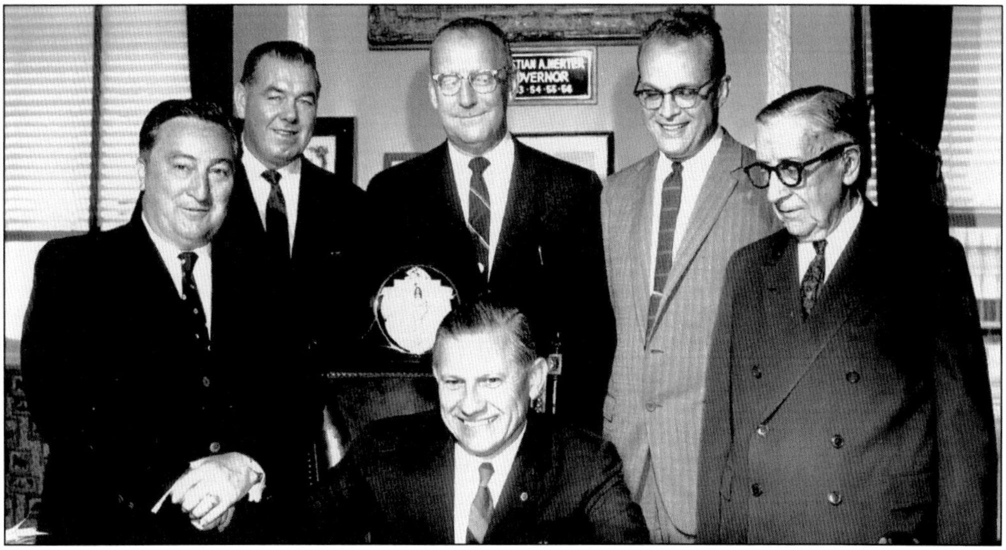

In 1962, Gov. John Volpe signed an important piece of legislation that gave President Lederle's administration the fiscal autonomy to hire faculty and staff and purchase supplies without state restrictions. Due to this legislation, Lederle was able to grow the University of Massachusetts Amherst campus from a cow college to a city in just 10 years. Pictured in this image, from left to right, are the following: Senate president John Powers, Speaker of the House John "Iron Duke" Thompson, minority leader Maurice Donahue, President Lederle, and trustee Frank L. Boyden. (Photograph courtesy of the Special Collections and Archives, W.E.B. Du Bois Library, University of Massachusetts Amherst.)

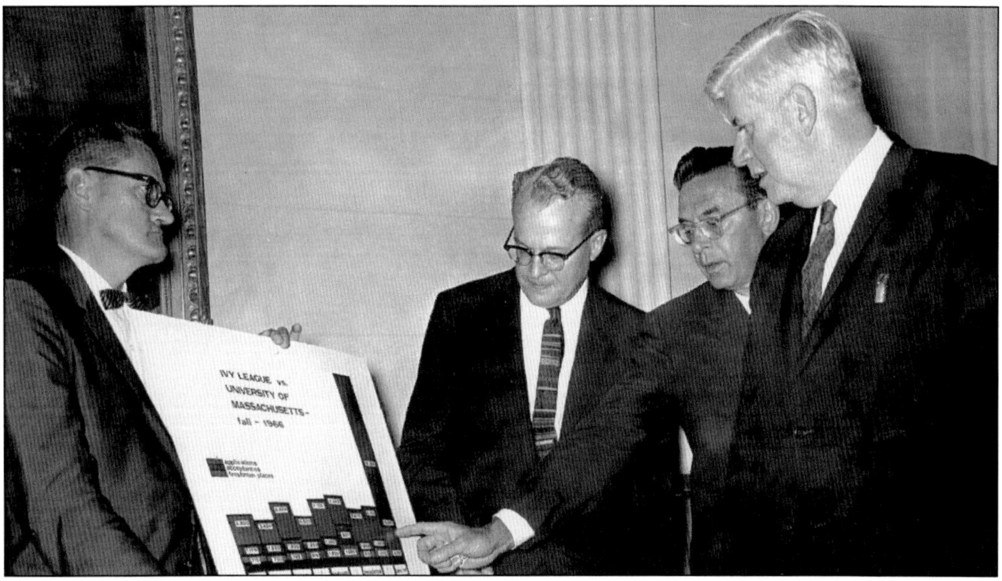

Leo Redfern, dean of university planning, holds a growth chart of the university campus while Pres. John Lederle (center) explains his needs to Congressmen Richard Boland and Thomas P. "Tip" O'Neill, both democrats from Massachusetts. During Lederle's tenure, 70 new buildings were constructed, bringing the number of buildings on campus to 300. (Photograph courtesy of the Special Collections and Archives, W.E.B. Du Bois Library, University of Massachusetts Amherst.)

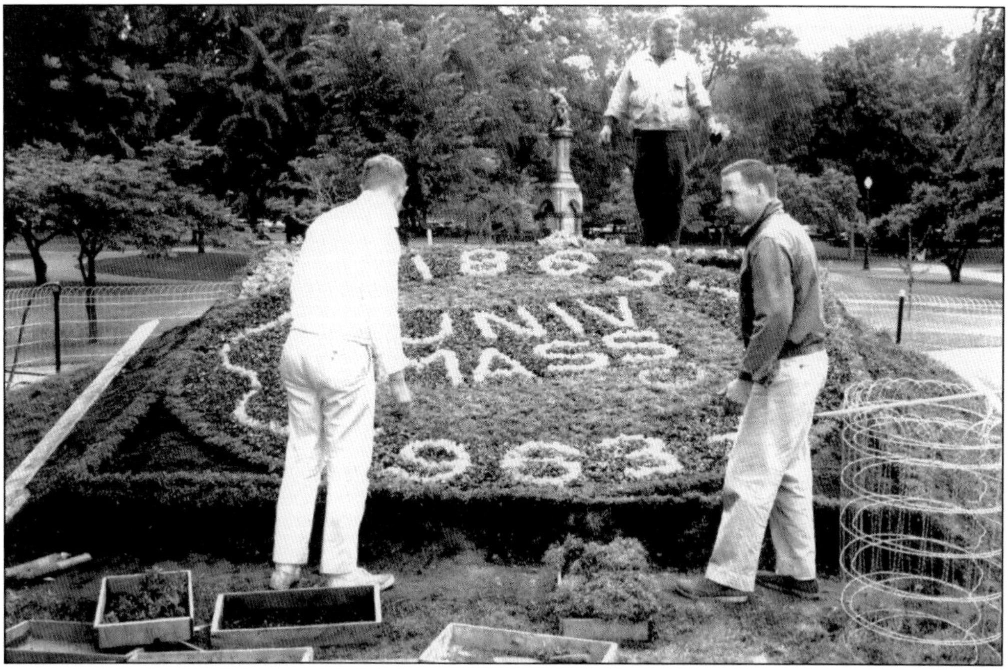

Campus physical plant personnel prepare a flower garden for the 100 year anniversary celebration on campus. The University of Massachusetts was established in 1863 as Massachusetts Agricultural College. It was one of the first institutions of its kind to be founded in the United States under the Morrill Land Grant Act of 1862. Mass Aggie was accepted by the Massachusetts Legislature on April 18, 1863. (Photograph courtesy of the Special Collections and Archives, W.E.B. Du Bois Library, University of Massachusetts Amherst.)

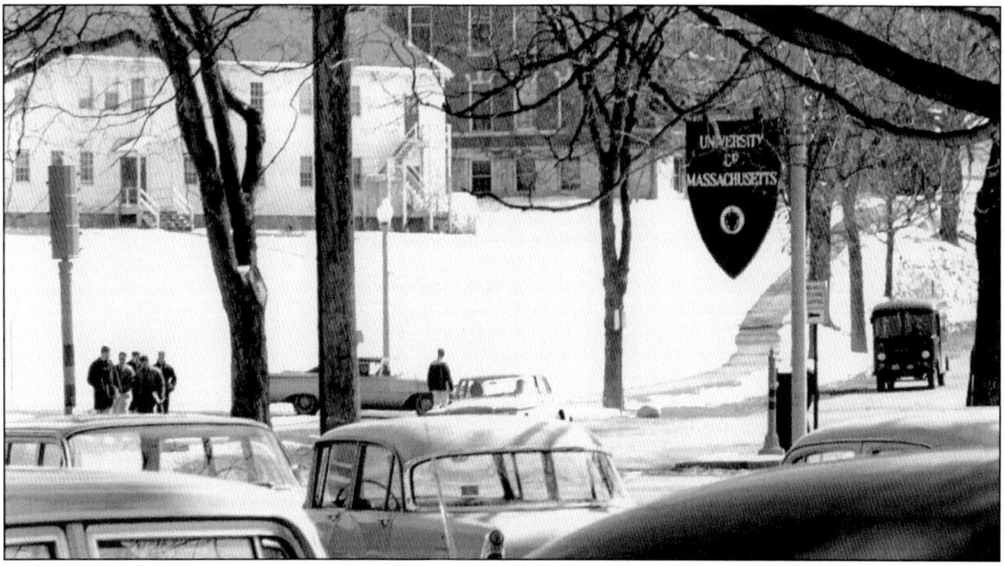

On April 18, 1963, the UMass campus was bustling with students, faculty, staff, and alumni, all celebrating the university's 1863 charter. (Photograph courtesy of the Special Collections and Archives, W.E.B. Du Bois Library, University of Massachusetts Amherst.)

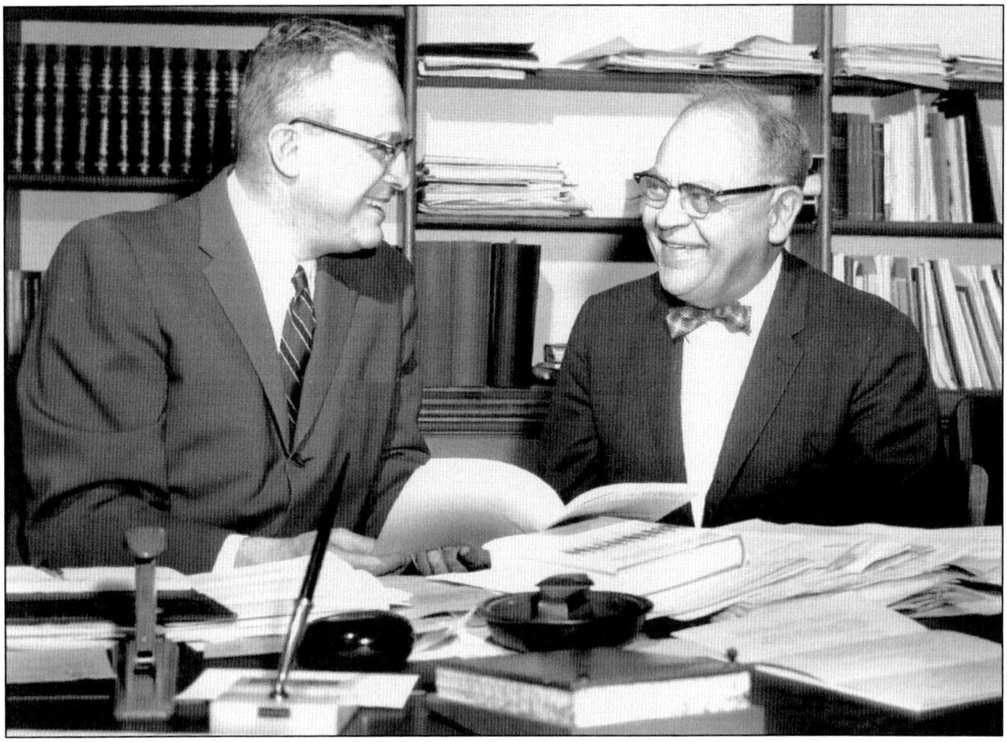

In this image, Pres. John W. Lederle shares a laugh with Philip L. Whitmore. Whitmore is an alumnus, the president of the alumni association, a university trustee, and a state representative from nearby Sunderland. The Whitmore Administration Building, built in 1967, is named after Philip Whitmore.

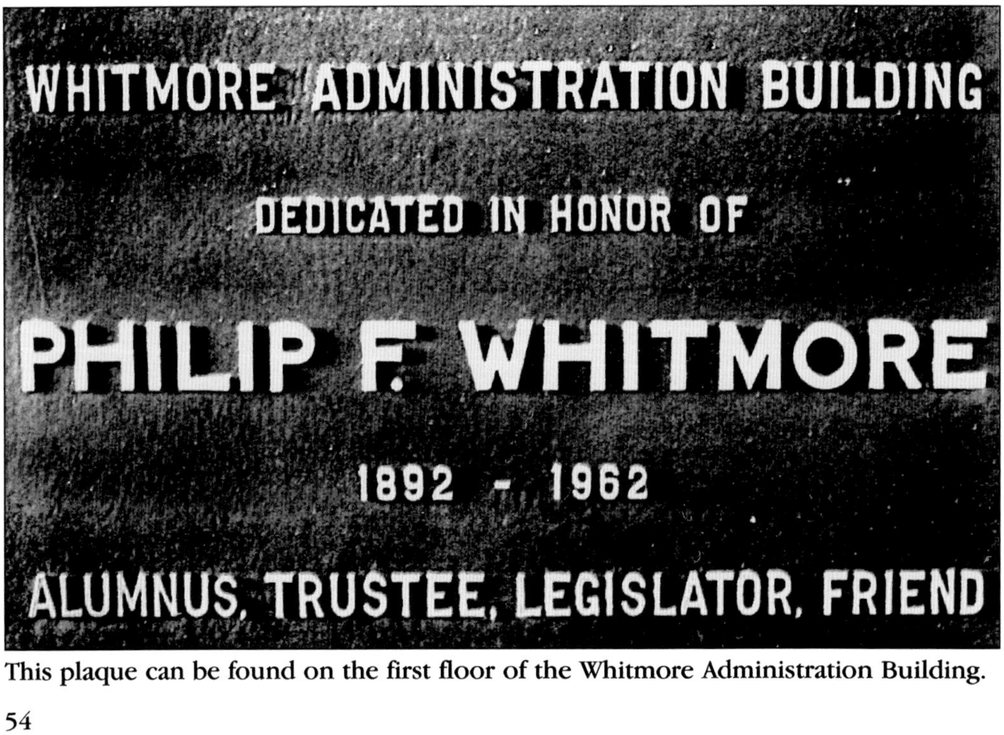

This plaque can be found on the first floor of the Whitmore Administration Building.

In the Lederle years, Massachusetts legislators constantly received invitations to visit campus. Given that the distance between the capital and campus was 100 miles, President Lederle used to send a bus to pick up legislators at 8:00 a.m. at the statehouse. The bus would bring them to campus and then drop them back in Boston by 4:00 p.m. Lederle felt strongly that members of the legislature needed to see and appreciate the "crown jewel of the west" if they were going to properly fund the institution. (Photograph courtesy of the Special Collections and Archives, W.E.B. Du Bois Library, University of Massachusetts Amherst.)

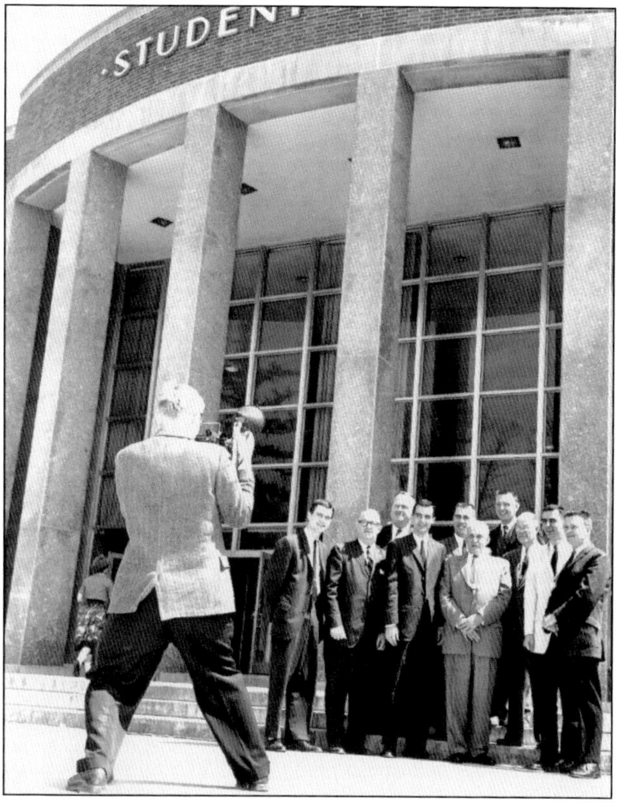

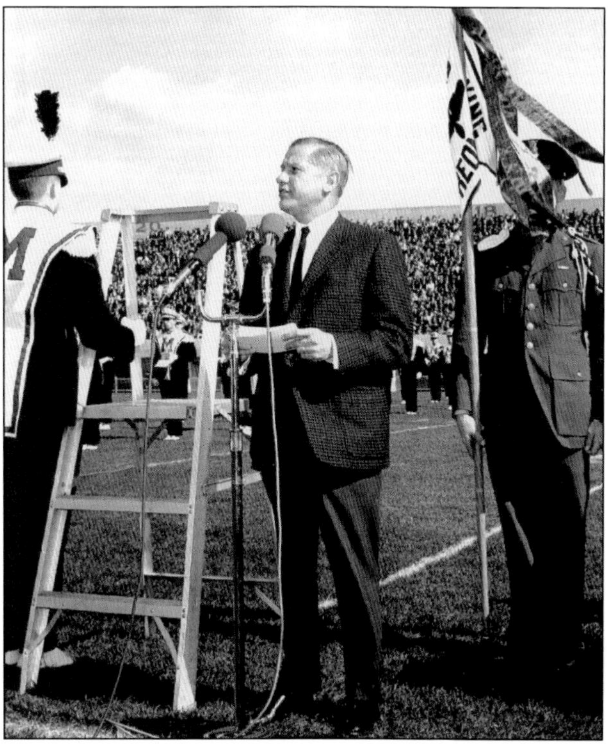

Gov. John Volpe was a frequent visitor to the UMass Amherst campus. President Lederle and wife Angie had a very cordial relationship with the Volpes. Pictured is Gov. John Volpe addressing the crowd at the 1962 homecoming football game. (Photograph courtesy of the Special Collections and Archives, W.E.B. Du Bois Library, University of Massachusetts Amherst.)

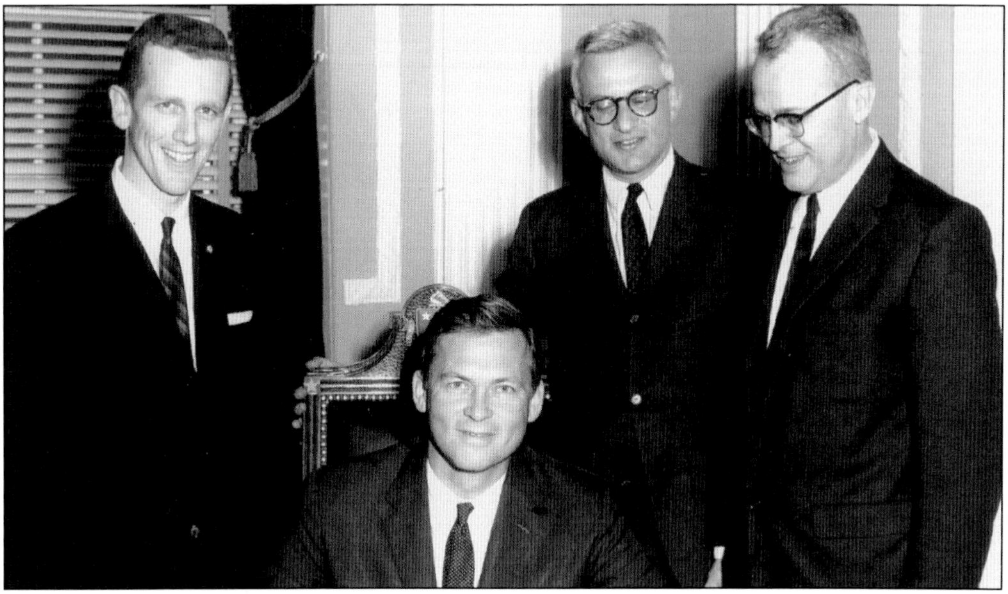

In June 1964, Gov. Endicott Peabody signed legislation to create the University of Massachusetts at Boston. Due to the demand of the new baby boomer generation (1945–1965), UMass Amherst was barraged with new applicants. In 1964 alone there were 20,000 applications for 3,500 slots. President Lederle, with the help of UMass Amherst alumnus David Bartley '56 (D-Holyoke) and Senators Maurice Donahue (D-Holyoke), George Kennealy (D-Dorchester), and house minority leader Bob Quinn (D-Dorchester) were able to secure a UMass Boston campus to relieve the applicant pool at UMass Amherst. Pictured above, from left to right, are the following: Rep. David Bartley, university administrator Robert Gordon, President Lederle, and Governor Peabody. (Photograph courtesy of the Special Collections and Archives, W.E.B. Du Bois Library, University of Massachusetts Amherst.)

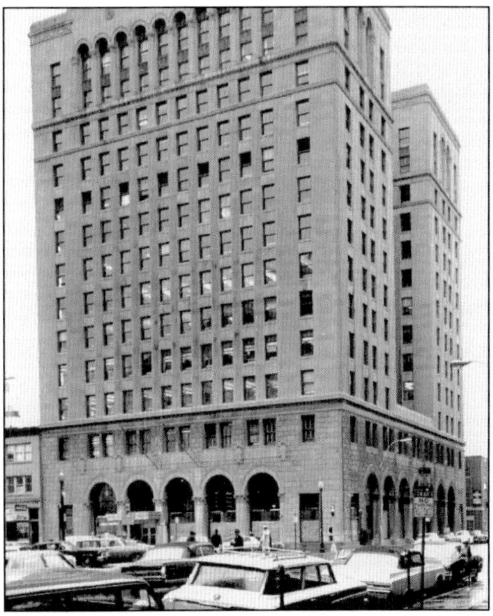

The old Boston Gas building in Park Square was the first home of UMass Boston, opening in September 1965. (Photograph courtesy of the Special Collections and Archives, W.E.B. Du Bois Library, University of Massachusetts Amherst.)

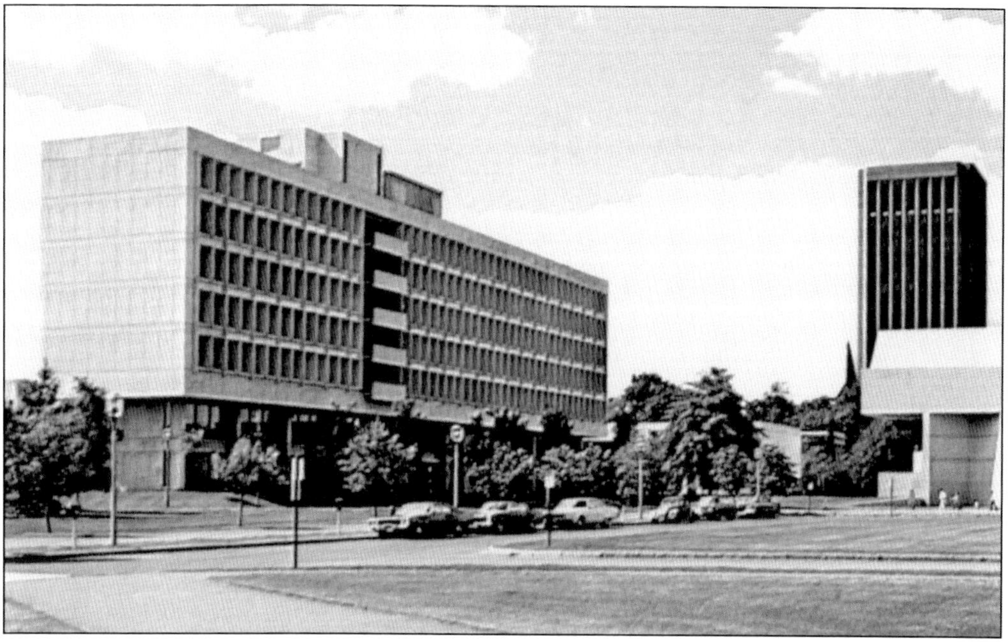

Herter Hall, named after Massachusetts governor Christian A. Herter (1953–1957), houses the history and language departments and the Herter Art Gallery. Commonly referred to by students as one of the concrete jungles on campus, Herter Hall was built in the early 1970s, the same era as the campus center, Whitmore, and the Fine Arts Center. (Photograph by Leonard Lorette.)

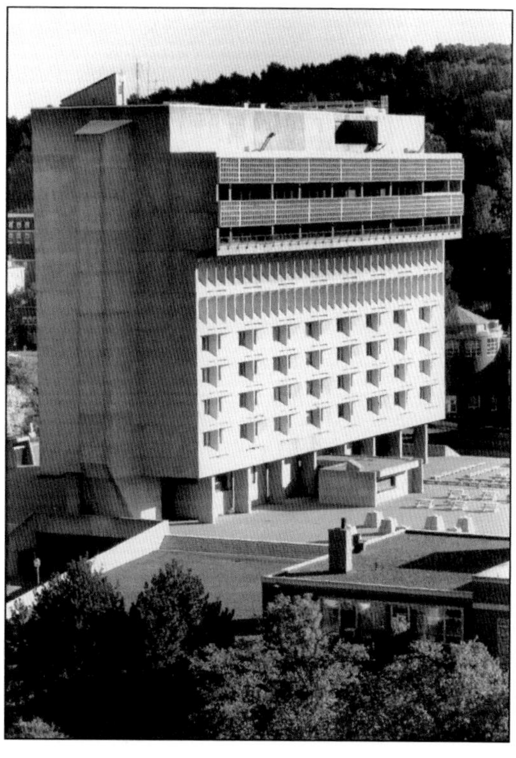

Named after Murray D. Lincoln of the Massachusetts Agricultural College class of 1914, the Murray D. Lincoln Campus Center serves as a hub for multiple activities. It houses a conference center and hotel for national institutes and associations. The Top of the Campus restaurant on the 10th floor offers the best view of the campus pond and Old Chapel. Lincoln served the university as the director of agriculture in the 1950s. (Photograph courtesy of the Special Collections and Archives, W.E.B. Du Bois Library, University of Massachusetts Amherst.)

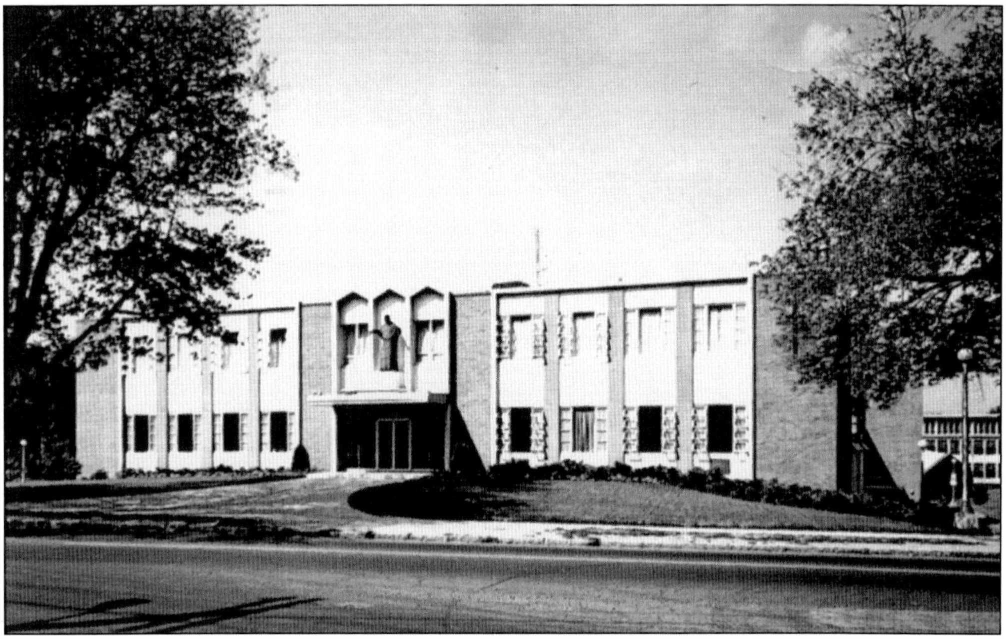

The Newman Center serves as the spiritual, educational, and social center for Catholic students. It was built by the Roman Catholic Diocese of Springfield in 1963.

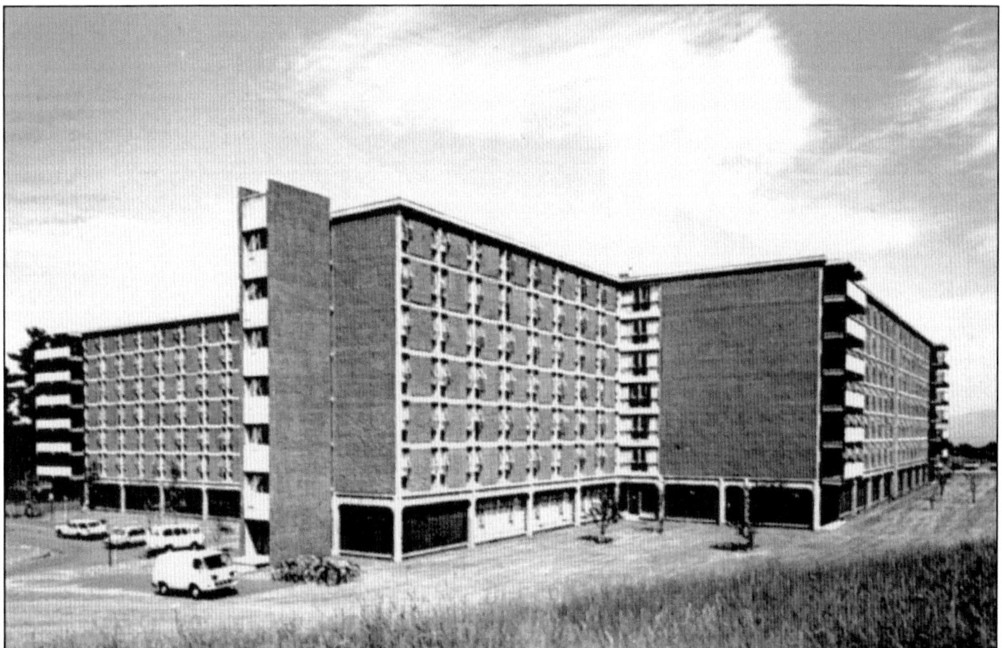

Referred to as Orchard Hill, these dorms were constructed in the middle of an apple orchard on the eastern part of the campus. Shown here are, from left to right, Grayson, Webster, and Field Halls, which all connect.

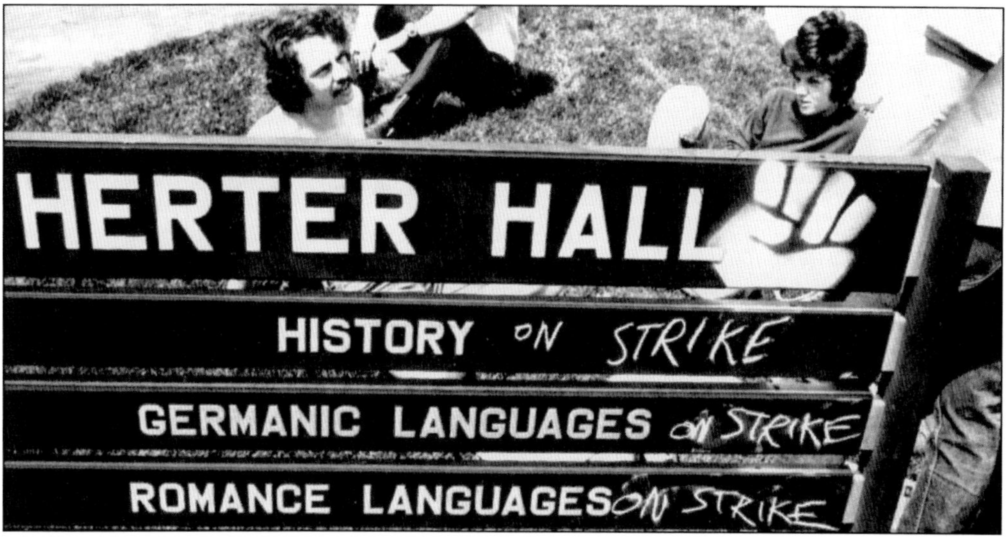

In the height of the Vietnam war, four students were killed by national guardsmen at Kent State in Ohio in May 1970. In the aftermath of the student killings, many college campuses went on strike to oppose the war. At UMass, students took over many buildings, and professors held classes outdoors. This photograph depicts the student strike in the spring of 1970, when students wrote on the campus sign at Herter Hall.

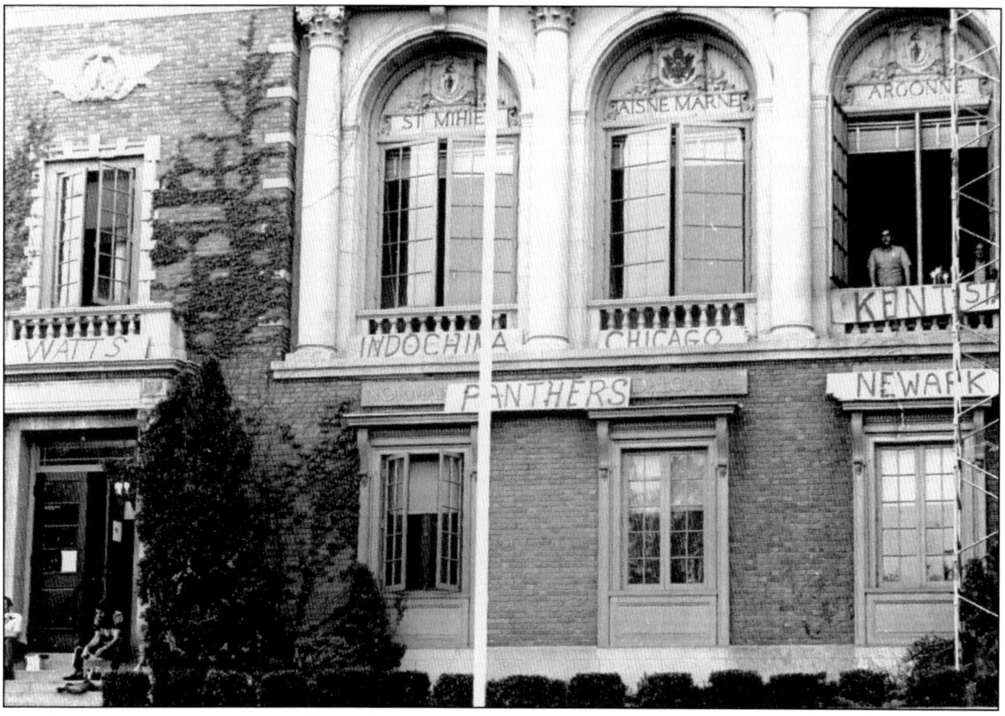

Students occupy Memorial Hall as a result of the 1970 Kent State massacre. Many students went on strike and refused to enter campus buildings. In the upper right corner, a student stands over a sign that reads "Kent State." (Photograph courtesy of the Special Collections and Archives, W.E.B. Du Bois Library, University of Massachusetts Amherst.).

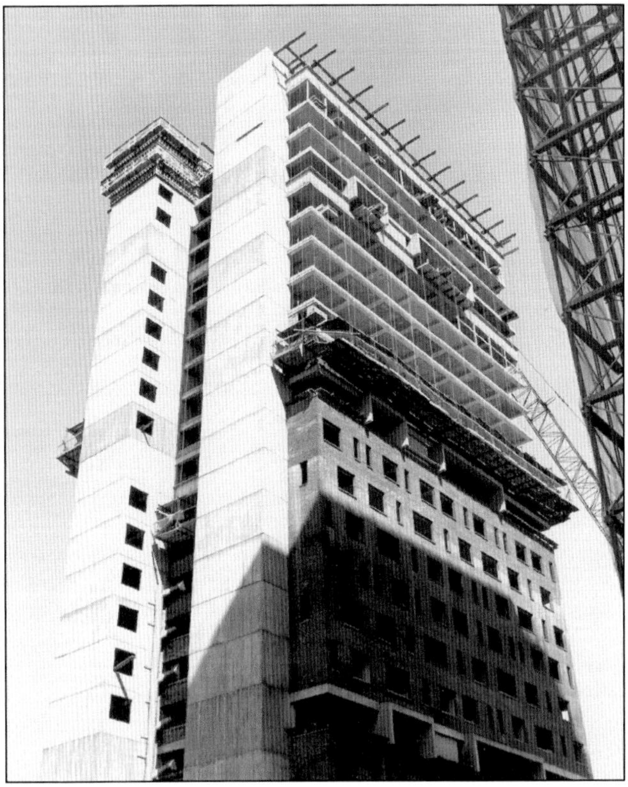

One of the Southwest residential towers is shown here under construction in 1965. Many of the building trade's union members logged in many miles to the Amherst campus in the 1960s. (Photograph courtesy of the Special Collections and Archives, W.E.B. Du Bois Library, University of Massachusetts Amherst.)

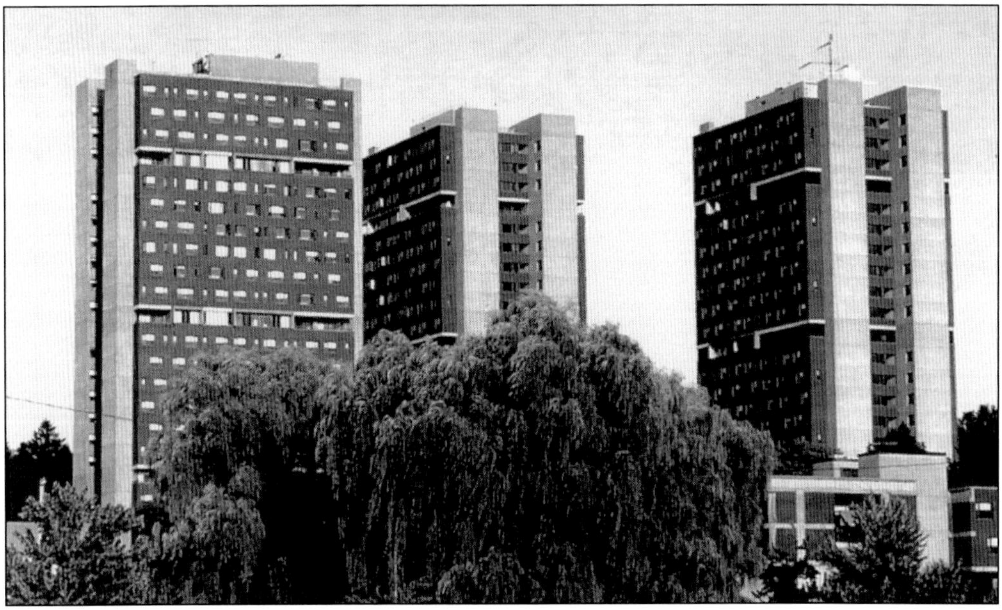

This view of campus shows the Southwest residential area, which was built to accommodate the huge influx of baby boomers demanding to attend college in Massachusetts. Southwest is made up of literally millions of yards of cement and countless miles of I-beams. There are five 22-story towers, twelve 3-story low-rise residence halls, and two dining commons. 5,400 students live in Southwest.

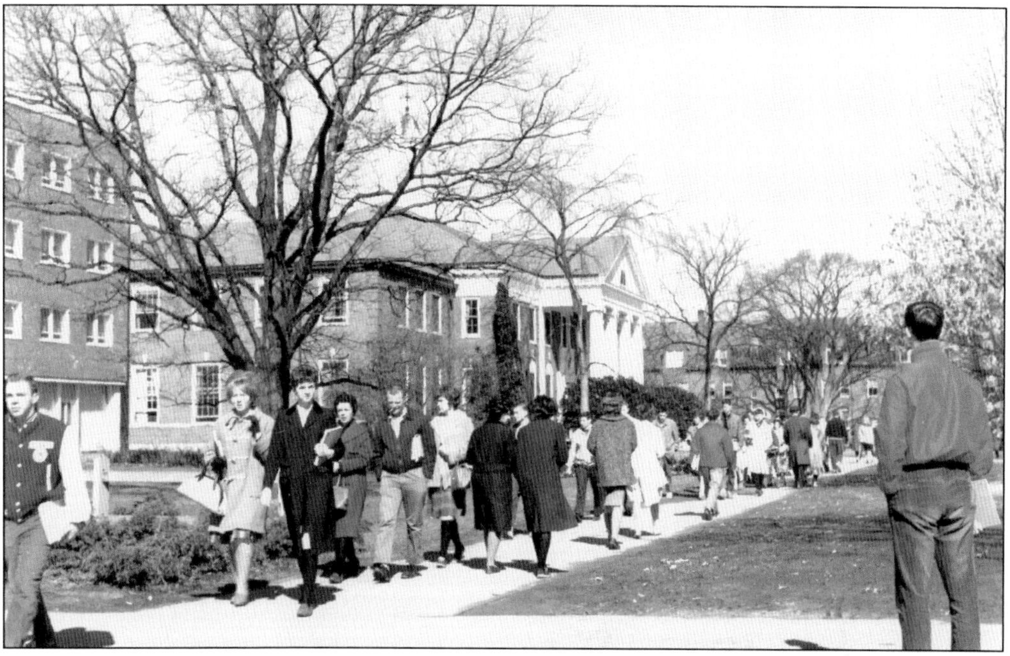

Students make their way from class to class between Goodell Library and Bartlett Hall on this beautiful fall day on campus in 1962. (Photograph courtesy of the Special Collections and Archives, W.E.B. Du Bois Library, University of Massachusetts Amherst.)

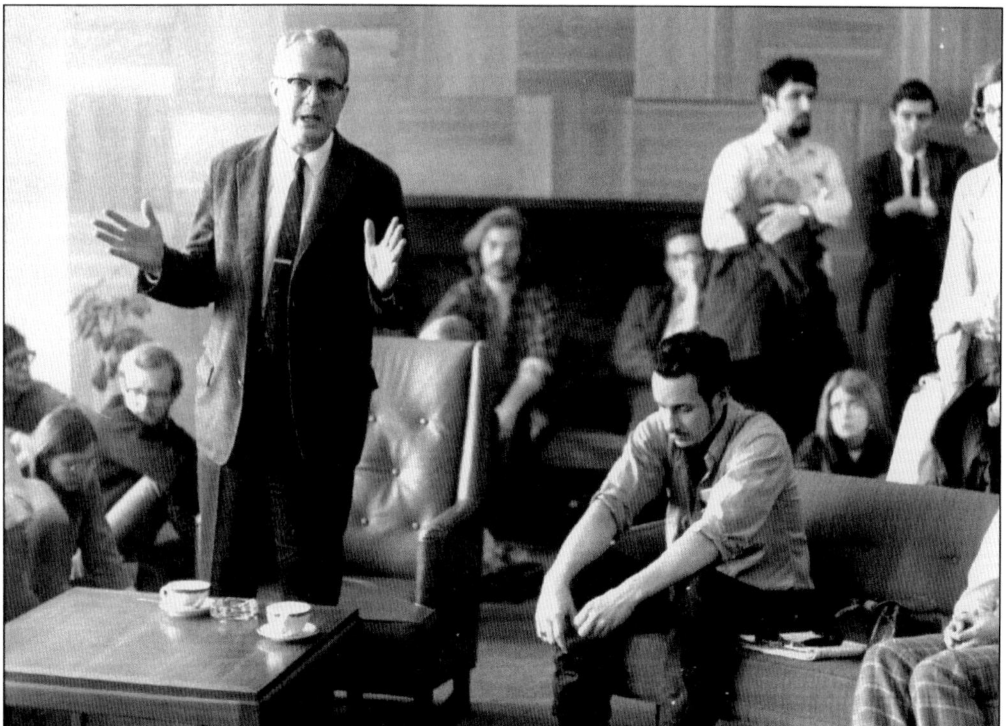

In this photograph, President Lederle speaks to students in the Student Union lounge. Lederle made it a point to be accessible to both the students and faculty.

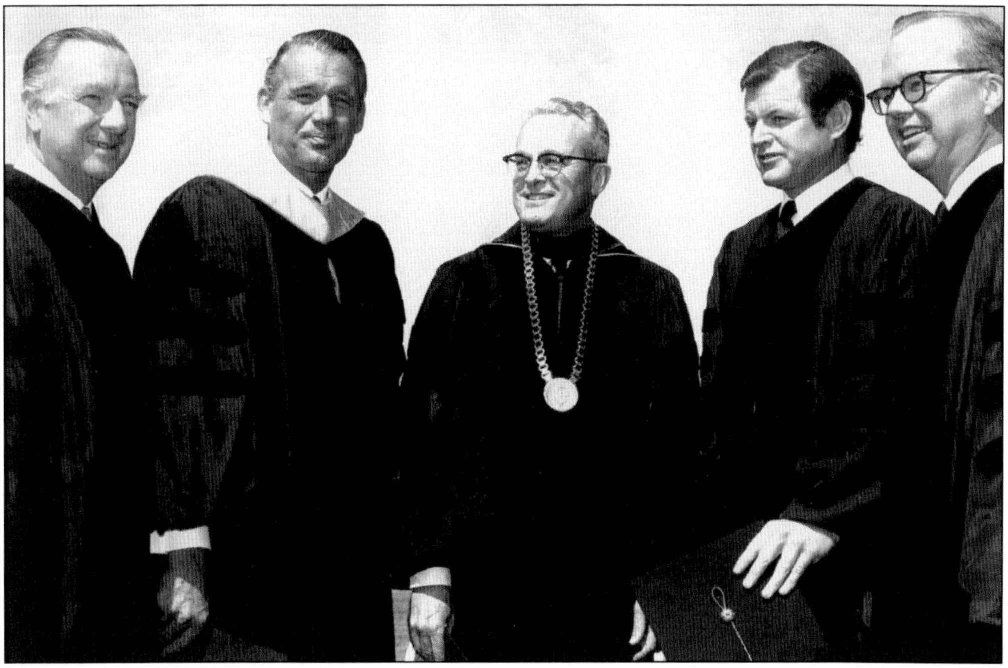

The commencement exercises of 1969 brought some heavy hitters to the campus. Shown in this image, from left to right, are the following: Walter Cronkite, Massachusetts governor Frank Sargent, President Lederle, Sen. Edward M. Kennedy, and an unidentified man. (Photograph courtesy of the Special Collections and Archives, W.E.B. Du Bois Library, University of Massachusetts Amherst.)

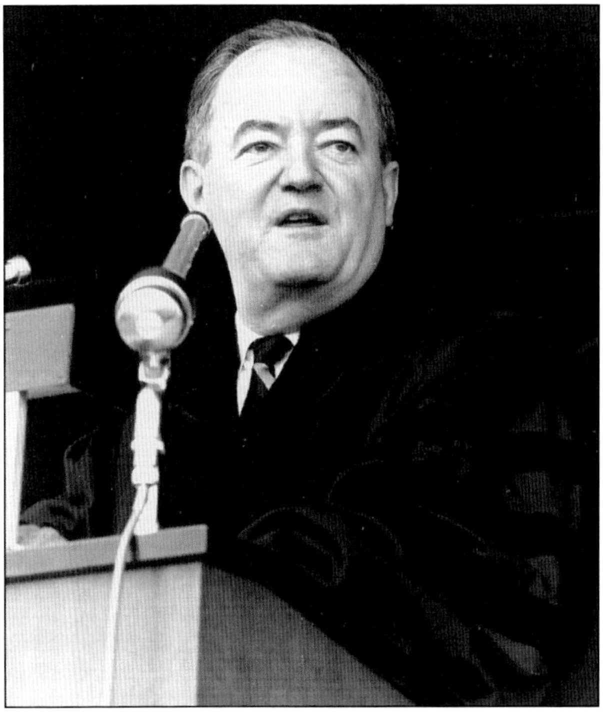

Minnesota senator Hubert H. Humphrey is shown here speaking at commencement in 1964. University president John W. Lederle was very politically astute and invited politicians to campus for various reasons. (Photograph courtesy of the Special Collections and Archives, W.E.B. Du Bois Library, University of Massachusetts Amherst.)

Five

ATHLETICS

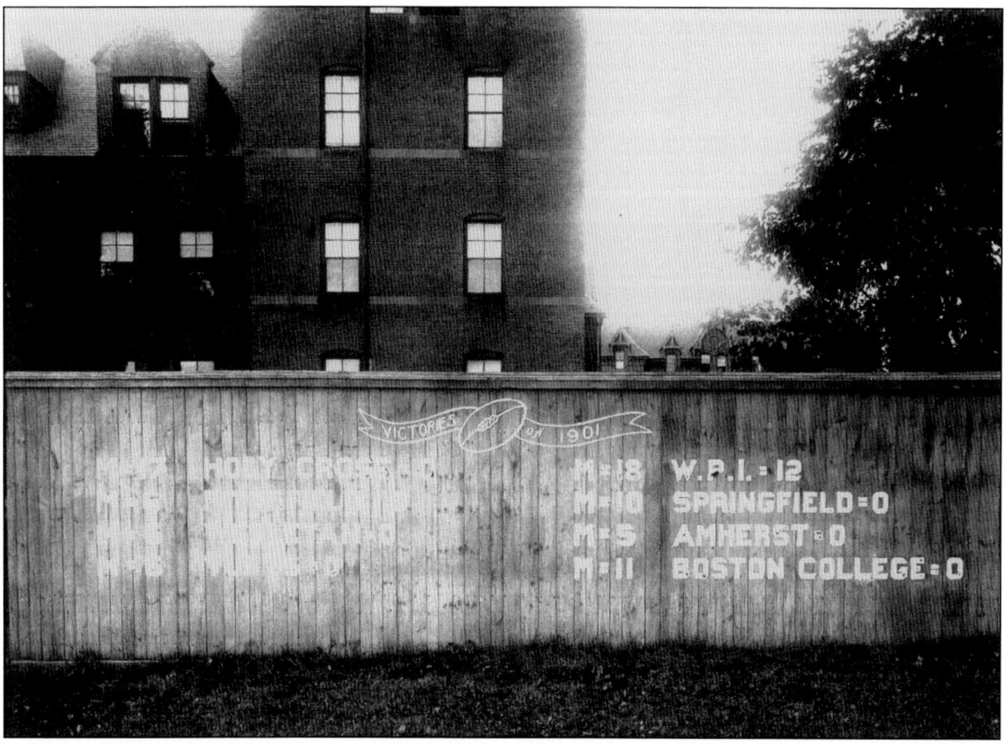

A little campus boasting is accomplished by displaying the record of the 1901 football team on a billboard in front of South College. Note the 11-0 score over Boston College. (Photograph courtesy of the Special Collections and Archives, W.E.B. Du Bois Library, University of Massachusetts Amherst.)

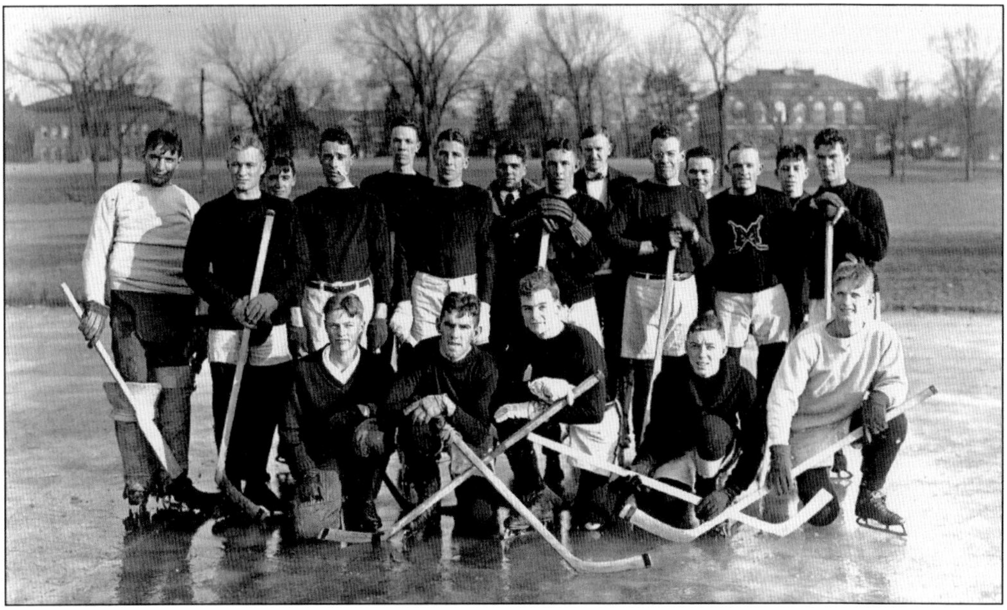

Men's ice hockey has been part of the athletic program since 1908. All of the hockey games were played on the campus pond in the month of January due to the cold weather. Many games were interrupted by foul weather or melting ice. It was not uncommon for some of the hockey games to end before all three periods were finished. In the early days, Massachusetts Agricultural College played all of the powerhouses of New England hockey: teams such as Dartmouth College, Bowdoin College, Colby College, Amherst College, Tufts, and Harvard. This is a photograph of the 1911 men's hockey team. (Photograph courtesy of the Special Collections and Archives, W.E.B. Du Bois Library, University of Massachusetts Amherst.)

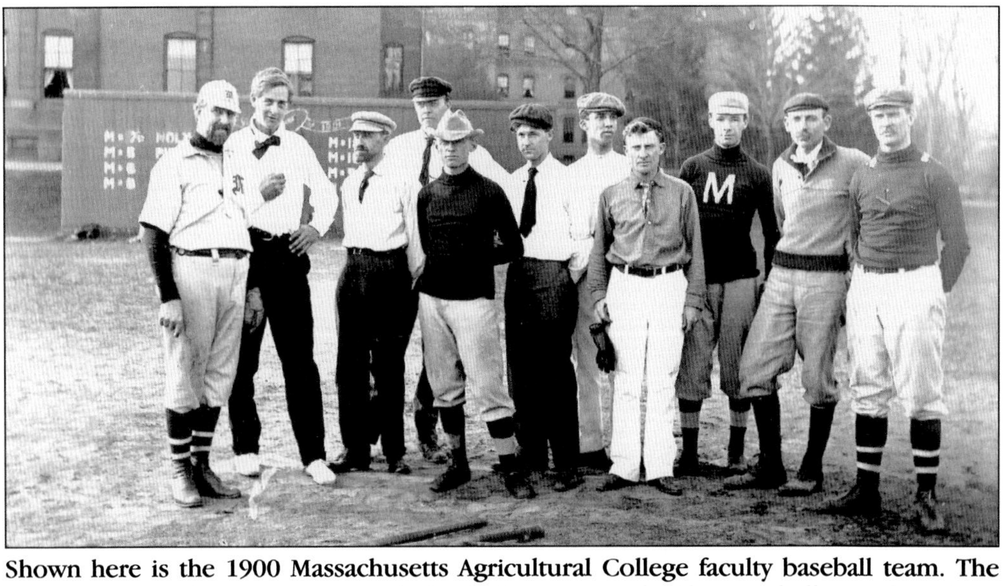

Shown here is the 1900 Massachusetts Agricultural College faculty baseball team. The members of the faculty team would play ball against each other or challenge their rivals from across town, the Amherst College faculty. (Photograph courtesy of the Special Collections and Archives, W.E.B. Du Bois Library, University of Massachusetts Amherst.)

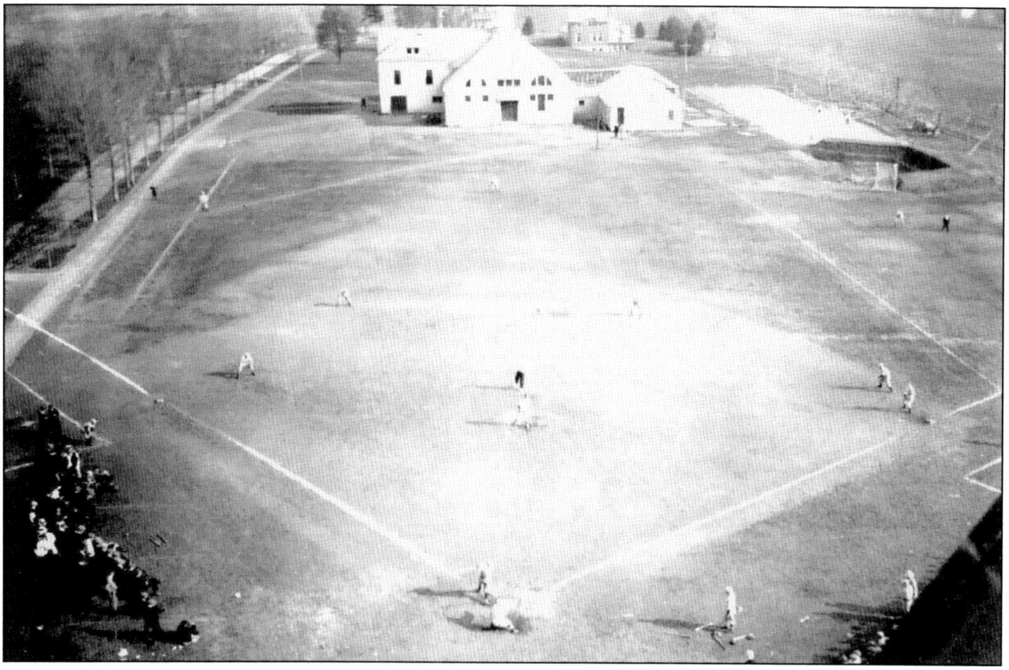

In the early days, both baseball and football games were played in the quad section of campus outside the Old Chapel. The parameters of the field would cover what is now Bartlett Hall, Curry Hicks Cage, and Herter Hall. (Photograph courtesy of the Special Collections and Archives, W.E.B. Du Bois Library, University of Massachusetts Amherst.)

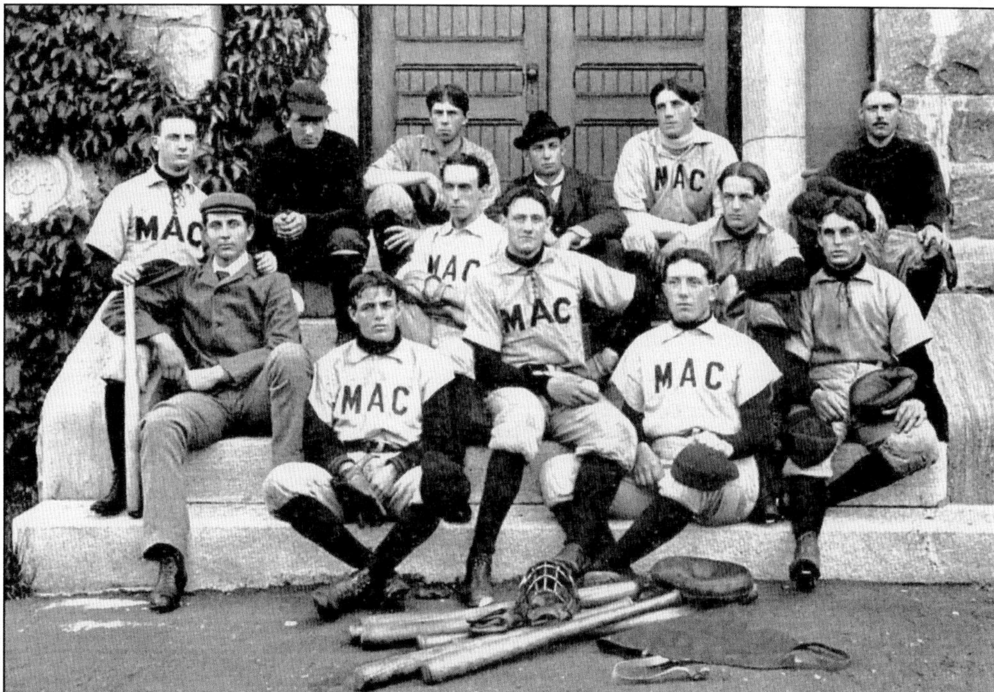

The 1900 baseball team poses for its annual photograph on the steps of the Old Chapel.

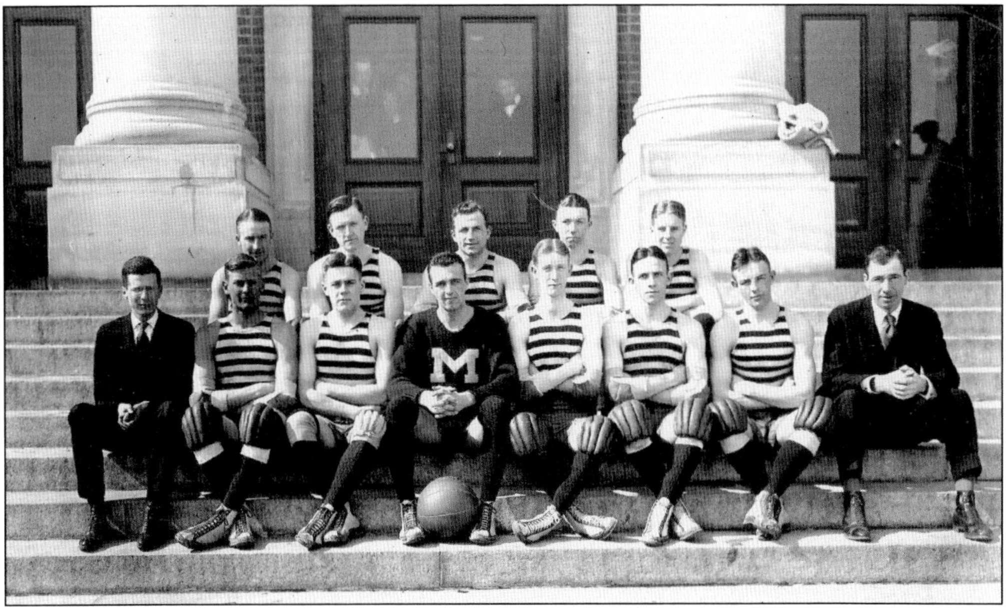

The 1920 Massachusetts Agricultural College basketball team is shown here sitting on the steps of Stockbridge Hall. The team had a record of seven wins and nine losses. Basketball started on campus in the 1899–1900 school year. (Photograph courtesy of the Special Collections and Archives, W.E.B. Du Bois Library, University of Massachusetts Amherst.)

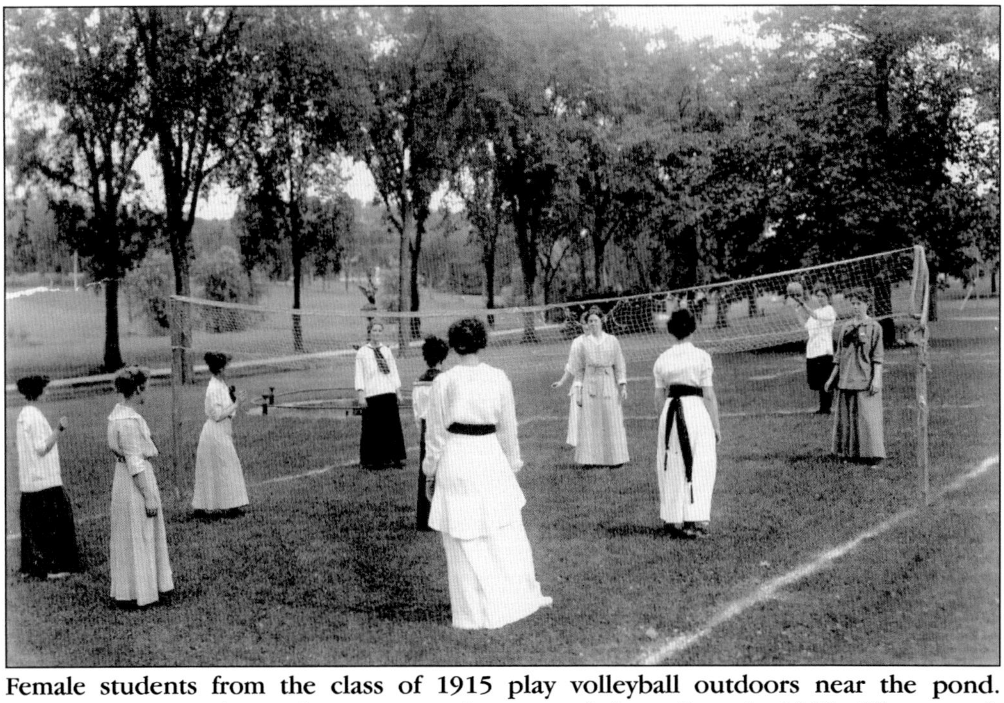

Female students from the class of 1915 play volleyball outdoors near the pond. Women were starting to become a major part of the college in 1915. (Photograph courtesy of the Special Collections and Archives, W.E.B. Du Bois Library, University of Massachusetts Amherst.)

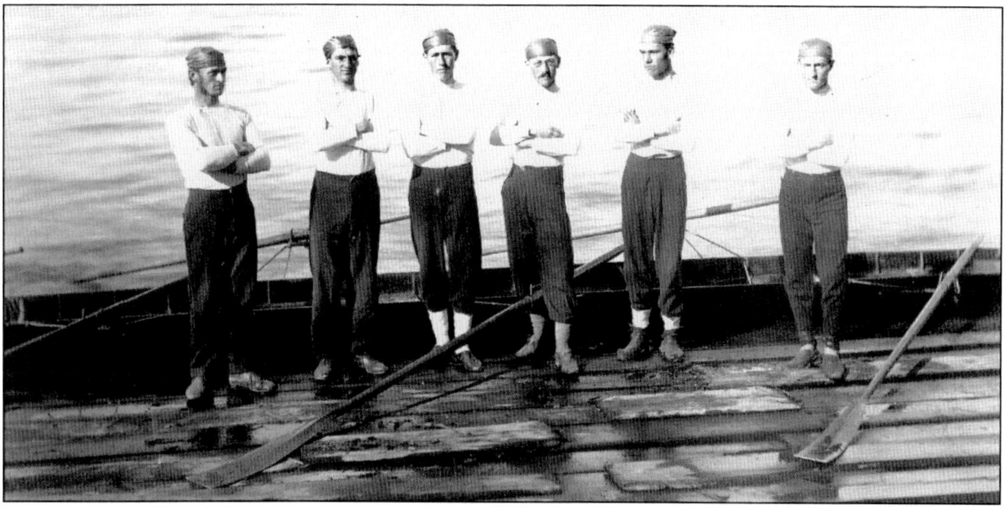

The crew team of 1871 poses in front of the famous shell that defeated both Harvard and Brown Universities in the much-publicized regatta of 1871. Shown in this image, from left to right, are the following: Eldred '73, Duncan '74, Allen '71, Leonard '71, Simpson, '73, and Hardy '74. With much hype and fanfare, three colleges entered the regatta. Harvard was the favorite due the fact that they had lost a close race to Oxford in England the year before. Brown was always a very tough contender. And there was a late entry: Massachusetts Agricultural College in Amherst. The banks of the Connecticut River were freckled with spectators; some 3,000 people paid the toll to cross the Chicopee Bridge. When it was over, the six unassuming college kids from Amherst had defeated the powerhouses of Harvard and Brown. President Clark, astride his horse, galloped into Amherst Center and informed the townspeople, "We won, folks. We won." (Photograph courtesy of the Special Collections and Archives, W.E.B. Du Bois Library, University of Massachusetts Amherst.)

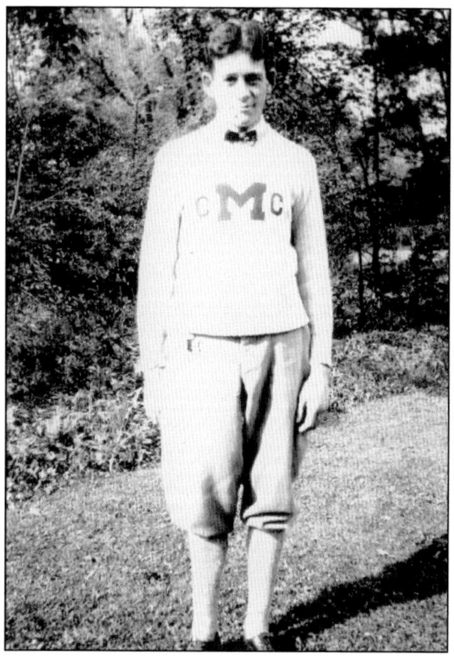

Senior running sensation Red Nottebart '27 proudly wears his varsity lettermen's sweater. Nottebart was one of the best cross-country runners ever at Massachusetts Agricultural College. (Photograph courtesy of the Special Collections and Archives, W.E.B. Du Bois Library, University of Massachusetts Amherst.)

Massachusetts State College

VARSITY BASKETBALL

	SCORE	
	MSC	Opp
December		
17 Middlebury at M.S.C., 8:00		
18 M.I.T. at Boston, 8:15		
January		
9 Williams at Williamstown		
13 Connecticut State at M.S.C., 8:00		
16 Amherst at M.S.C., 8:00		
20 Wesleyan at M.S.C., 8:00		
23 Boston University at M.S.C., 8:00		
February		
10 Rhode Island at Kingston		
12 Norwich at M.S.C., 7:00		
13 Springfield at Springfield, 8:15		
17 Amherst at Amherst		
19 Coast Guard at M.S.C., 8:00		
24 W.P.I. at M.S.C., 8:00		
March		
3 Tufts at Medford		

Isadore Barr '37, *Captain*

John Kabat '37, *Manager*

Wilho Frigard '34, *Coach*

Massachusetts State College

VARSITY HOCKEY

	SCORE	
	MSC	Opp
January		
6 Union at M.S.C., 3:30		
9 Army at West Point		
11 M.I.T. at M.S.C., 3:30		
14 Northeastern at Boston, 8:00		
16 Hamilton at Clinton, 8:15		
18 New Hampshire at M.S.C., 3:30		
21 Amherst at Amherst, tentative		
23 Middlebury at Middlebury		

Allan S. Ingalls '37, *Captain*

Paul H. Rosberry '37, *Manager*

Lorin E. Ball '21, *Coach*

This pocket schedule and scorecard from the 1936–1937 season helped students keep track of the schedule and the wins and loses of their favorite varsity teams. Note that all of the hockey games were played in the month of January due to the fairly predictable cold New England weather. The Massachusetts State College hockey games were played at 3:30 p.m. because the team played outside on the campus pond. Many games were either postponed or forced to end early due to inclement weather or darkness.

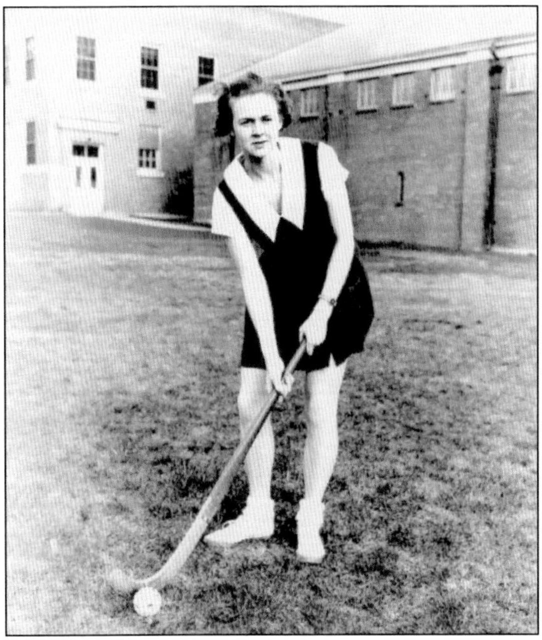

Student-athlete Phyllis Louise Nelson poses with her field hockey stick and ball. Women's sports were integrated into the Massachusetts State College athletic programs as more women started to attend the college. (Photograph courtesy of the Special Collections and Archives, W.E.B. Du Bois Library, University of Massachusetts Amherst.)

Student-athlete Eleanor D. Fahey swings her tennis racket in 1936. (Photograph courtesy of the Special Collections and Archives, W.E.B. Du Bois Library, University of Massachusetts Amherst.)

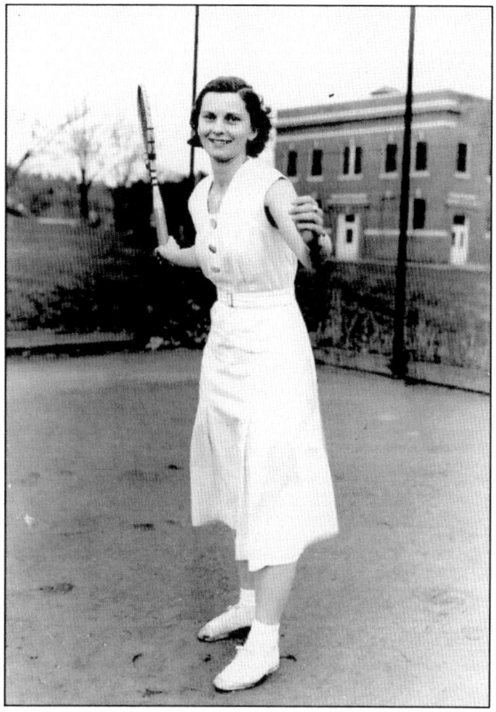

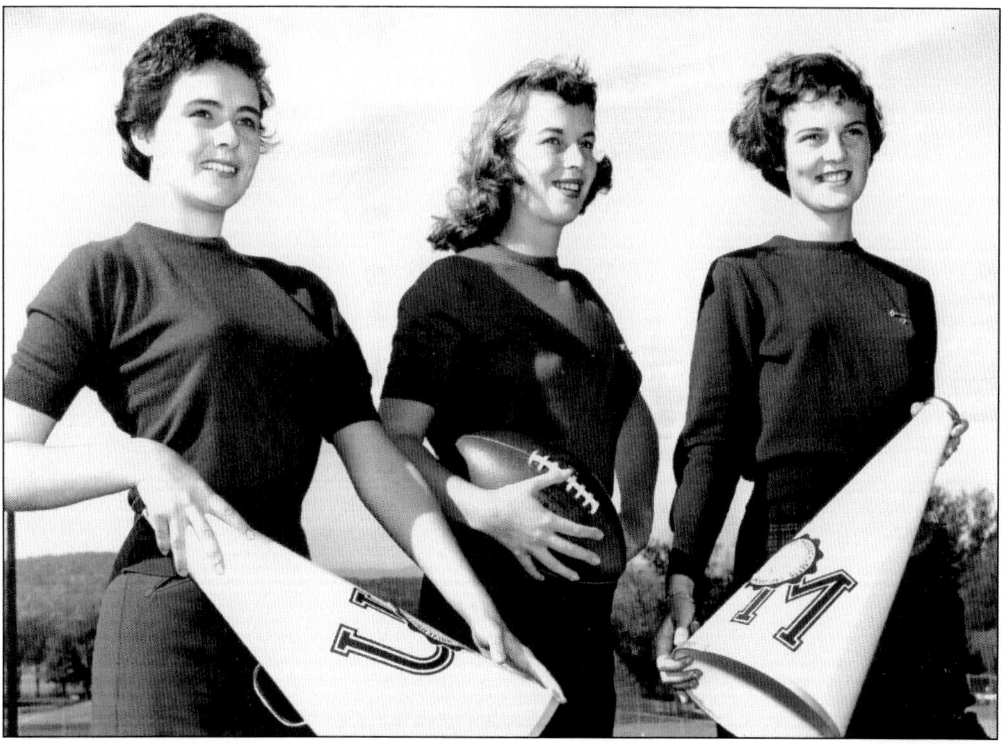

University of Massachusetts football cheerleaders are shown here *c.* 1962. (Photograph courtesy of the Special Collections and Archives, W.E.B. Du Bois Library, University of Massachusetts Amherst.)

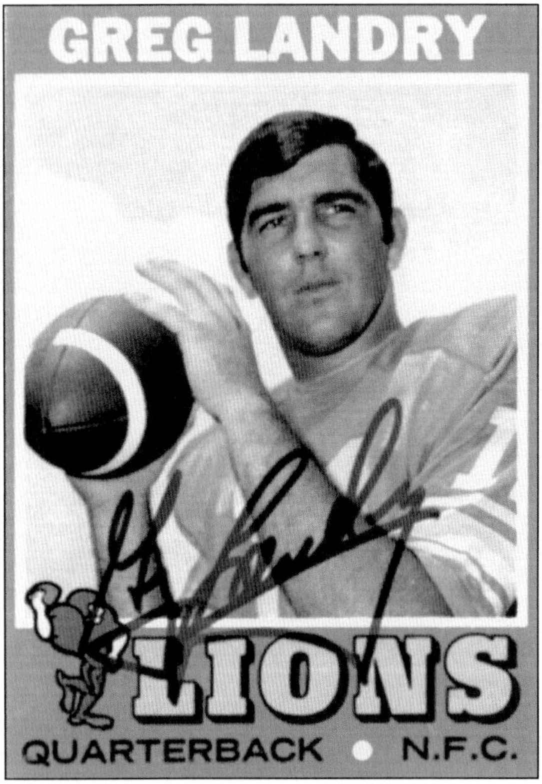

Greg Landry '68 is arguably the greatest quarterback in UMass football history. Landry earned three varsity letters between 1965 and 1967, and he played for the Detroit Lions after he left UMass. He is married to UMass Women's gymnastics Hall-of-Famer Jeannine Burger.

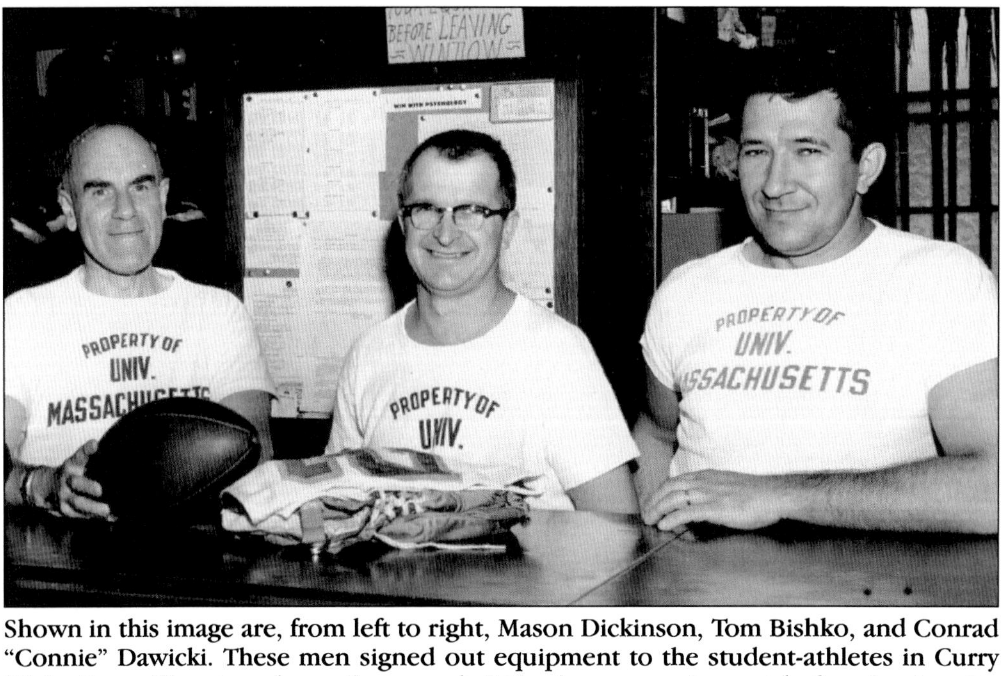

Shown in this image are, from left to right, Mason Dickinson, Tom Bishko, and Conrad "Connie" Dawicki. These men signed out equipment to the student-athletes in Curry Hicks Cage. The sign above them reads "Check your equipment before leaving the window." (Photograph courtesy of the Special Collections and Archives, W.E.B. Du Bois Library, University of Massachusetts Amherst.)

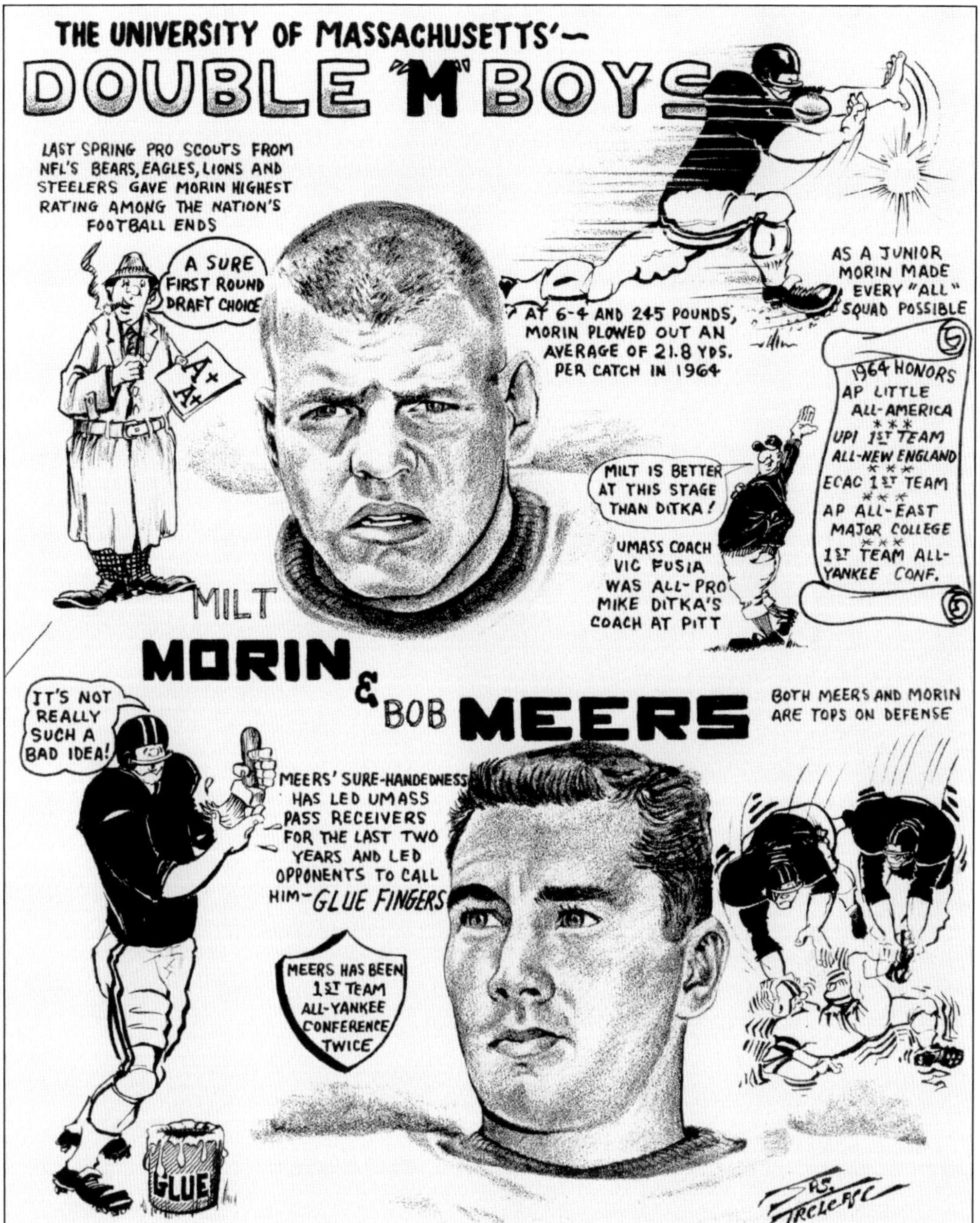

This poster, created by the *Springfield Union* newspaper, highlights two of UMass's greatest football players, Milt Morin '67 and Bob Meers '66. Both players were dominant forces on the gridiron; they were known as the Double M Boys. (Photograph courtesy of the Special Collections and Archives, W.E.B. Du Bois Library, University of Massachusetts Amherst.)

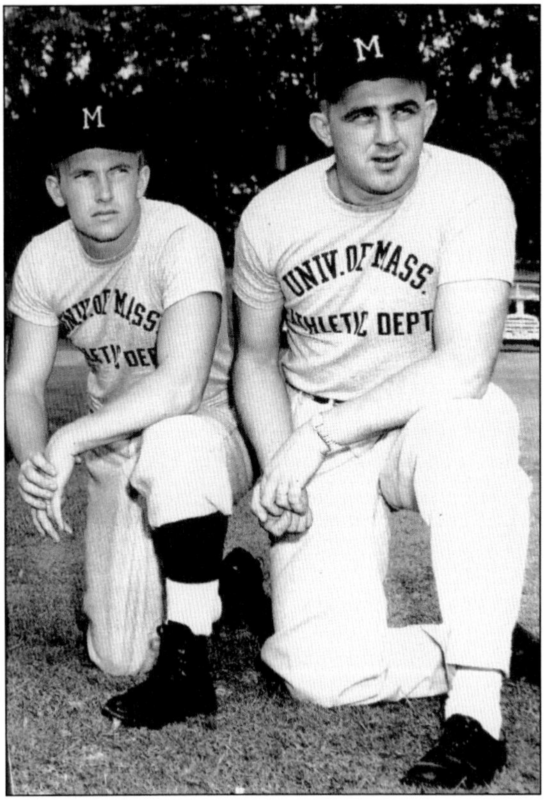

Coach Noel Reebenocker (on the left) and football trainer Vic Keedy (on the right) intently watch football practice in 1957. (Photograph courtesy of the Special Collections and Archives, W.E.B. Du Bois Library, University of Massachusetts Amherst.)

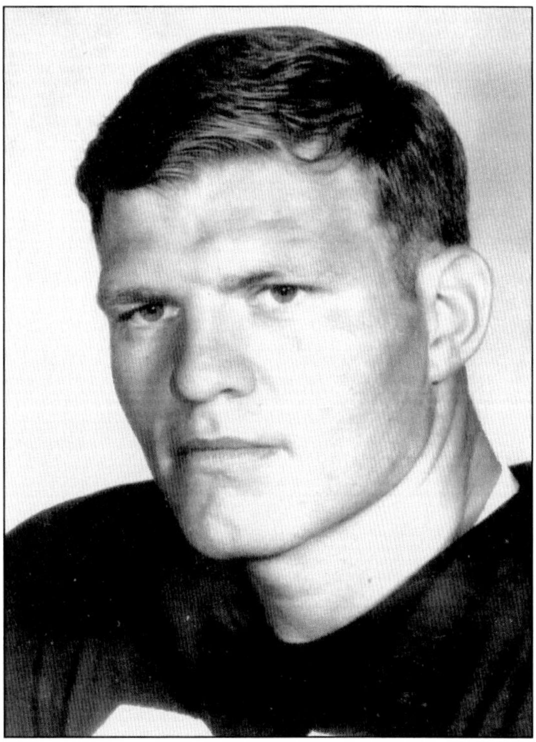

Milt Morin was a three-time letter winner in football from 1963 to 1965. Morin was a versatile athlete and was crowned the New England Heavyweight Wrestling Champion in 1965. He also played lacrosse for Dick Garber. Morin played 10 years for the Cleveland Browns, where he was named to the All-Pro Team in 1966, 1968, and 1969. (Photograph courtesy of the Special Collections and Archives, W.E.B. Du Bois Library, University of Massachusetts Amherst.)

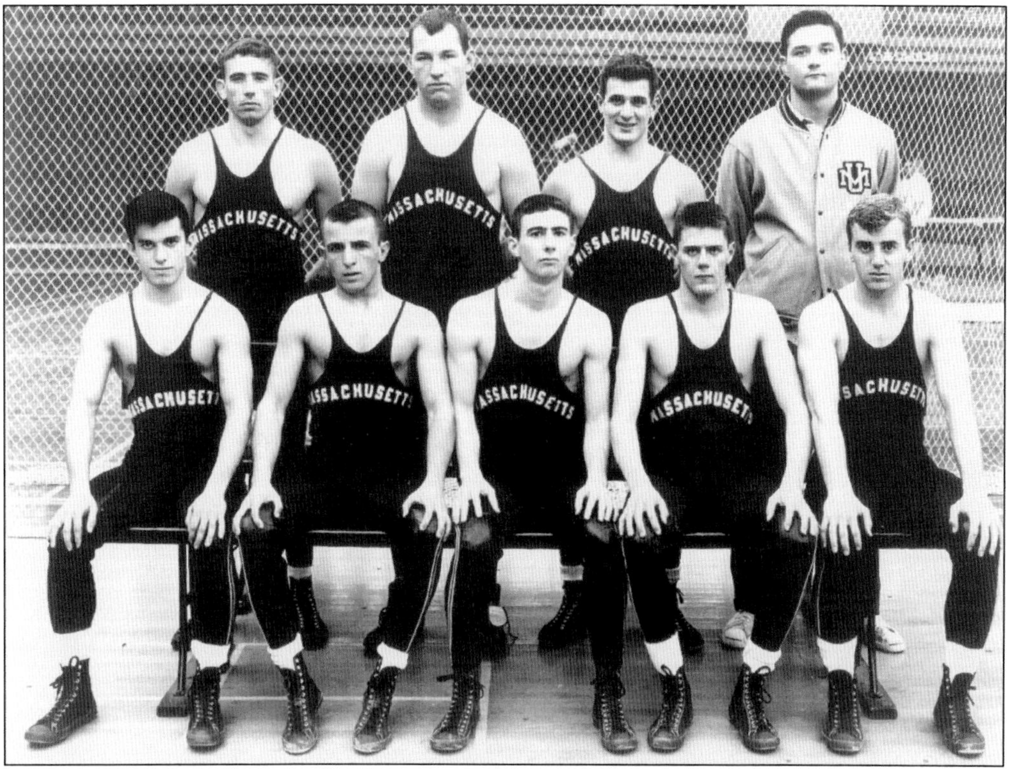

This is the 1961 wrestling team. (Photograph courtesy of the Special Collections and Archives, W.E.B. Du Bois Library, University of Massachusetts Amherst.)

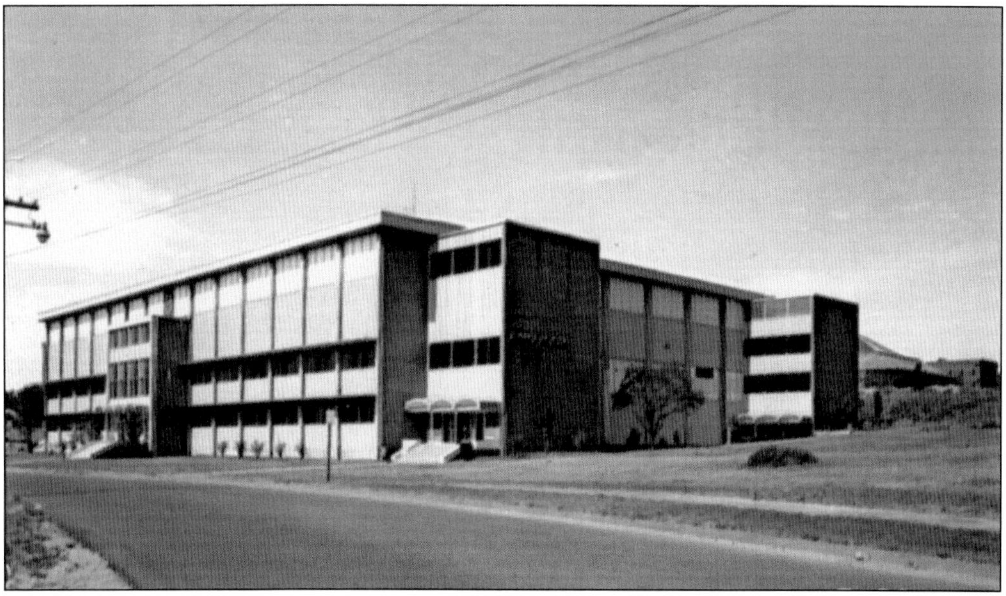

In its day, the Boyden Gym was a state-of-the-art recreational facility with more than an acre of running track inside. It also served as the athletic offices for coaches and staff. It was named after Dr. Frank L. Boyden, headmaster of Deerfield Academy and chairman of the University of Massachusetts Board of Trustees. It was built in 1963.

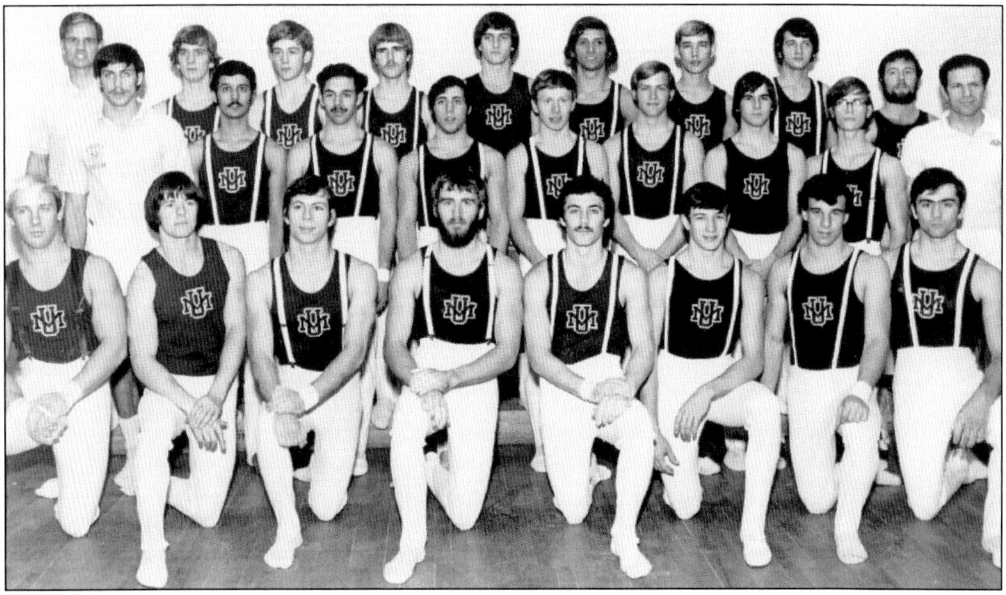

Here, the members of the men's 1971–1972 gymnastics team pose for their annual photograph. (Photograph courtesy of the Special Collections and Archives, W.E.B. Du Bois Library, University of Massachusetts Amherst.)

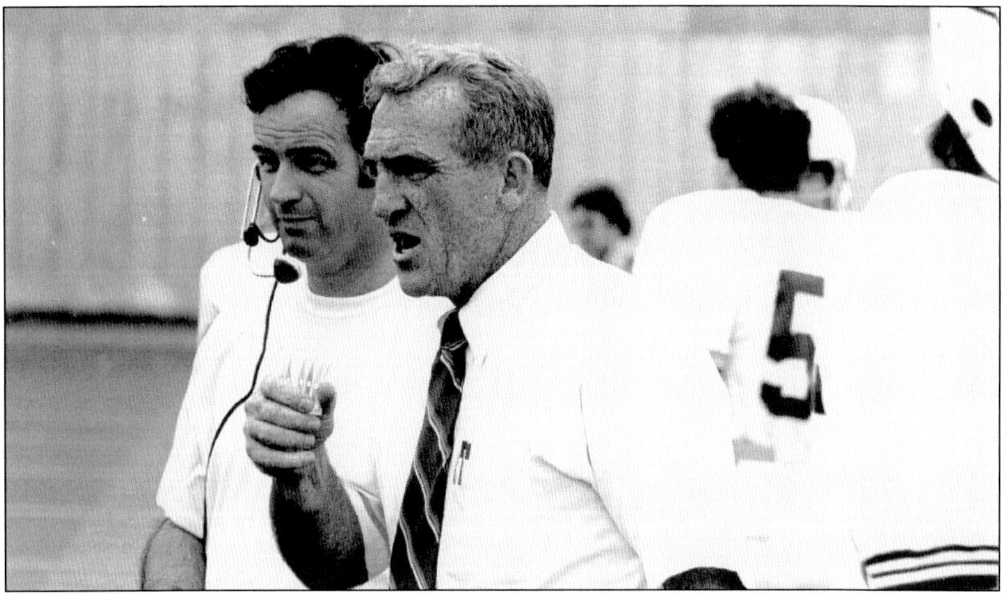

Dick MacPherson (on the right) took over the helm of the Minuteman football team from Vic Fusia in 1971 and coached through the 1977 season. He led UMass to four Yankee Conference Championships and a 35-14 victory in the 1972 Boardwalk Bowl over California at Davis. McPherson was also head coach of the New England Patriots between 1991 and 1992. His assistant coach and successor, Bob Pickett (on the left), coached from 1978 to 1983 and compiled a 35 and 28 record in his tenure, including four Yankee Conference Championships. (Photograph courtesy of the Special Collections and Archives, W.E.B. Du Bois Library, University of Massachusetts Amherst.)

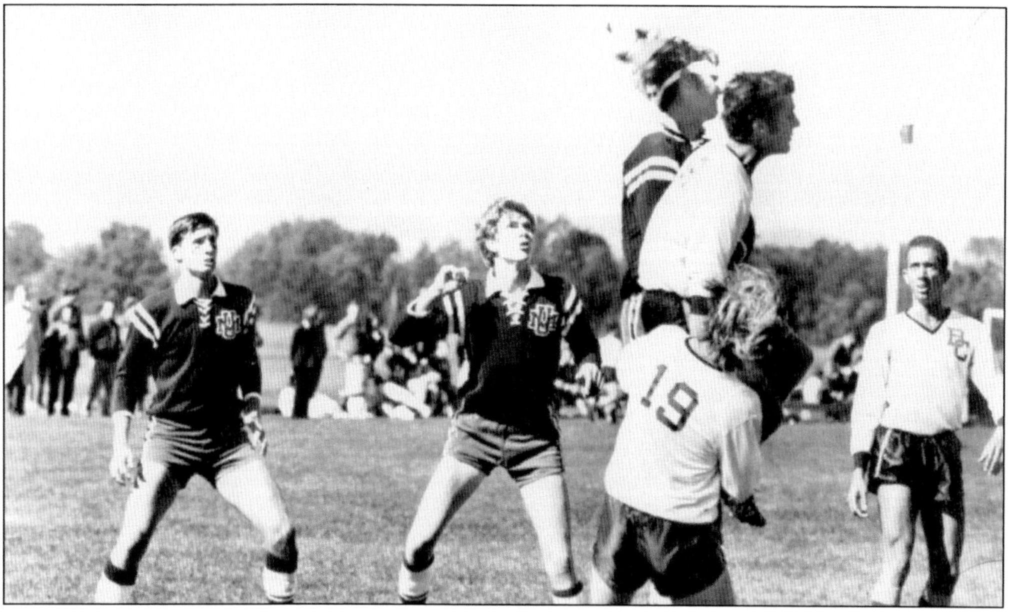

The 1969 UMass men's soccer team finished the season with six wins and four losses. The team's victories came over Boston College (3-0), UConn (2-1), Tufts (5-4), URI (2-1), Coast Guard (6-2), and UNH (1-0). Led by co-captains Rich Matuszcak and Dick Meyer, the team's defense only allowed 17 goals in 10 contests. Men's soccer has been played on campus since 1930.

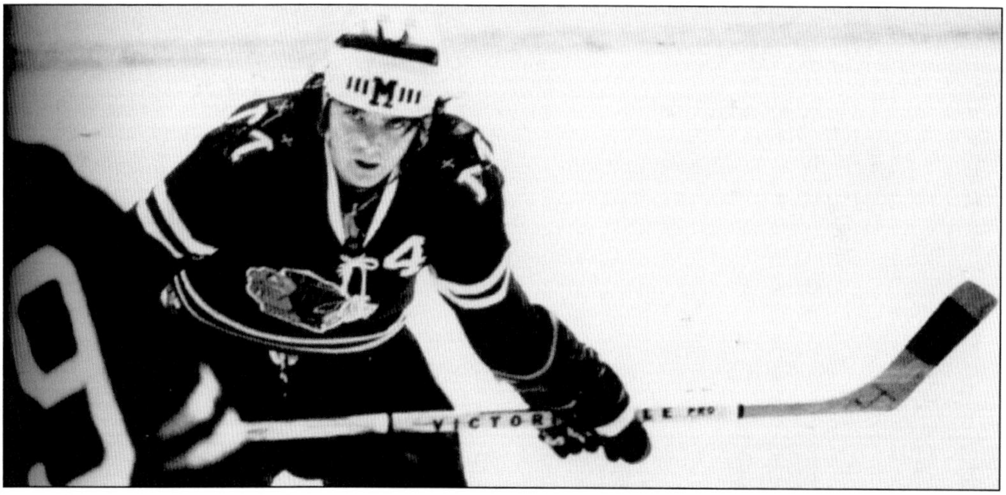

Patrick Keenan earned three varsity letters in ice hockey at UMass between 1970 and 1973 and was twice chosen as a first-team all-American selection for Coach Jack Canniff. A member of the Minutemen's 1971–1972 ECAC Division II national championship squad, which finished 19-7 overall (a school record at the time), Keenan still ranks as the all-time leading scorer in school history with 180 points. He also holds school records for goals scored (105) and ranks third in assists (75). In addition to his career marks, Keenan holds the three best single-season marks for points and goals scored: 65 points and 43 goals in 1972–1973, 59 points and 43 goals in 1971–1972, and 56 points and 28 goals in 1970–1971. He also still holds the UMass single-game record for points: he earned nine against Holy Cross in 1970.

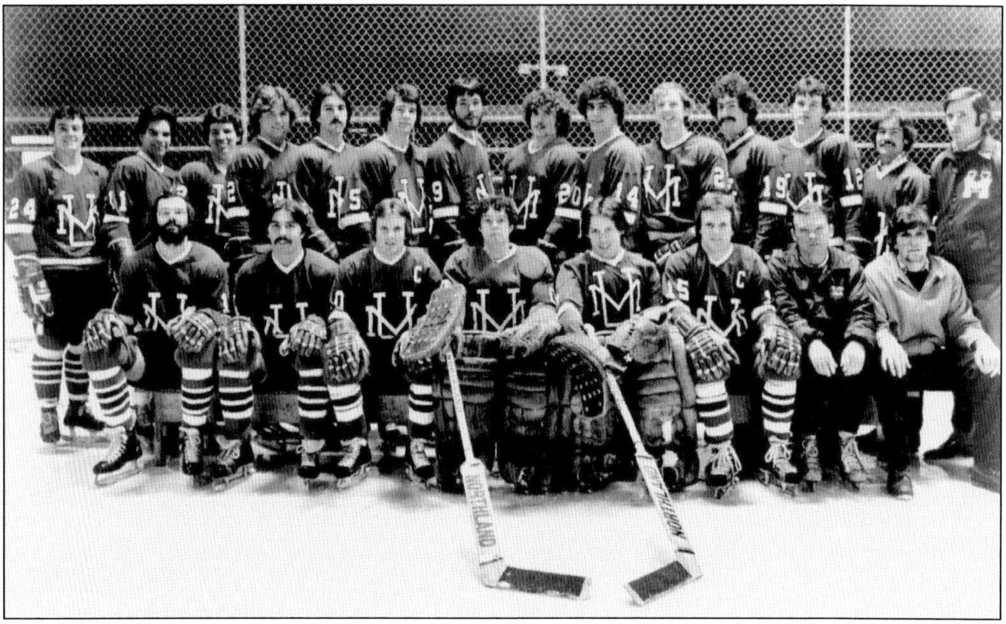

This team photograph marked the near end of UMass hockey in 1978. Due to NCAA Title IX regulations, colleges had to offer as many sports for women as they did for men, and the hockey team was forced to take a hiatus from 1980 to 1993. (Photograph courtesy of the Special Collections and Archives, W.E.B. Du Bois Library, University of Massachusetts Amherst.)

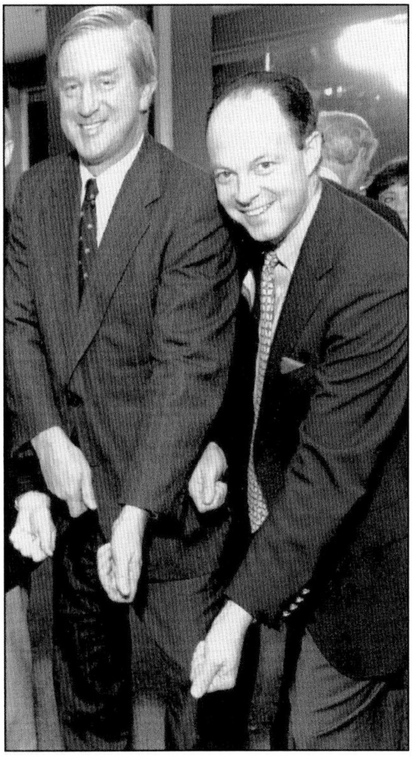

Massachusetts governor William Weld (on the left) and former goalie John Riley '78 (on the right) pose with make-believe hockey sticks in 1993 before the first UMass hockey game since 1980. On October 30, 1993, Governor Weld dropped the ceremonial first puck as UMass took on and beat Villanova 9-1.

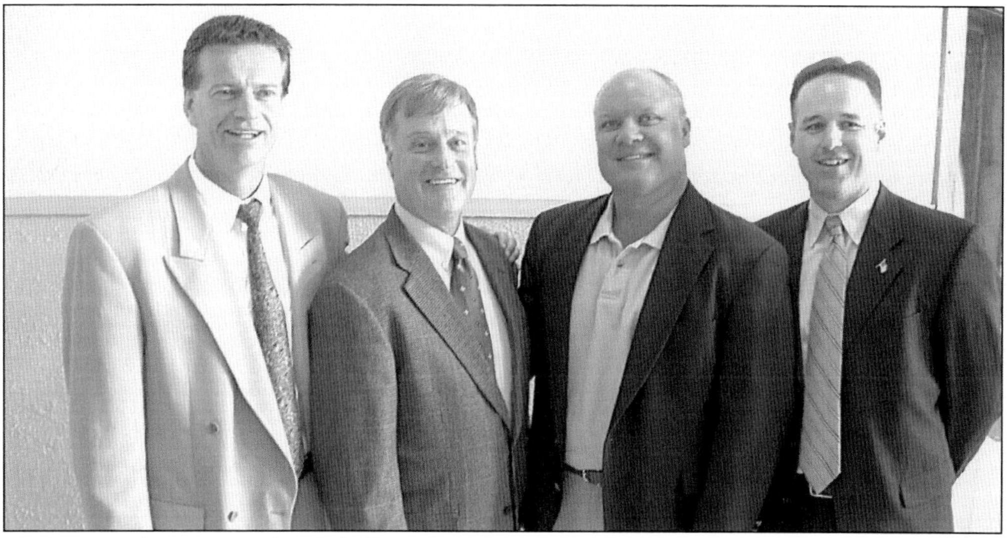

Shown in this image, from left to right, are Bill Gilligan, Don "Toot" Cahoon, Jim Stewart, and Mark Dennehy. In 2004, UMass has what is arguably the very best coaching staff in all of Hockey East. Gilligan is a graduate of Brown University, where he still holds the title of all-time leading goal scorer and assist leader. Cahoon, a Boston University graduate, won national championships in 1971 and 1972 and has celebrated esteemed coaching careers at Princeton and Norwich Universities. Cahoon was named Hockey East coach of the year in 2003. Jim Stewart is a volunteer assistant goalie coach and a Holy Cross graduate. He played goalie for the Boston Bruins and is one of only five hockey players in the Holy Cross hall of fame. Mark Dennehy is a 1991 graduate of Boston College, where he played hockey with some of the NHL's best: Bill Guerin, Marty McInnis, and Steve Heinze. Mark is a defensive specialist for the staff.

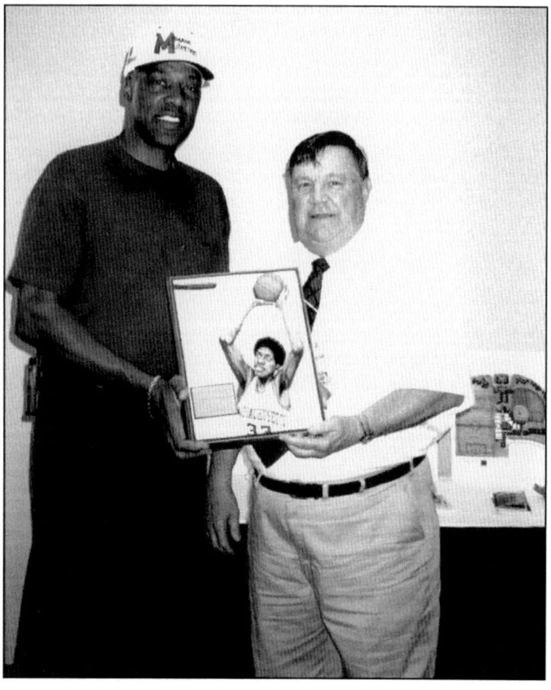

Basketball great Julius Erving and his coach Jack Leaman proudly display Dr. J's UMass Athletic Hall of Fame photograph.

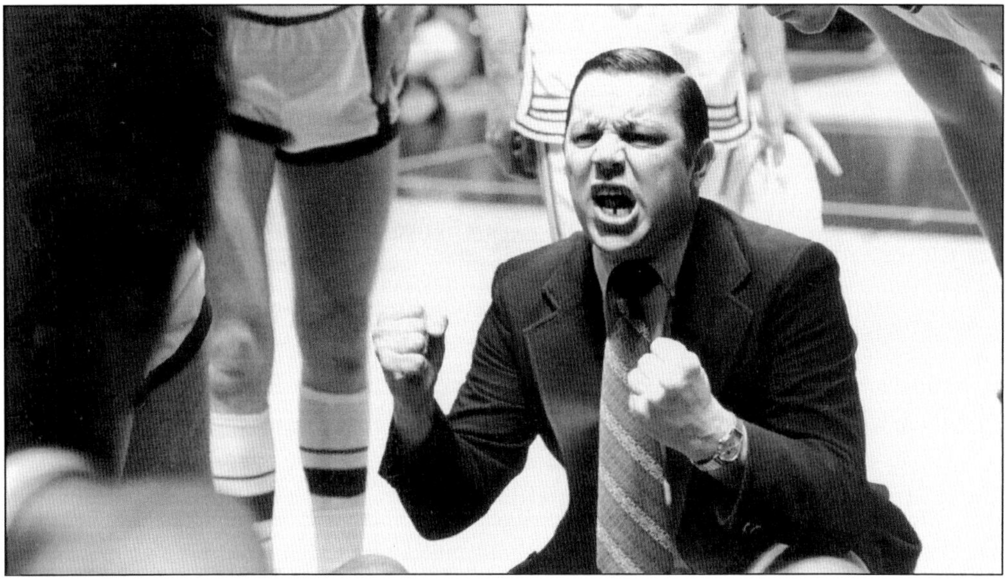

Jack Leaman was head coach of the men's basketball team from 1966 to 1979, compiling a record of 217-126. The two-time New England coach of the year coached some of the university's best: Julius Erving, Rick Pitino, Al Skinner, Bill Tindall, and Joe DiSarcina. Leaman also served as the athletic director of the Stockbridge School of Agriculture. (Photograph courtesy of the Special Collections and Archives, W.E.B. Du Bois Library, University of Massachusetts Amherst.)

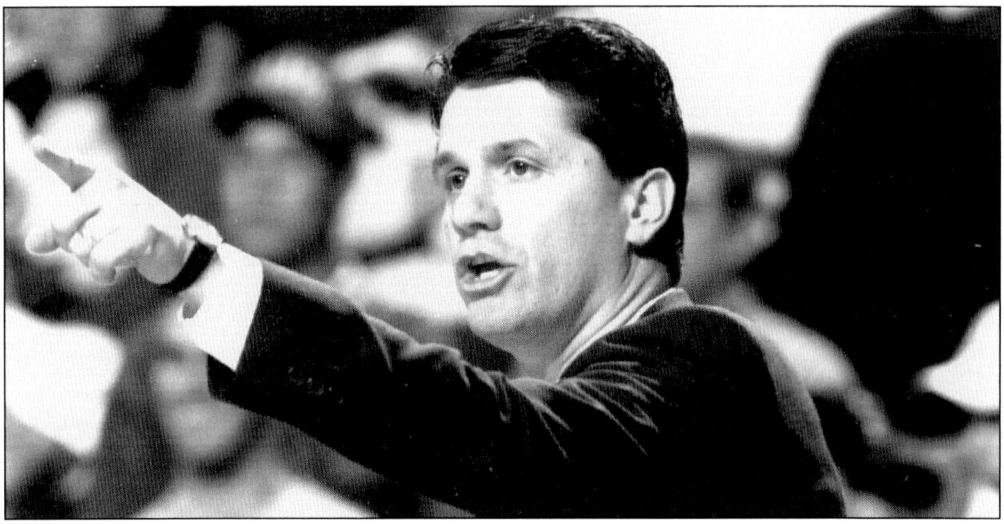

During his eight-year stint at UMass, John Calipari transformed the Minutemen from a team that had struggled in the Atlantic 10 Conference into a national powerhouse. UMass went to five straight NCAA Tournaments from 1992 to 1996, advancing to the Final Four in Calipari's last season. UMass advanced to the NCAA Sweet 16 on three occasions and advanced to two Elite Eights. The school became only the second NCAA Division I program to win five straight regular-season and conference tournament championships. Calipari compiled a 193-71 record (.731) during his career at Massachusetts, including a 108-44 mark (.684) in Atlantic 10 Conference play. (Photograph courtesy of UMass Athletic Media Relations.)

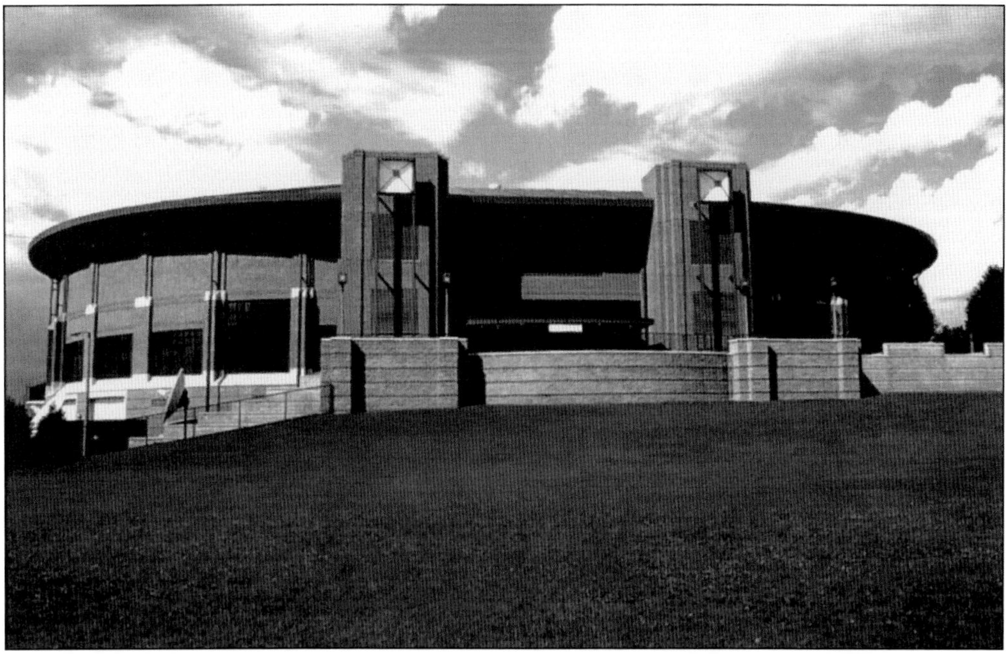

The Mullins Center, built in 1993, is named after William D. Mullins, a state representative from Ludlow who secured the almost $52 million to build this state-of-the-art sports and entertainment center. The Mullins Center is the home of UMass men's ice hockey, basketball, a public skating rink, and concert hall.

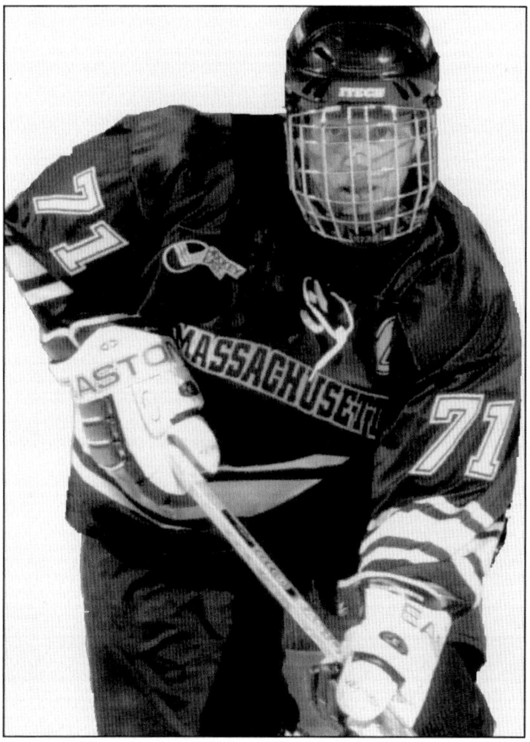

Austrian-born Thomas Pöck was selected as a first-team All-American by *Inside College Hockey* and was named the nation's defenseman of the year by the same organization. He had a stellar senior season in which he became UMass' all-time leading scoring defenseman and shattered nearly every offensive blue-liner record. The Hobey Baker Top Ten finalist played in all 37 games in the 2003–2004 season, scoring 41 points (16 goals, 25 assists), a nation's best for defensemen. He finished his UMass career tied for sixth on the all-time scoring list with 102 points (44 goals, 58 assists). Over the 2002–2003 and 2003–2004 seasons, Pöck accumulated a remarkable 78 points (33 goals, 45 assists) as a defenseman. Pöck signed a free-agent contract on March 23, 2004, with the New York Rangers and has become an instant success with the team. He netted his first career goal in his first NHL game, which came on the same day that he signed with the Rangers.

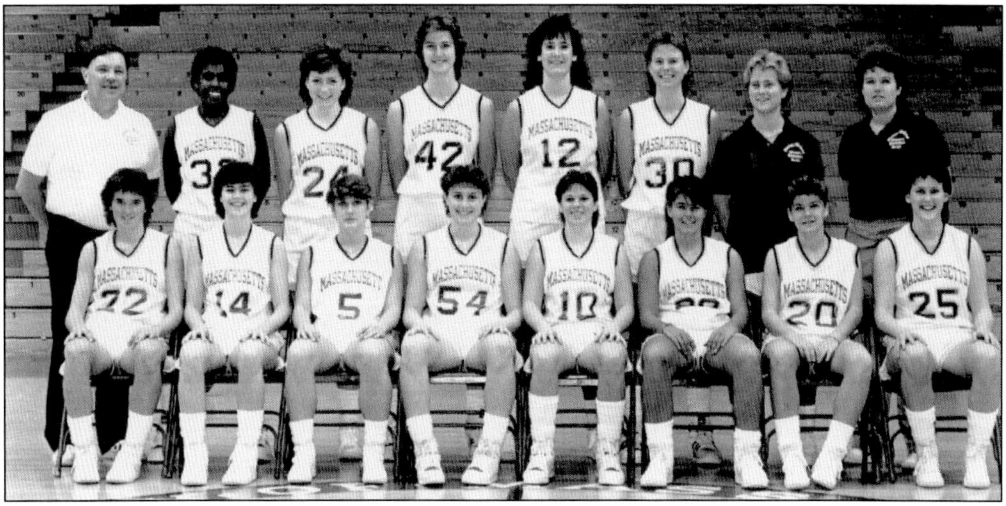

Pictured here is the 1986–1987 women's basketball team, led by head coach Jack Leaman. The team finished 14-12. Women's basketball started in the 1968–1969 season, and the team went 13-2. After the first four years without a head coach, Jane Farr took over the reins in the 1972–1973 season and celebrated an 8-6 record. In the 1983–1984 season, the Minutewomen joined the Atlantic 10 Conference under coach Barbara Stevens. (Photograph courtesy of the Special Collections and Archives, W.E.B. Du Bois Library, University of Massachusetts Amherst.)

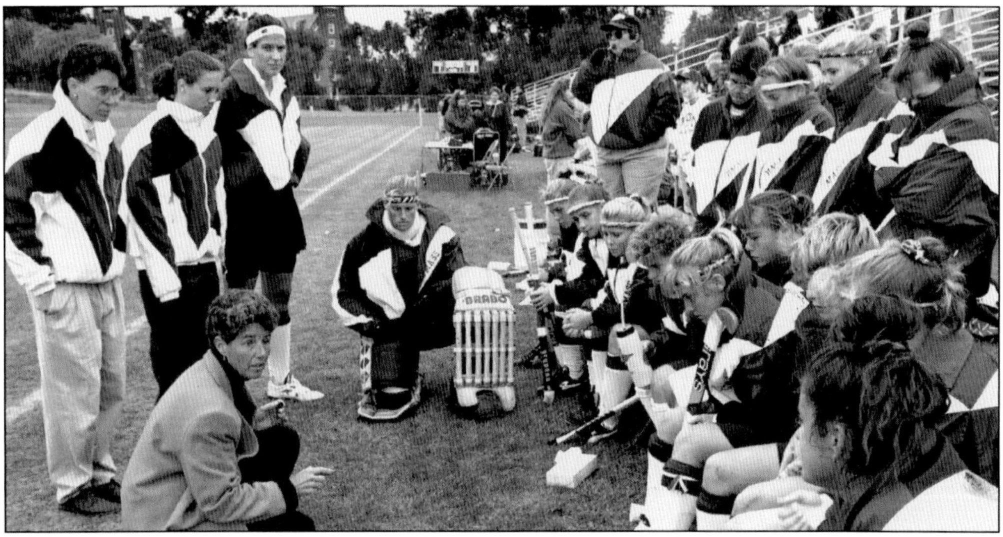

Pam Hixon (kneeling at the left) coached UMass women's field hockey for 17 seasons. She left in 1999 to take over as full-time coach of the national women's field hockey team, which she led during the 1996 Olympics. National coach of the year in 1981, Hixon took UMass to the final four a total of four times and racked up a 272-75-18 record. Hixon ranks not only as one of UMass' greatest coaches ever but also as one of field hockey's finest. She is the fifth most-winning coach in collegiate field hockey history. Hixon directed the Massachusetts field hockey program for 17 seasons (from 1978 to 1993 and again in 1996) and led her team to postseason play every year. She took the Minutewomen to 14 NCAA tournaments, one AIAW tournament, and a pair of EAIAW tournaments. (Photograph courtesy of UMass Athletic Media Relations.)

UMass field hockey goaltender Christine Tocco '05 is seen here in action defending her goal. Field hockey has been played at UMass since 1975. In 29 years of competition, the program has yielded 19 NCAA appearances and nine A-10 Championships. Reading native Tocco has been named captain for the upcoming 2004 season. (Photograph courtesy of UMass Athletic Media Relations.)

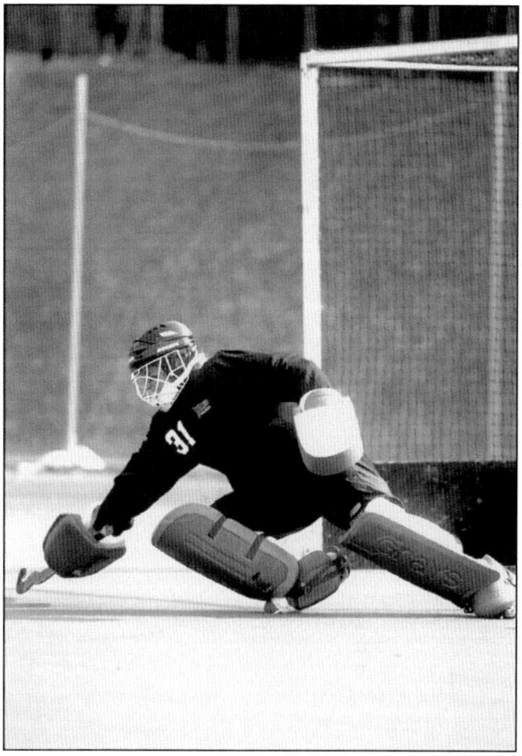

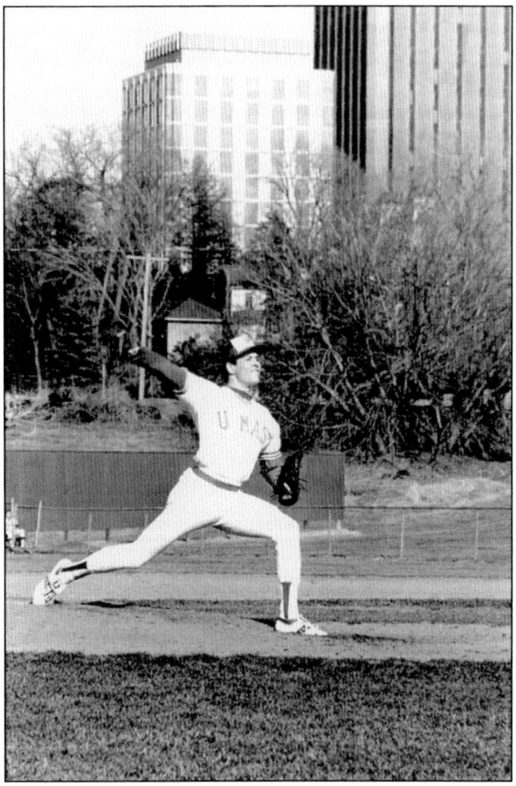

UMass has been playing baseball on campus since 1877. The program has yielded 60 players who have played professional baseball. Household names like Jeff Reardon '77, Mike Flanagan '73, Gary DiSarcina '88, and Dave Telgheder '89 were some of the notable UMass alumni who played pro ball. (Photograph courtesy of the Special Collections and Archives, W.E.B. Du Bois Library, University of Massachusetts Amherst.)

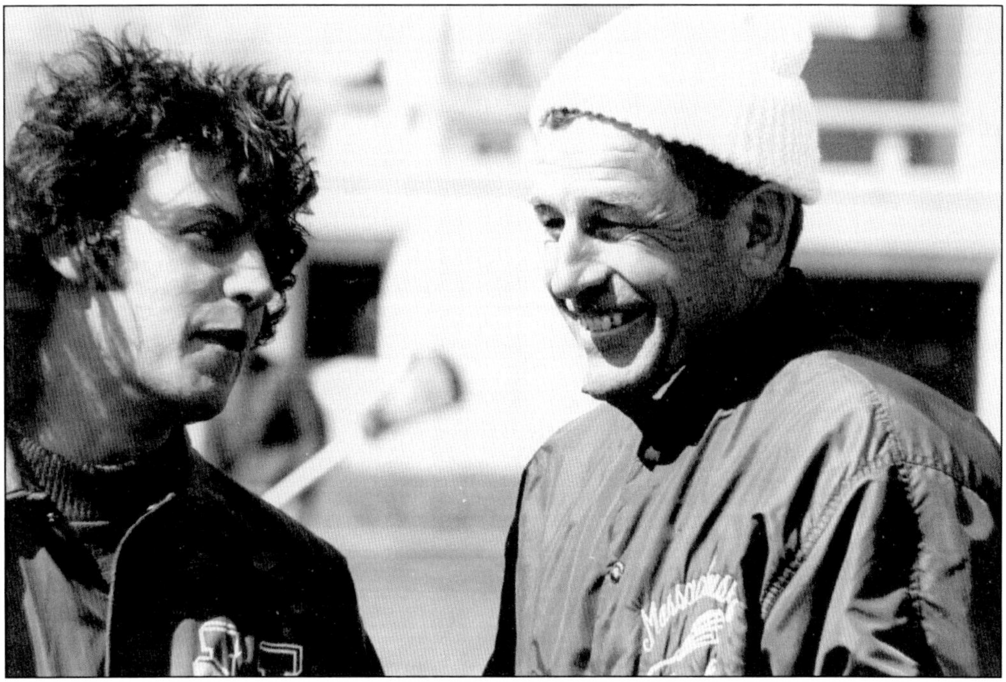

Coach Dick Garber (on the right) is a legend on campus. He coached the always-competitive UMass men's lacrosse team from 1955 to 1990. Garber compiled a 300-142-3 record in 36 seasons as coach. He led his Garber's Gorillas to 9 NCAA tournament appearances and 13 New England championships. In 1992, Upper Boyden Field was renamed Richard F. Garber Field. (Photograph courtesy of the Special Collections and Archives, W.E.B. Du Bois Library, University of Massachusetts Amherst.)

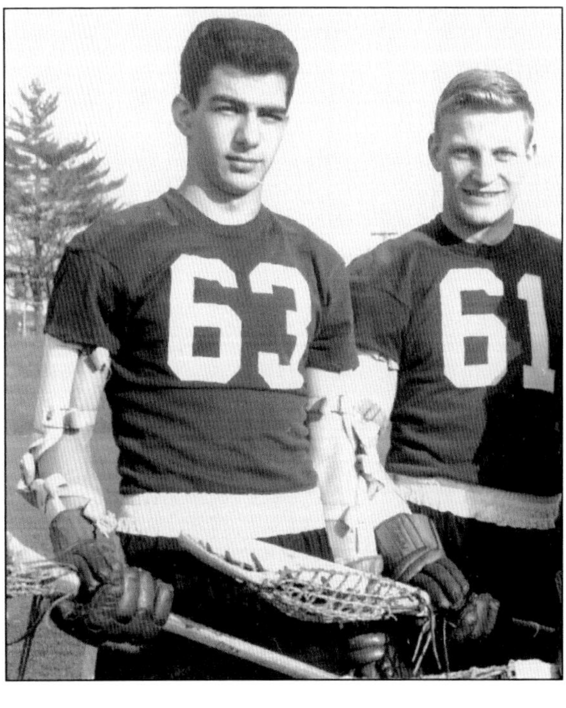

Charles Avakian and Dave Jarrett were both lettermen in 1964, 1965, and 1966. As UMass lacrosse folklore has it, in 1965 the girlfriend of heavily recruited player Kevin O'Connor from New York came up indirectly with the nickname of Garber's Gorillas. She had drawn a picture of a gorilla holding a lacrosse stick and wearing a helmet. She was poking fun at the small size of the UMass players. Members of the team liked the picture so much they made stickers of it and stuck them on their helmets, and the name Garber's Gorillas was born. (Photograph courtesy of the Special Collections and Archives, W.E.B. Du Bois Library, University of Massachusetts Amherst.)

Noel Reebenacker was a walk-on quarterback who earned three varsity letters in football from 1951 to 1953. At the completion of his UMass career, Reebenacker had established school records for passing yards (1,865), completions (132), touchdown passes (20), and total offense yards (2,080). Noel Reebenacker was inducted into the UMass Athletic Hall of Fame in 1982.

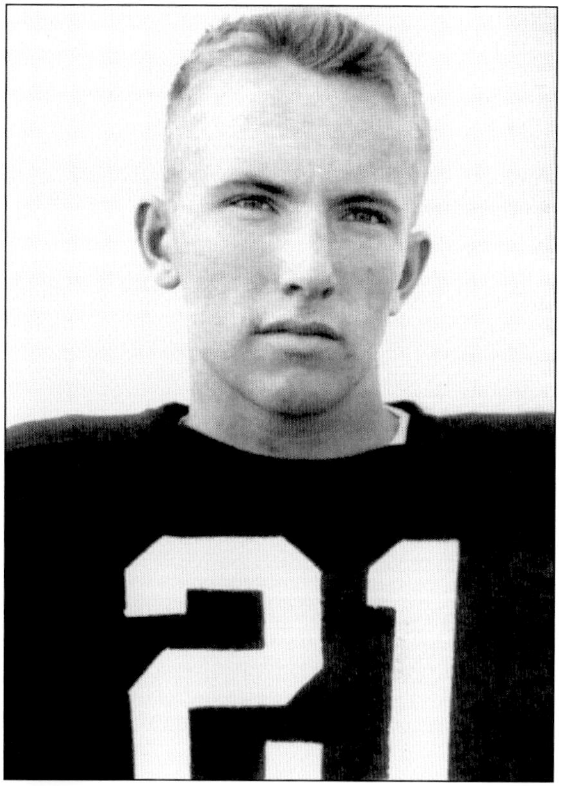

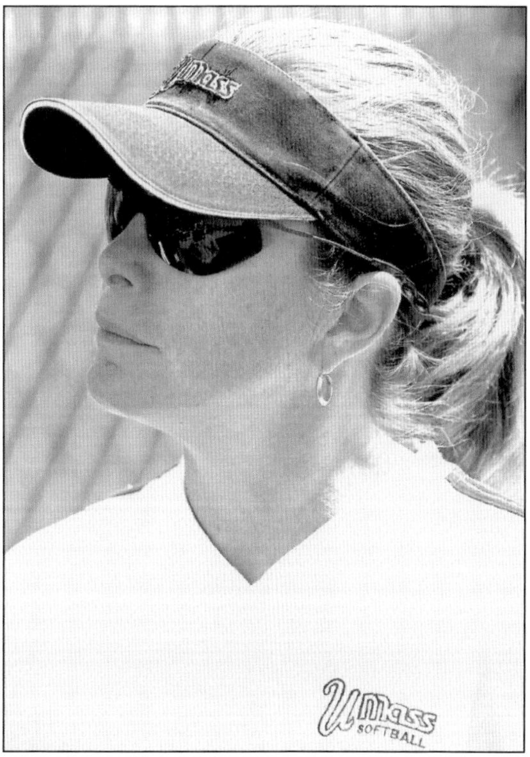

Elaine Sortino is a living dynasty. She has been coaching the UMass women's softball team for 24 years. She ranks ninth in the active most-winning NCAA softball coaches, with 824 wins and 355 loses. Sortino has led UMass to 16 Atlantic 10 conference titles, 13 NCAA regional appearances, and 3 trips to the NCAA college world series. (Photograph courtesy of UMass Athletic Media Relations.)

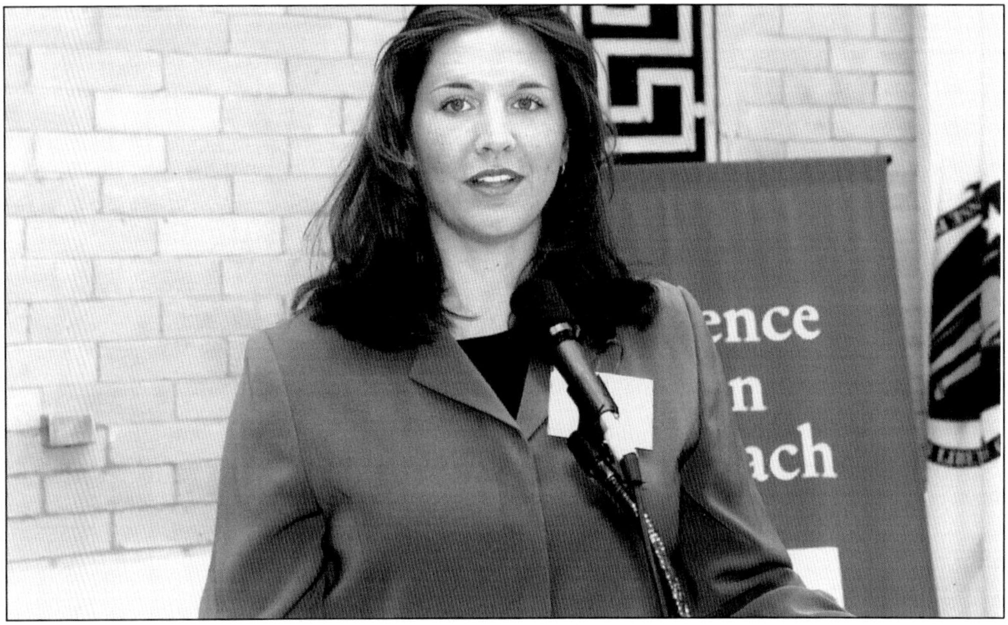

Danielle Henderson '99 basically rewrote the Minutewoman record book by smashing almost every pitching record. She finished her career with 1,343 strikeouts and led the nation in strikeouts in 1998 and 1999. In the 2000 Summer Olympics, Danielle won a gold medal in women's softball.

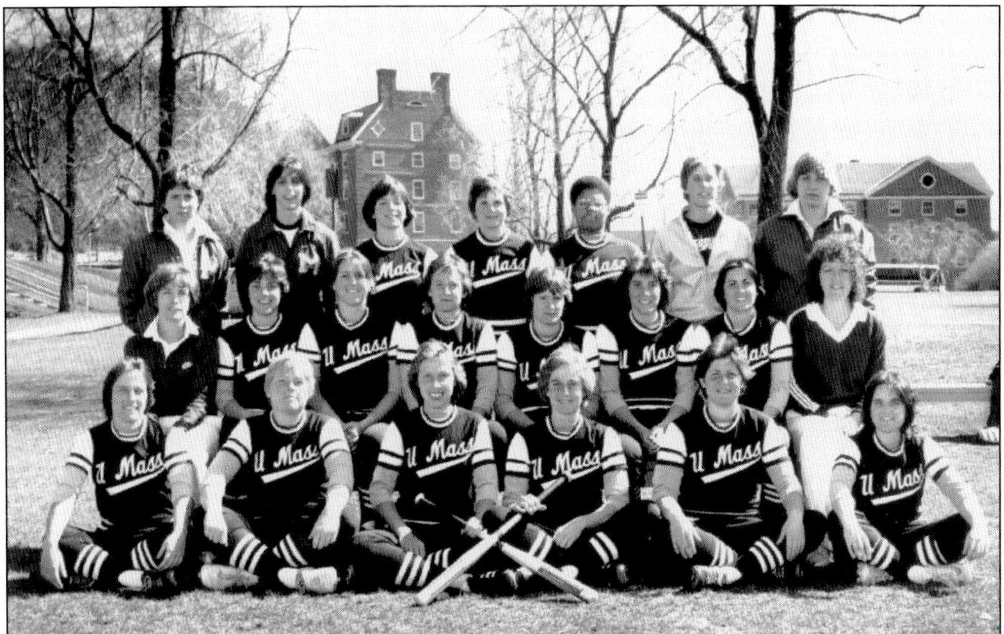

The 1981 women's varsity softball team enjoyed a 16-8 record and was led by All-American Jackie Gaw. (Photograph courtesy of the Special Collections and Archives, W.E.B. Du Bois Library, University of Massachusetts Amherst.)

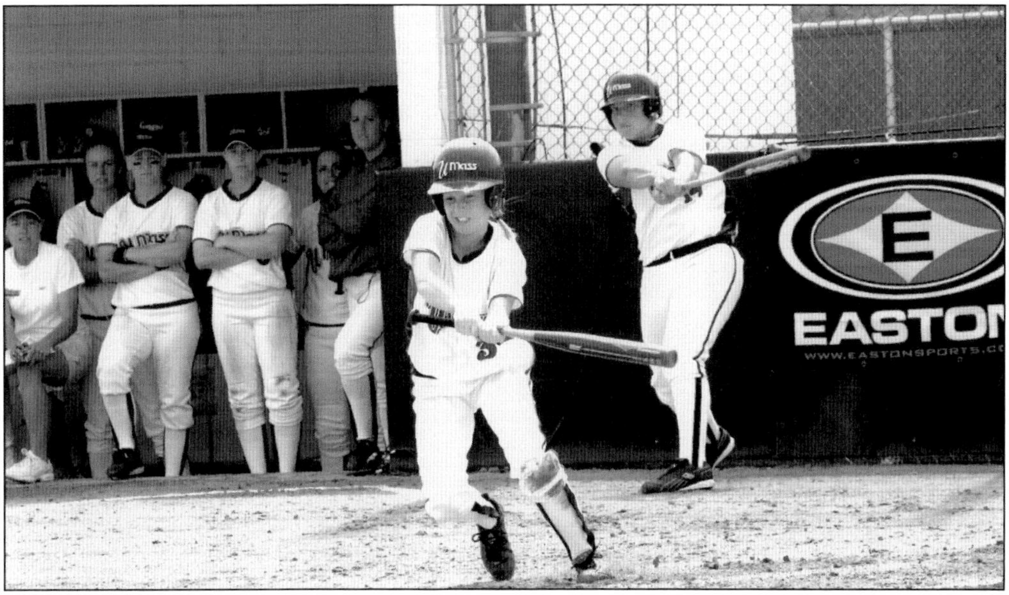

Freshman outfielder Candice Molinari hits one to the opposite field in a 2004 game against Fordam University. Katie Jo Kelley swings a bat in the on-deck circle. (Photograph courtesy of Karen Winger '00.)

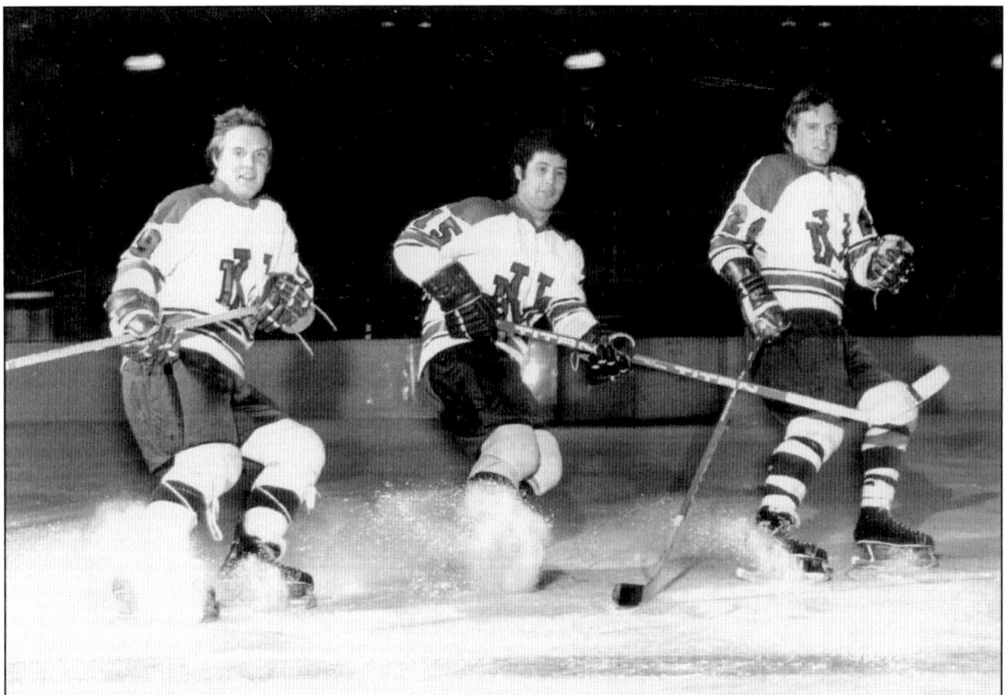

Shown in this image are, from left to right, Bobby White '78, Chris Lamby '77, and Bill White '78. (Photograph courtesy of the Special Collections and Archives, W.E.B. Du Bois Library, University of Massachusetts Amherst.)

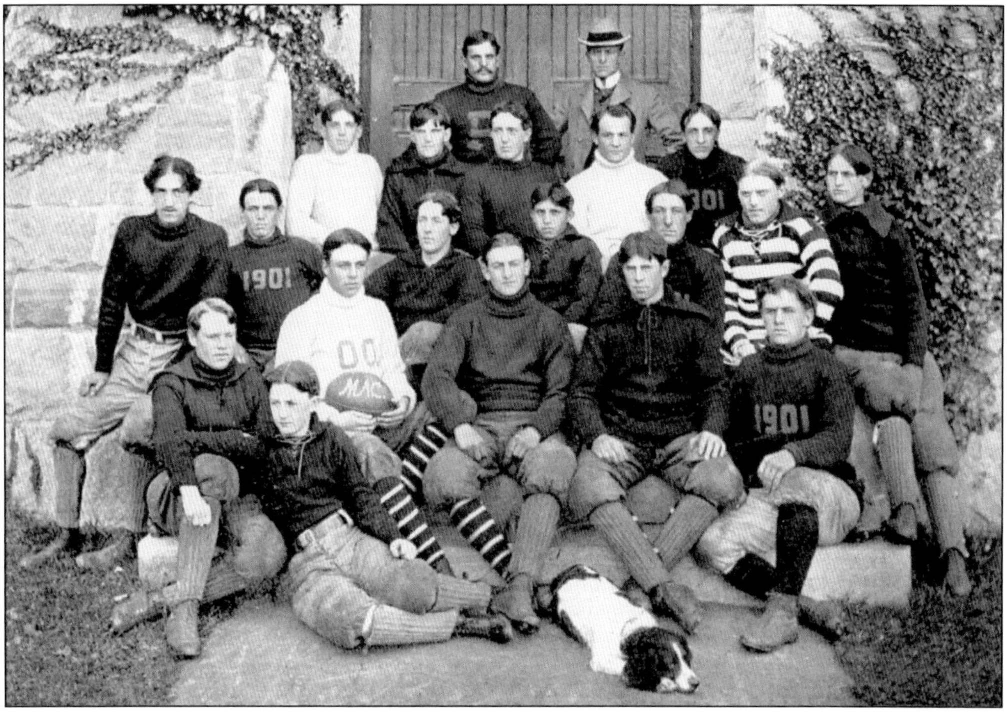

Pictured are the members the 1900 football team posing for their annual team photograph. Their mascot looks unenthused.

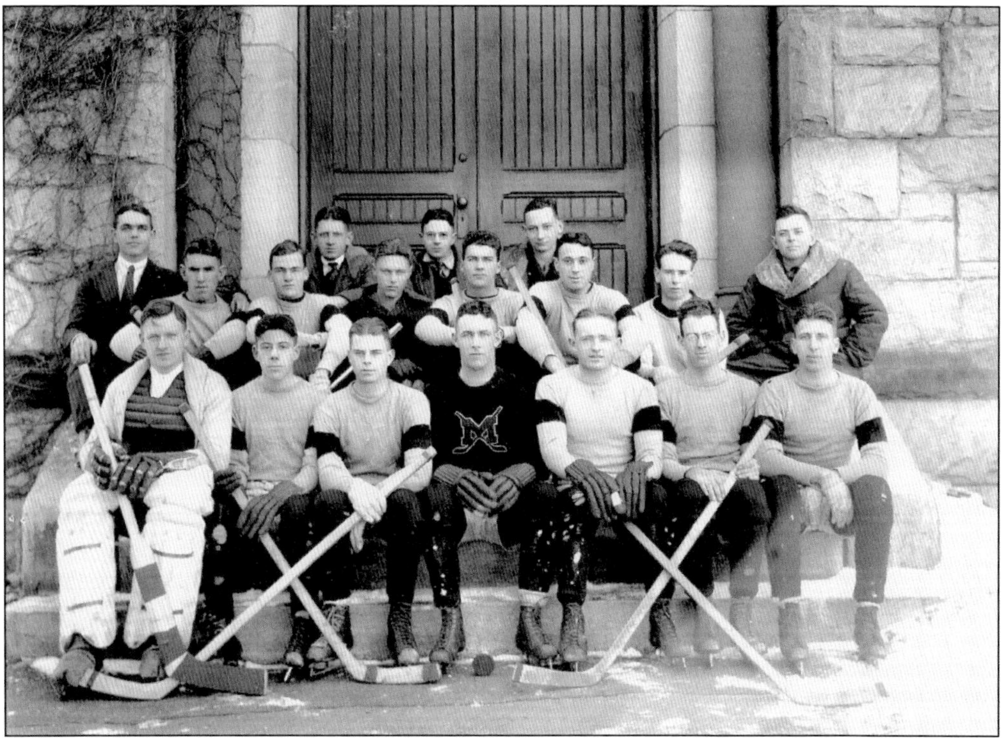

The 1919 hockey team poses for its annual photograph on the steps of the Old Chapel.

Six

Traditions

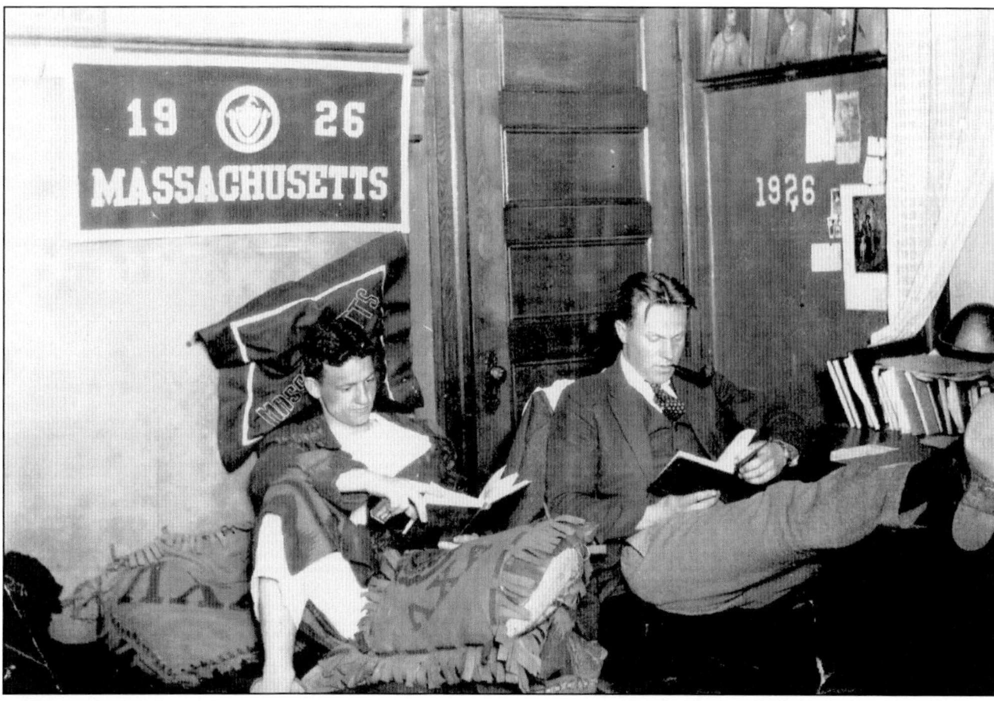

James E. Burnham and Roy Norcross are seen here in 1925, their junior year, at the Lambda Chi Alpha house at 84 North Pleasant Street in Amherst . (Photograph courtesy of the Special Collections and Archives, W.E.B. Du Bois Library, University of Massachusetts Amherst.)

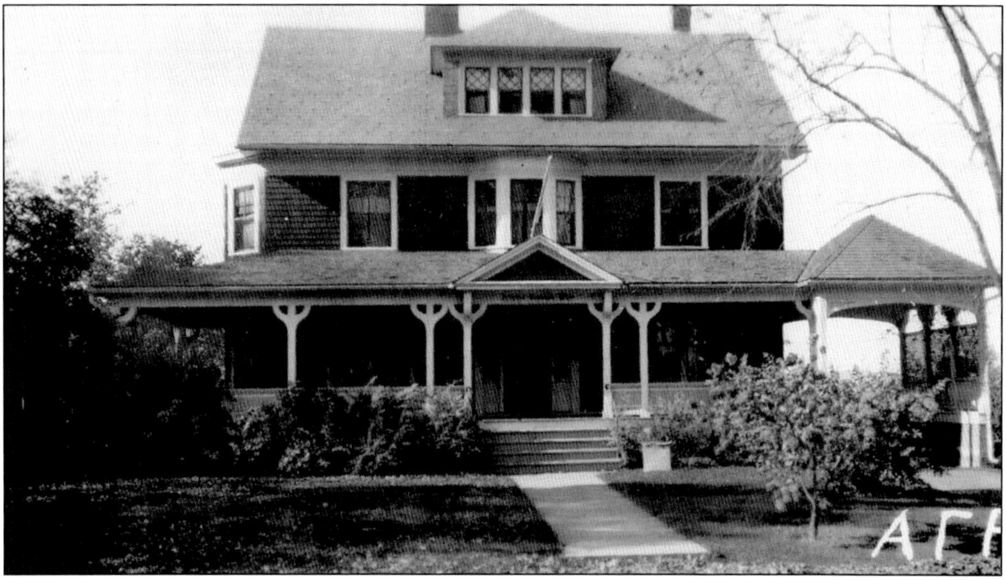

Alpha Gamma Rho Fraternity was founded nationally in 1908 and locally in Amherst in 1910. Fraternities and sororities were a big part of campus life in the early days of the college. Before the huge influx of students onto campus in the 1960s, a high percentage of students were part of Greek life. Existing mainly as social organizations, these groups seek to foster a healthy and balanced development of the individual through comradeship and mutual undertakings.

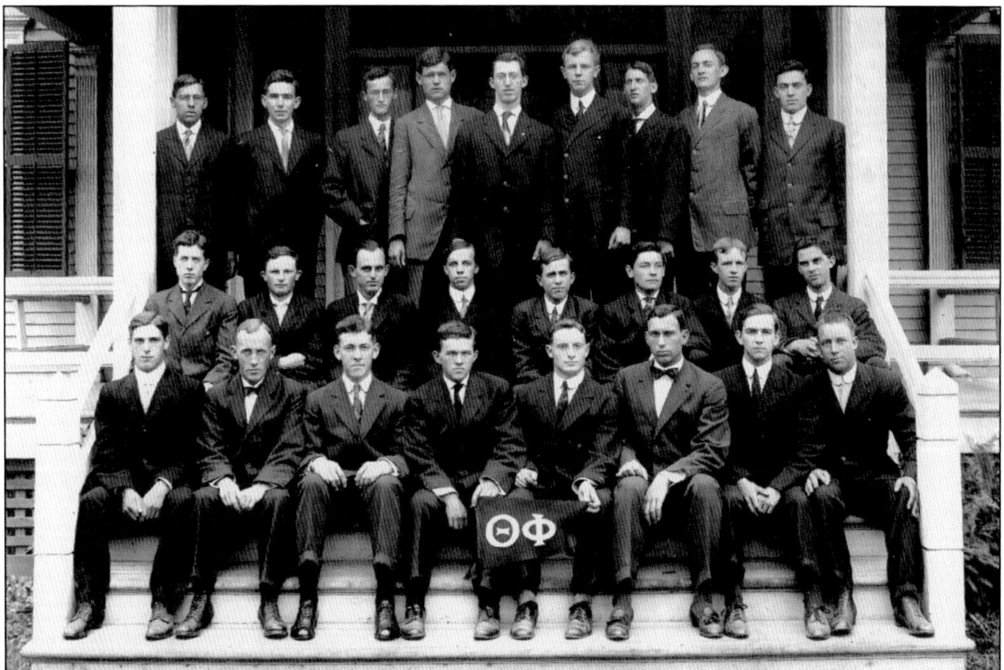

Members of Theta Phi pose on the steps of the fraternity house in 1919. (Photograph courtesy of the Special Collections and Archives, W.E.B. Du Bois Library, University of Massachusetts Amherst.)

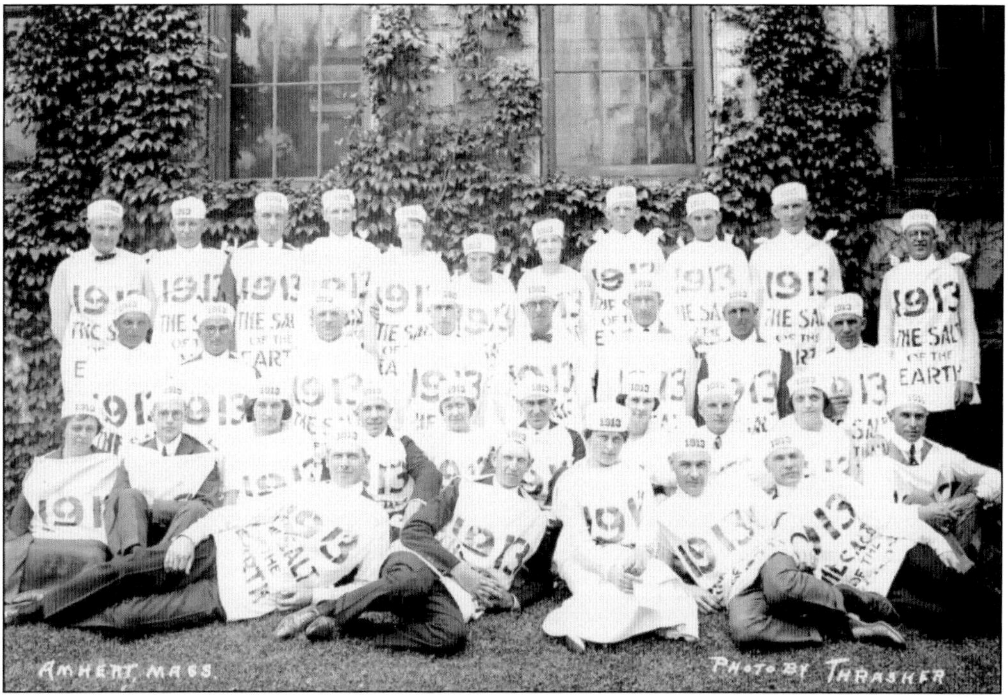

Members of the class of 1913 returned for the annual reunion weekend on June 13, 1921, wearing outfits that read "The Salt of the Earth." (Photograph courtesy of the Special Collections and Archives, W.E.B. Du Bois Library, University of Massachusetts Amherst.)

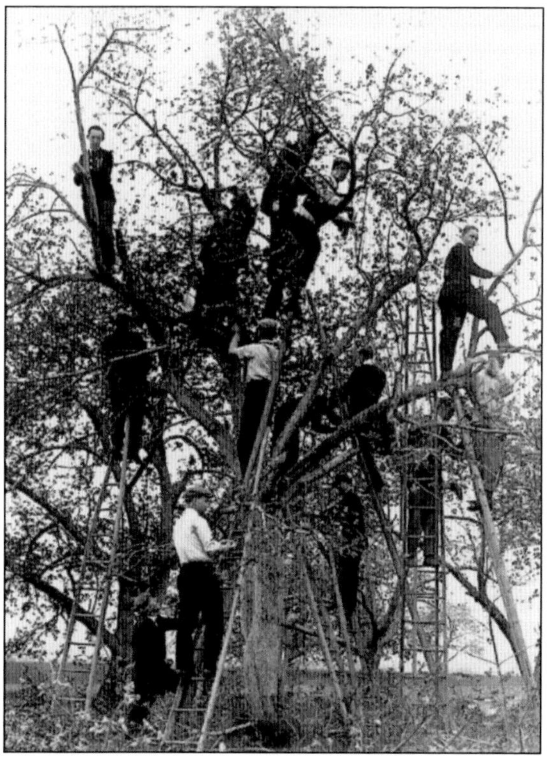

In this 1909 image, students of the class of 1910 work on pruning an apple tree. Part of the curriculum of the Massachusetts Agricultural College in the early days was agronomy and polomony. (Photograph courtesy of the Special Collections and Archives, W.E.B. Du Bois Library, University of Massachusetts Amherst.)

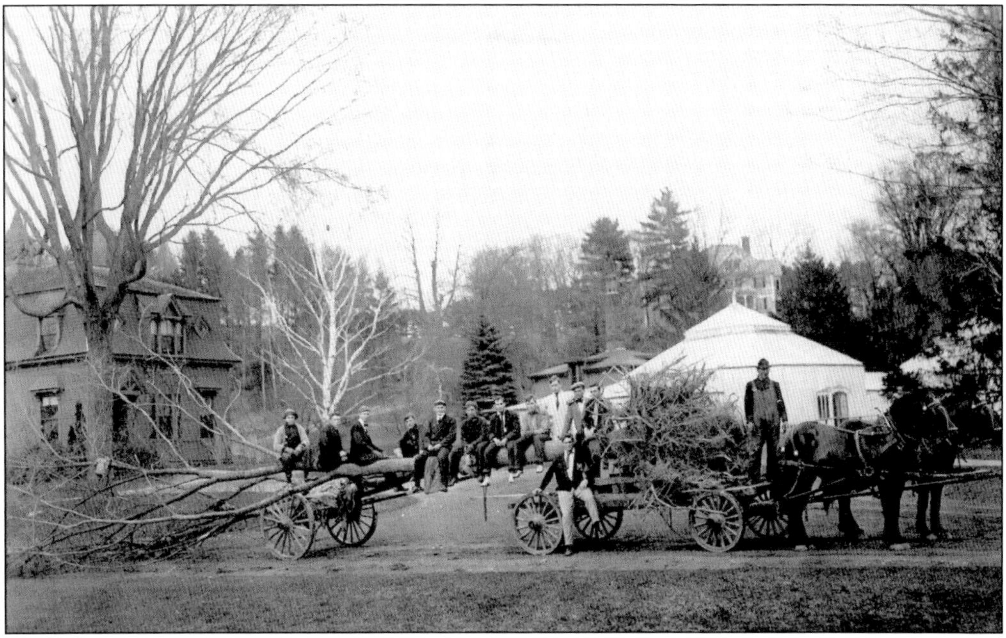

A horse-drawn carriage is shown here pulling the class tree of 1909, seen lying on its side. A dozen students sit on the tree. In the background are the Botanic Museum, the Durfee Conservatory, and the president's house. (Photograph courtesy of the Special Collections and Archives, W.E.B. Du Bois Library, University of Massachusetts Amherst.)

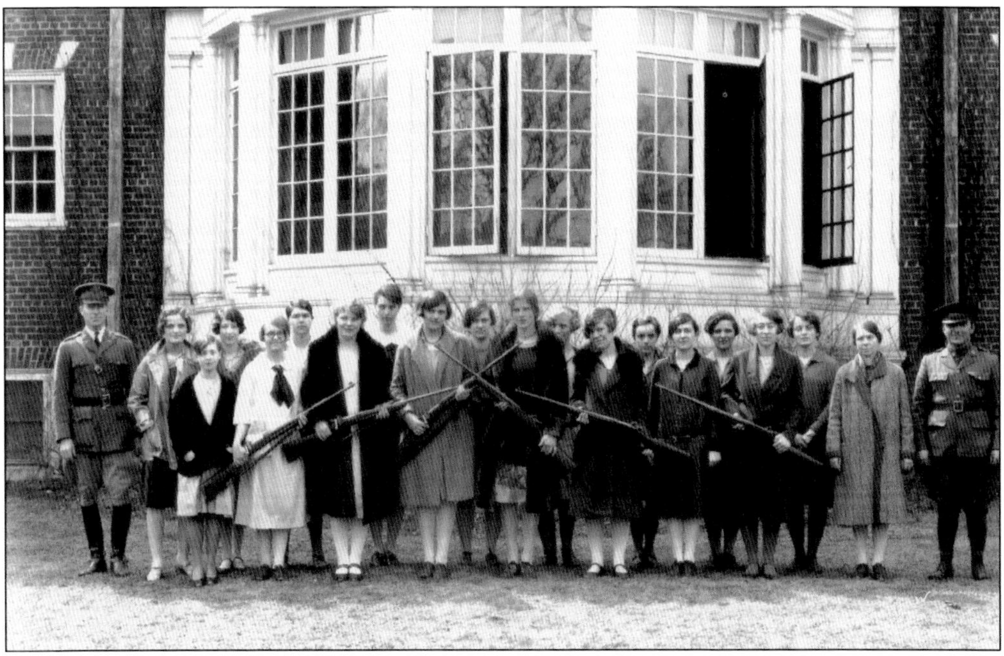

Members of the Women's Rifle Club stand in front of the all-female dorm, the Abigail Adams House, in 1920. (Photograph courtesy of the Special Collections and Archives, W.E.B. Du Bois Library, University of Massachusetts Amherst.)

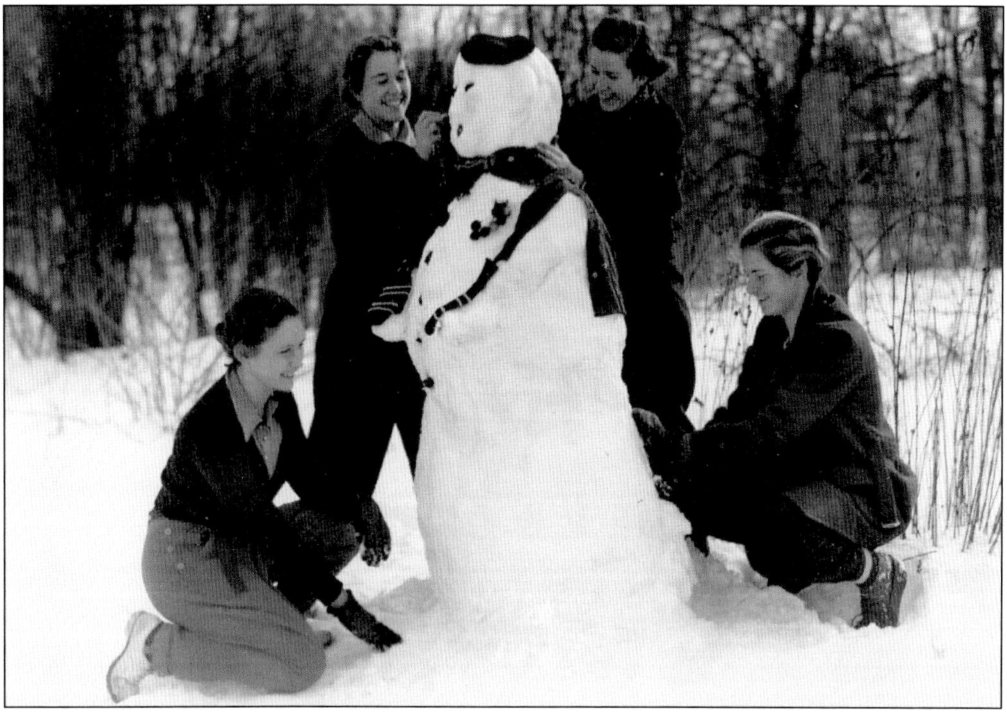

Shown here building a snowman on campus in 1934 are, from left to right, Edith Mildred Parsons '36 of Turners Falls; Constance Hathaway Hall '36 of Sharon; Beatrice "Bebe" Norma Rafter '36 of Sharon; and Eleanor Clarke Fillmore '36 of Melrose. (Photograph courtesy of Mary Taylor Barnhard '34.)

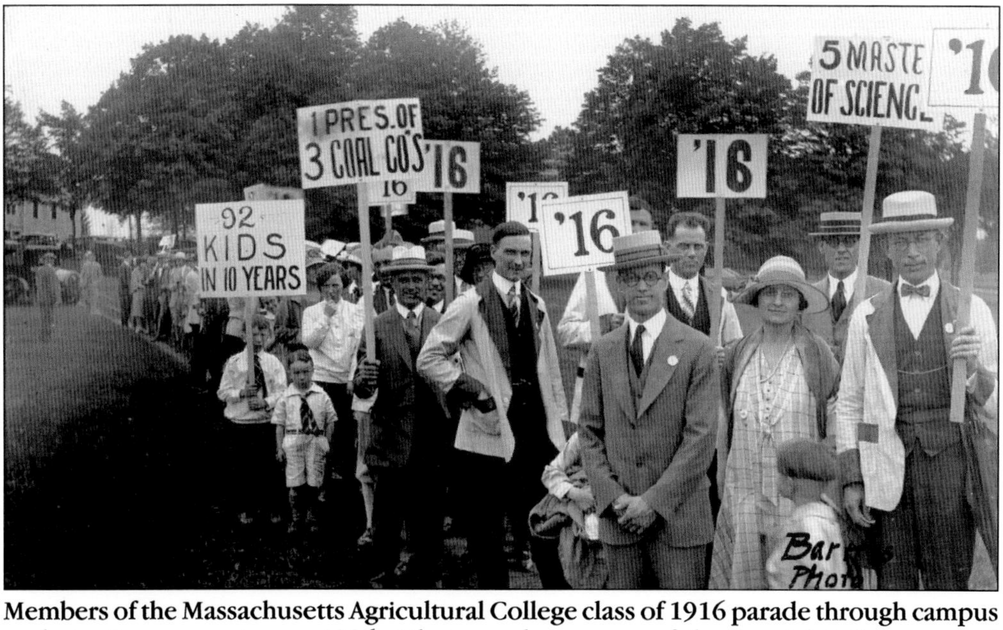

Members of the Massachusetts Agricultural College class of 1916 parade through campus at their 10-year reunion in 1926. (Photograph courtesy of the Special Collections and Archives, W.E.B. Du Bois Library, University of Massachusetts Amherst.)

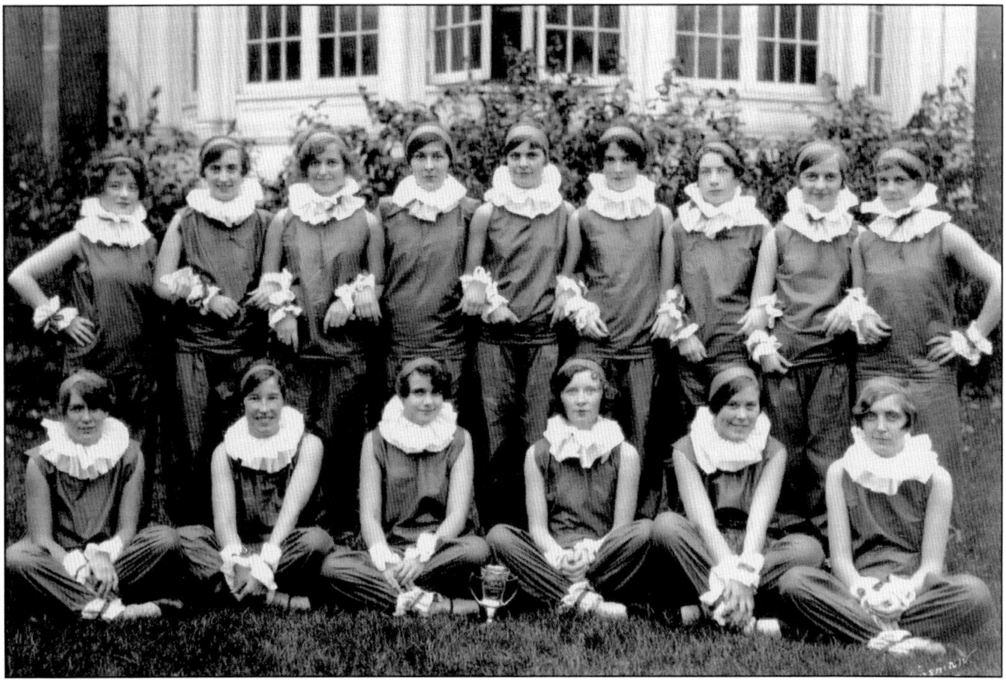

These sorority sisters from Delta Phi Gamma are getting ready for the Intra-fraternity Sing Competition of 1928. They are posing in front of the Abigail Adams House. Established in 1916, Delta Phi Gamma was the first sorority on campus. (Photograph courtesy of the Special Collections and Archives, W.E.B. Du Bois Library, University of Massachusetts Amherst.)

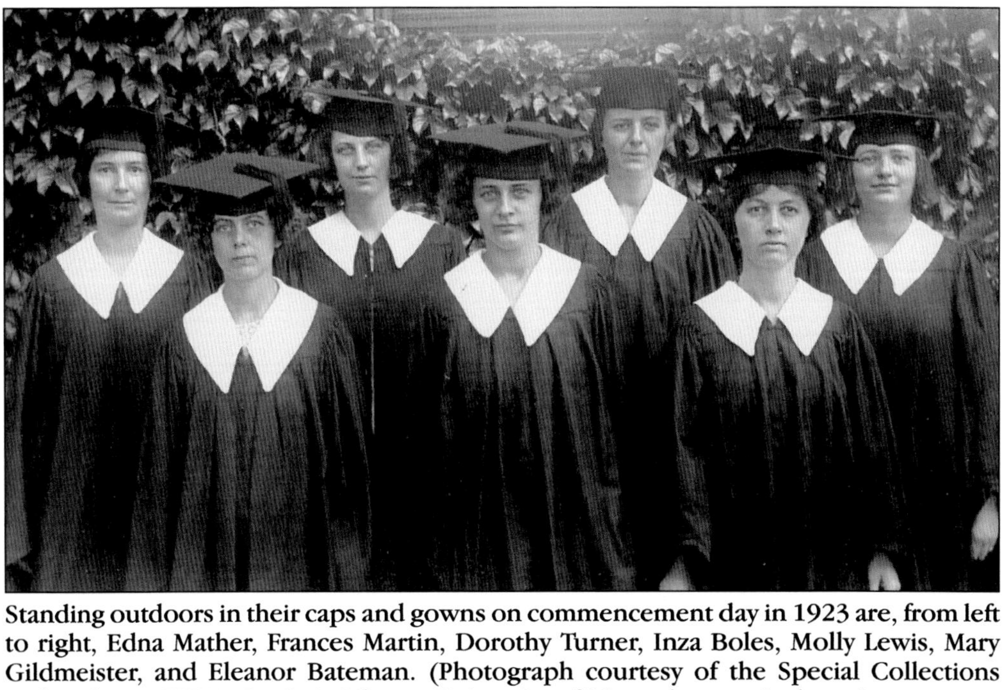

Standing outdoors in their caps and gowns on commencement day in 1923 are, from left to right, Edna Mather, Frances Martin, Dorothy Turner, Inza Boles, Molly Lewis, Mary Gildmeister, and Eleanor Bateman. (Photograph courtesy of the Special Collections and Archives, W.E.B. Du Bois Library, University of Massachusetts Amherst.)

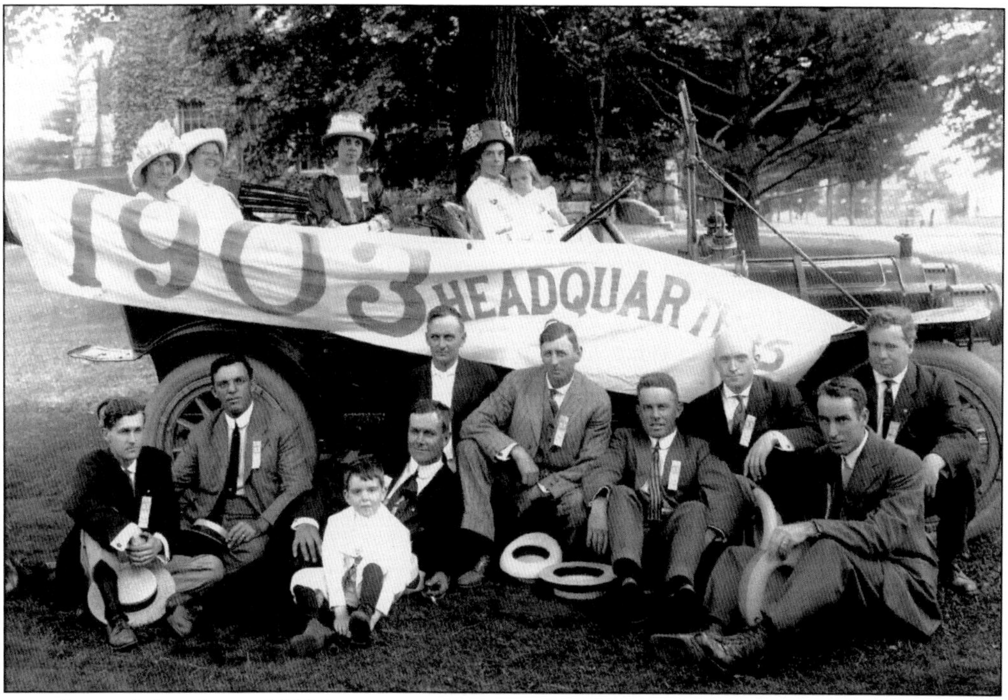

Members of the class of 1903 pose outdoors on an automobile with a banner that reads "1903 Headquarters." (Photograph courtesy of the Special Collections and Archives, W.E.B. Du Bois Library, University of Massachusetts Amherst.)

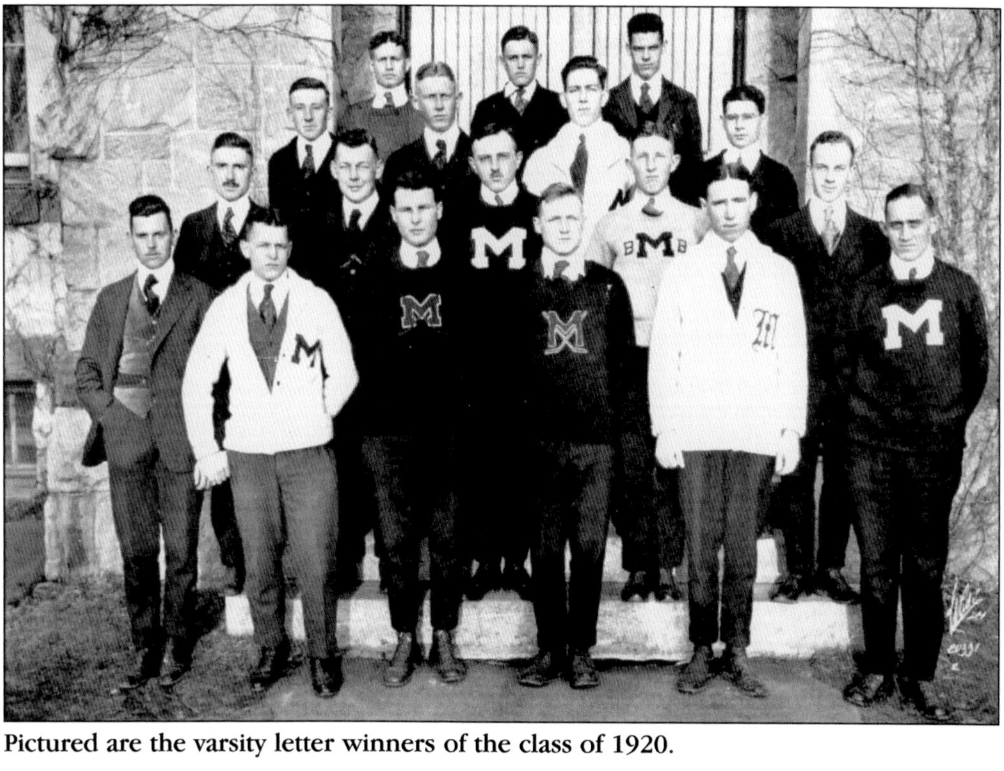

Pictured are the varsity letter winners of the class of 1920.

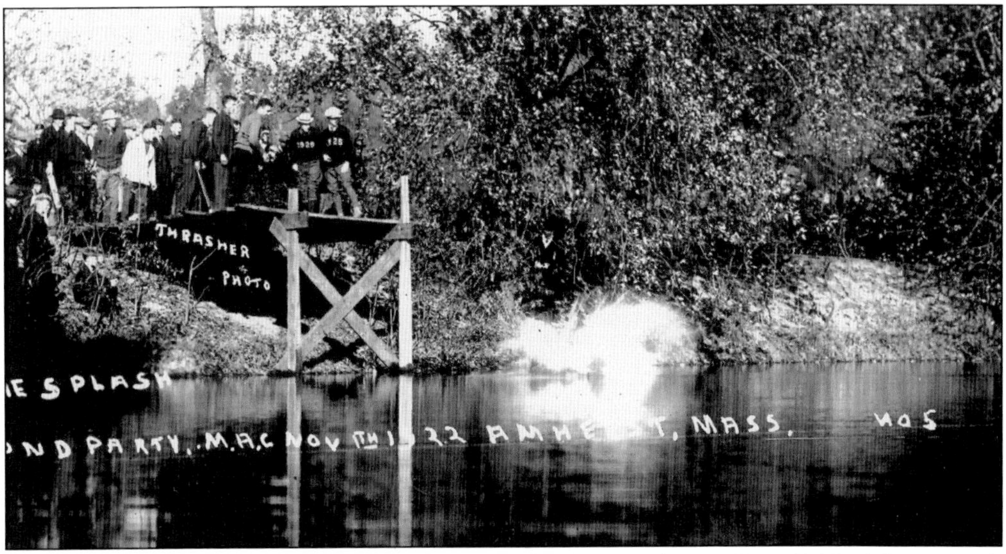

The student making the splash was sentenced to a "pond party" in 1922. (Photograph courtesy of the Special Collections and Archives, W.E.B. Du Bois Library, University of Massachusetts Amherst.)

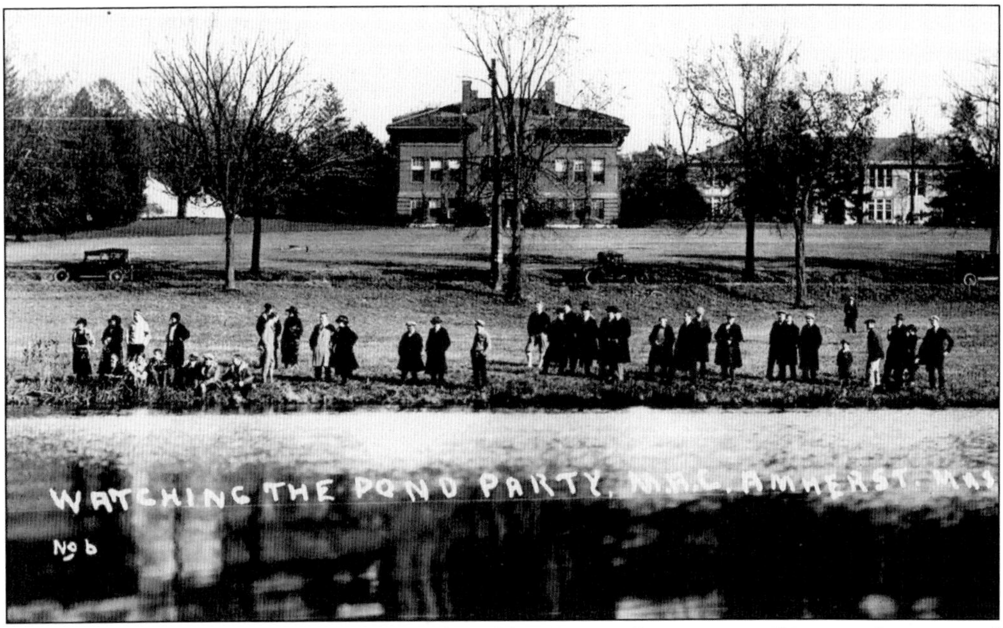

The penalty of a "pond party" was ordered by the student senate if it was determined that a student had broken the laws of the campus. According to campus rules, only upperclassmen could smoke and only seniors could wear mustaches. Underclassmen were required to carry matches to light the upperclassmen's cigarettes or pipes, were obligated to salute all faculty and members of the student senate, and were forbidden to walk around campus with their hands in their pockets. According to Ellsworth "Dutchy" Barnard '28, "In this established ritual, the victim would be heaved into the campus pond in front of the upperclassmen. Any freshman who was caught watching the procedure received the same treatment."

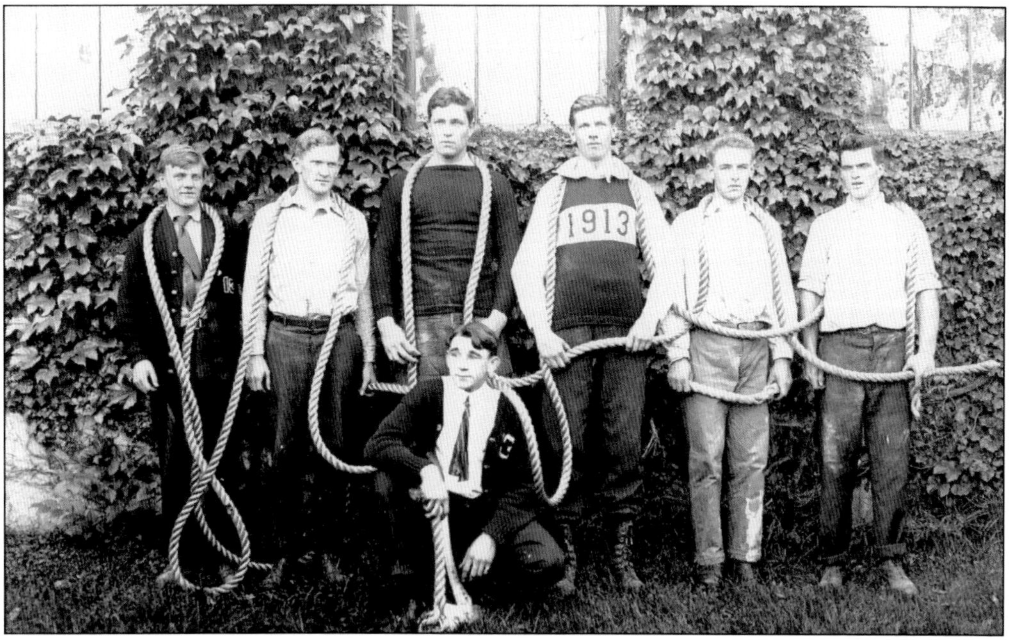

Standing proudly with a length of rope, members of the class of 1913 show off their hard work. The 60-man rope pull used to take place the first Saturday after college opened each year. Teams of 60 men from each class were placed on opposite sides of the pond with a 600-foot rope between them. Each team tried to pull the other through the pond within the time limit. The freshmen battled the sophomores and the juniors clashed with the seniors. The winning teams cut the rope in one-foot lengths and prominently displayed them in their dorm rooms. (Photograph courtesy of the Special Collections and Archives, W.E.B. Du Bois Library, University of Massachusetts Amherst.)

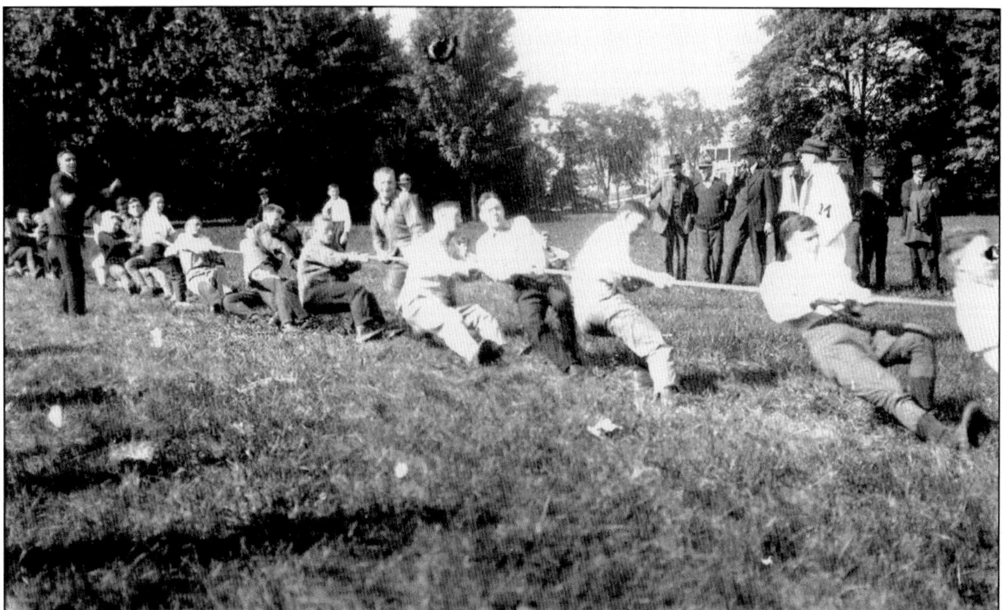

The rope pull is shown in action in 1922.

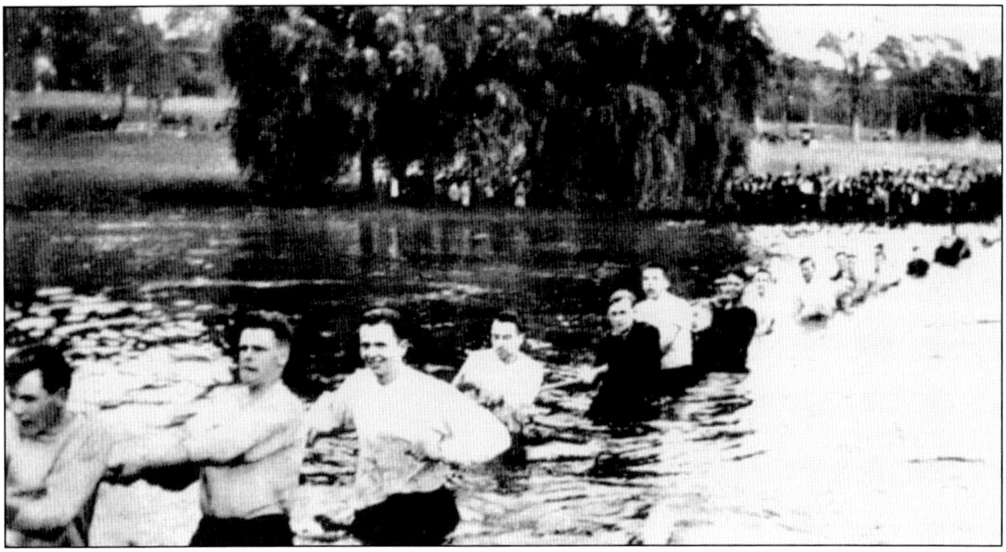

These students seem to be enjoying the rope pull, although it appears they have lost since they are in the water.

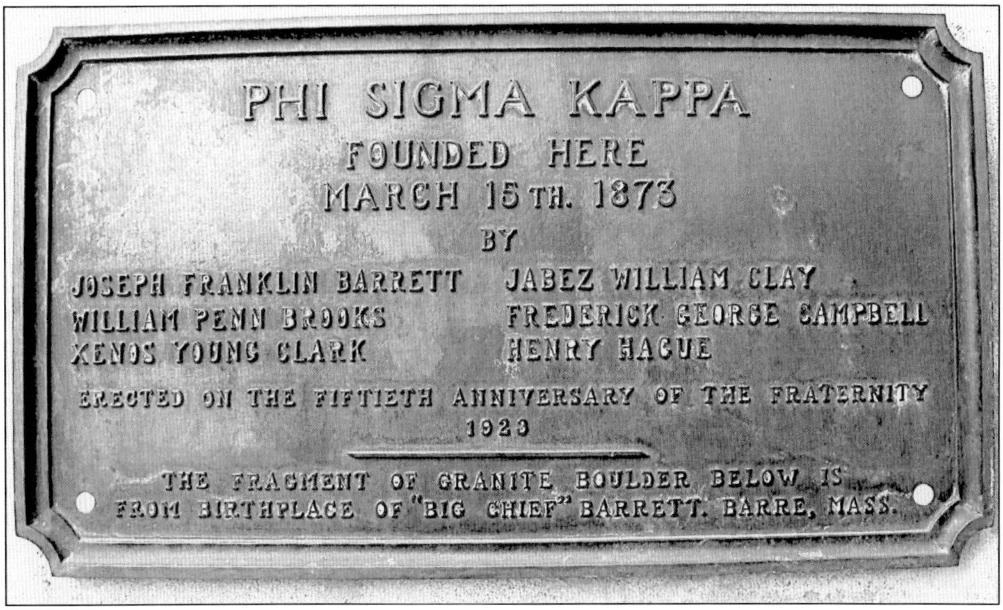

This plaque can be found on the wall of Machmer Hall. Phi Sigma Kappa was founded in 1873 at Massachusetts Agricultural College. As sophomores at MAC, six students banded together to form a "society to promote morality, learning and social culture." The six students were Jabez William Clay, Frederick George Campbell, Joseph Franklin Barrett, Xenos Young Clark, William Penn Brooks, and Henry Hague. Many years later, in 1957, a senior Phi Sigma Kappa brother from 15 Lovett Street in Salem graduated and became the most famous chief executive officer in the world. He worked for the General Electric Company and his name was John Francis Welch.

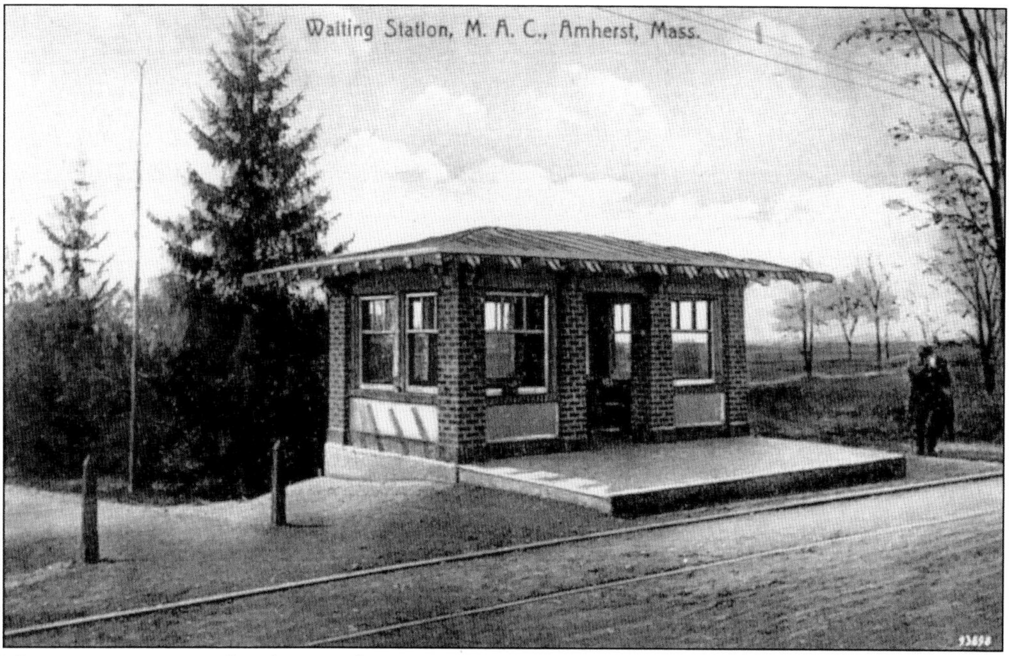

The waiting station has been a fixture on campus since 1911. Located next to Hasbrouck Laboratory on North Pleasant Street, it has kept students out of the elements for over 90 years.

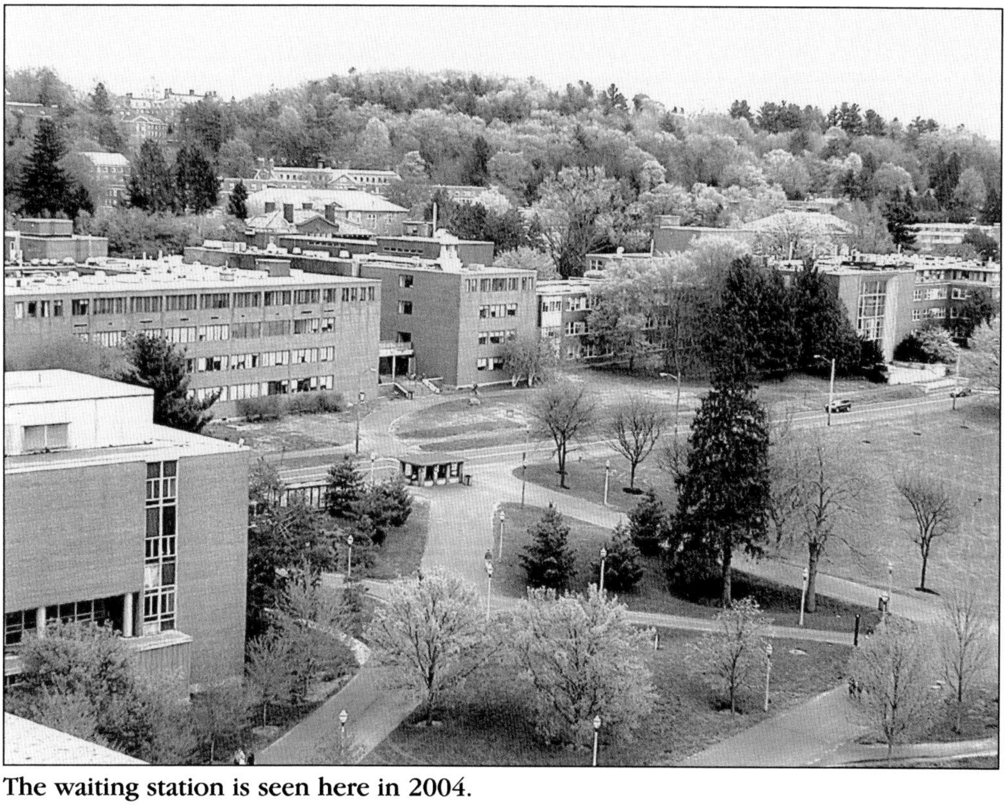

The waiting station is seen here in 2004.

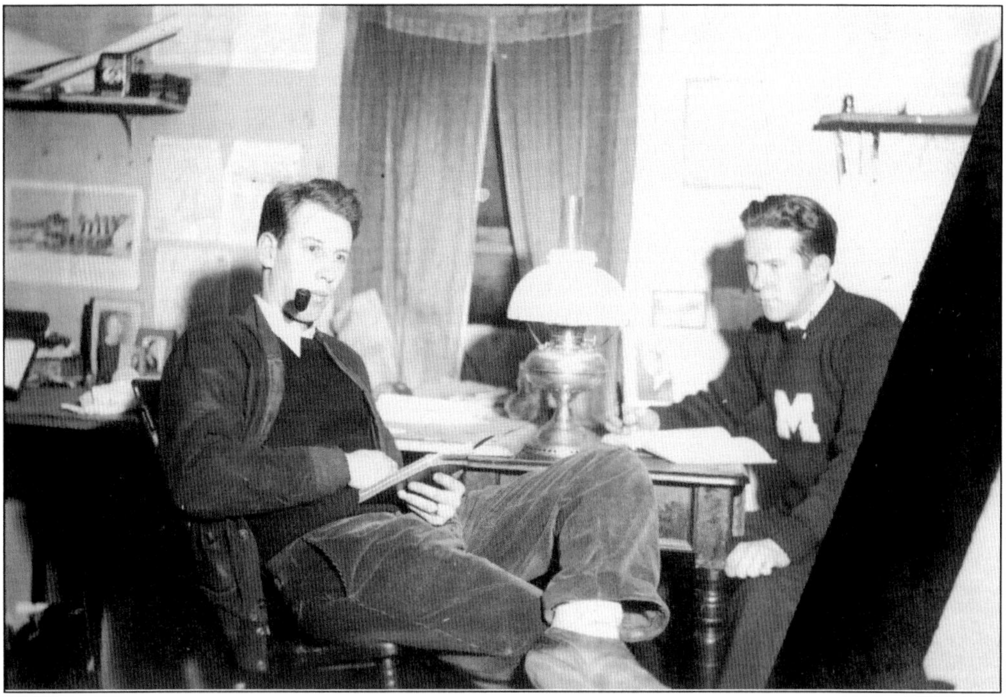

David Crosby and Gordon Ainsworth study in their dorm room at Massachusetts State College in 1932. (Photograph courtesy of the Special Collections and Archives, W.E.B. Du Bois Library, University of Massachusetts Amherst.)

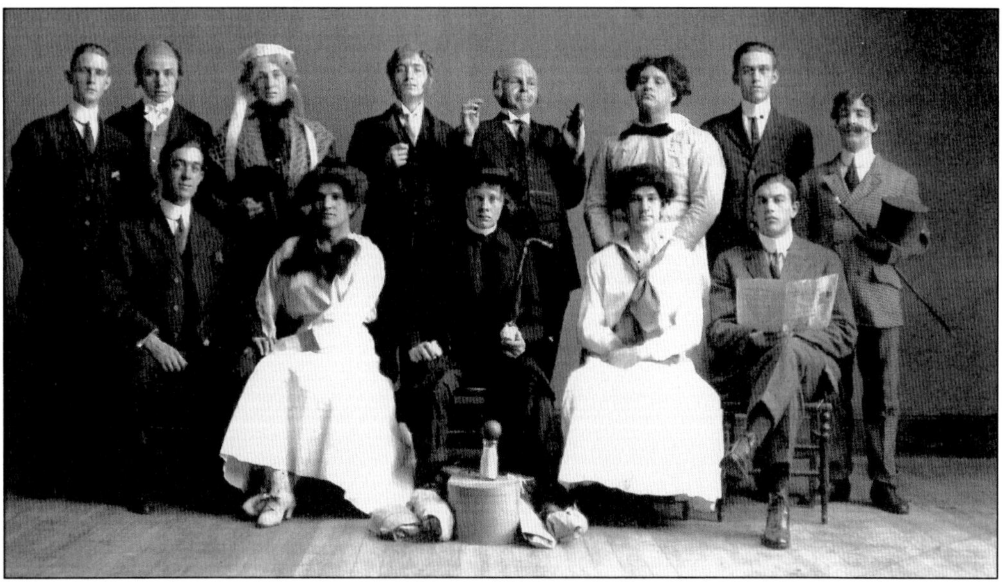

The cast of "The Private Secretary" poses indoors; some of the actors shown are identified as Reid, Nickerson, Sharpe, Hills, Goodnough, Moir, Jordan, Zabrieski, Wilde, Robinson, Dudley, Van Zwakenburg, and Simmons. During the 1910–1911 season, the theater program was an enormous success under director Frank Prentice Rand. (Photograph courtesy of the Special Collections and Archives, W.E.B. Du Bois Library, University of Massachusetts Amherst.)

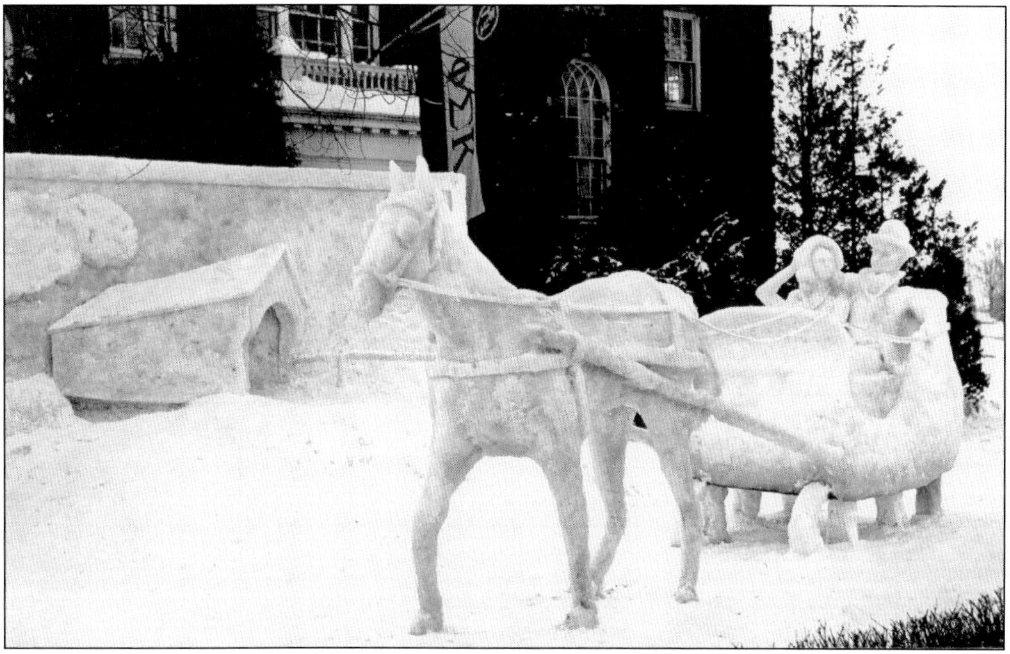

A longstanding tradition at the university, the winter carnival, gave the fraternities and sororities a chance to show off their creativity by building snow sculptures in front of their fraternity or sorority houses. The Greek council determined who the winner was. (Photograph courtesy of the Special Collections and Archives, W.E.B. Du Bois Library, University of Massachusetts Amherst.)

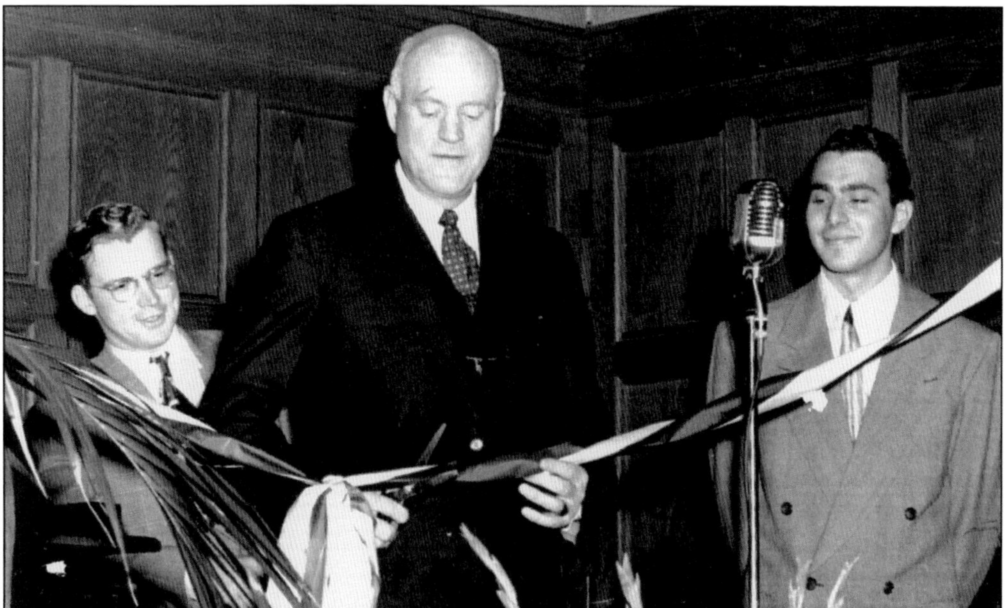

Shown here, from left to right, are Wayne Langill, UMass president Ralph A. Van Meter, and Irv Wasserman. President Van Meter is cutting the celebratory ribbon at the opening of the student radio station, WMUA, in 1949. (Photograph courtesy of the Special Collections and Archives, W.E.B. Du Bois Library, University of Massachusetts Amherst.)

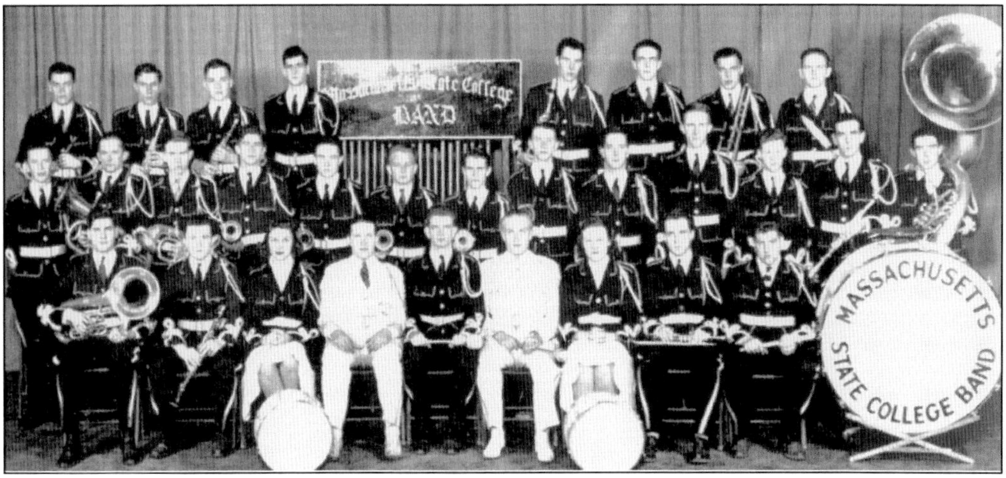

This is the annual photograph of the Massachusetts State College Marching Band in 1941.

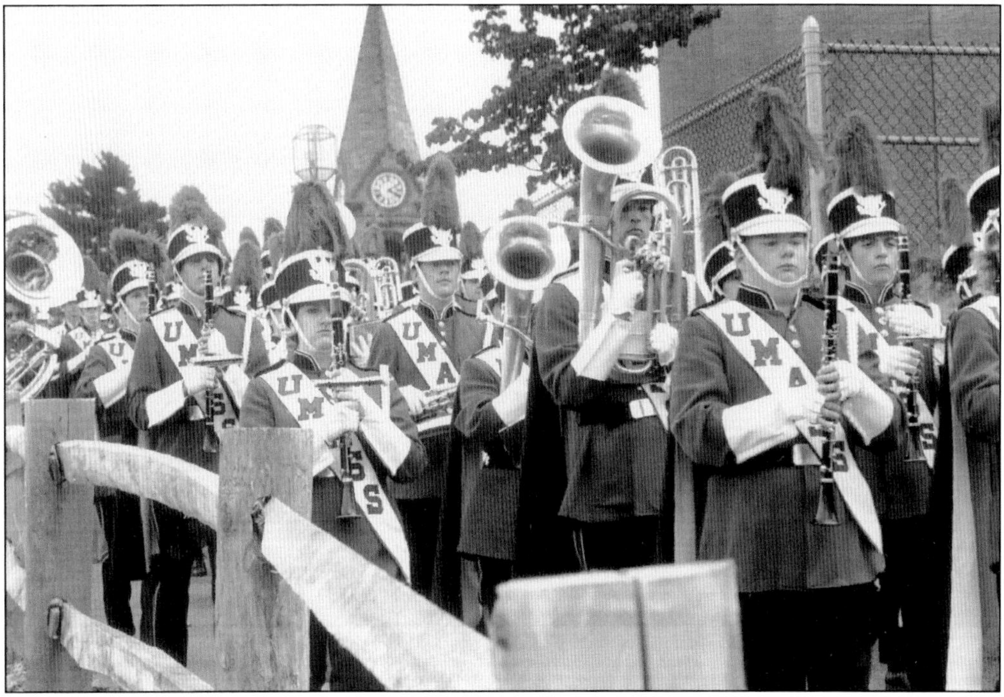

The marching band has enjoyed a long and rich history at the University of Massachusetts Amherst. The band as it is known today was officially organized in 1935 under the direction of Charles Farnum. The first leader of the Mass Aggie band was 1st Lt. Charles Morris, who started the Morris Drum Corps as a military band in the 1880s. (Photograph courtesy of the Special Collections and Archives, W.E.B. Du Bois Library, University of Massachusetts Amherst.)

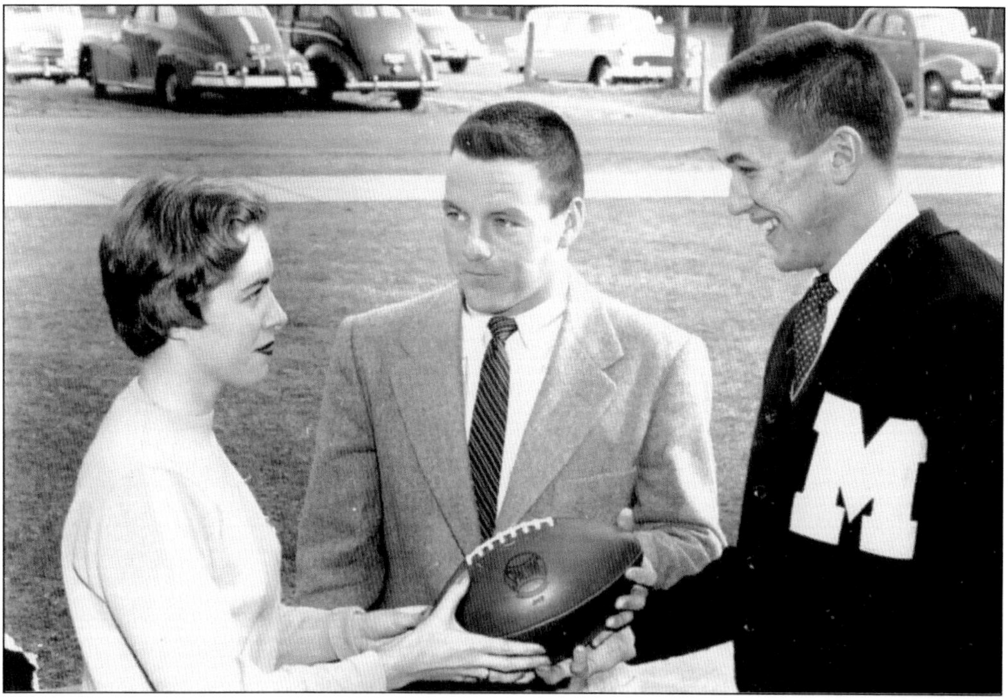

Homecoming has been a long-standing tradition on the Amherst campus, dating back to the early 1900s. With all its custom and ritual, homecoming at UMass Amherst started out on a Friday night with a pep rally and a bonfire beside the pond and ended Saturday with the crowning of homecoming queen at the football game. The photograph above shows the homecoming queen accepting a football from the coach and captain in 1950. (Photograph courtesy of the Special Collections and Archives, W.E.B. Du Bois Library, University of Massachusetts Amherst.)

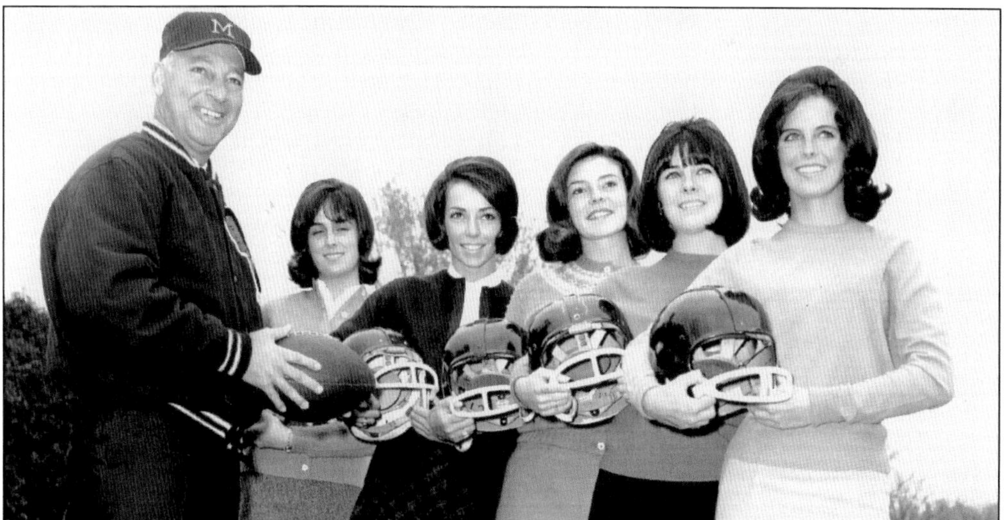

Head football coach Vic Fusia poses with the homecoming queen finalists in 1963. (Photograph courtesy of the Special Collections and Archives, W.E.B. Du Bois Library, University of Massachusetts Amherst.)

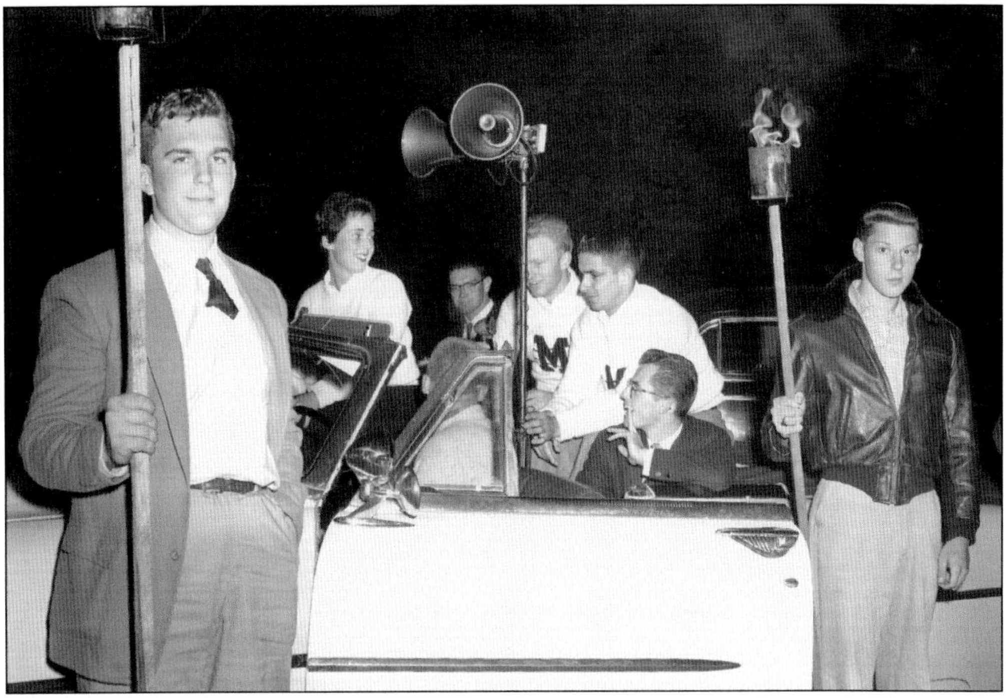

Football pep rallies were an annual fall tradition on campus and were held near the campus pond. The students in this photograph in 1956 seem content in this convertible sedan, despite the fall temperatures. (Photograph courtesy of the Special Collections and Archives, W.E.B. Du Bois Library, University of Massachusetts Amherst.)

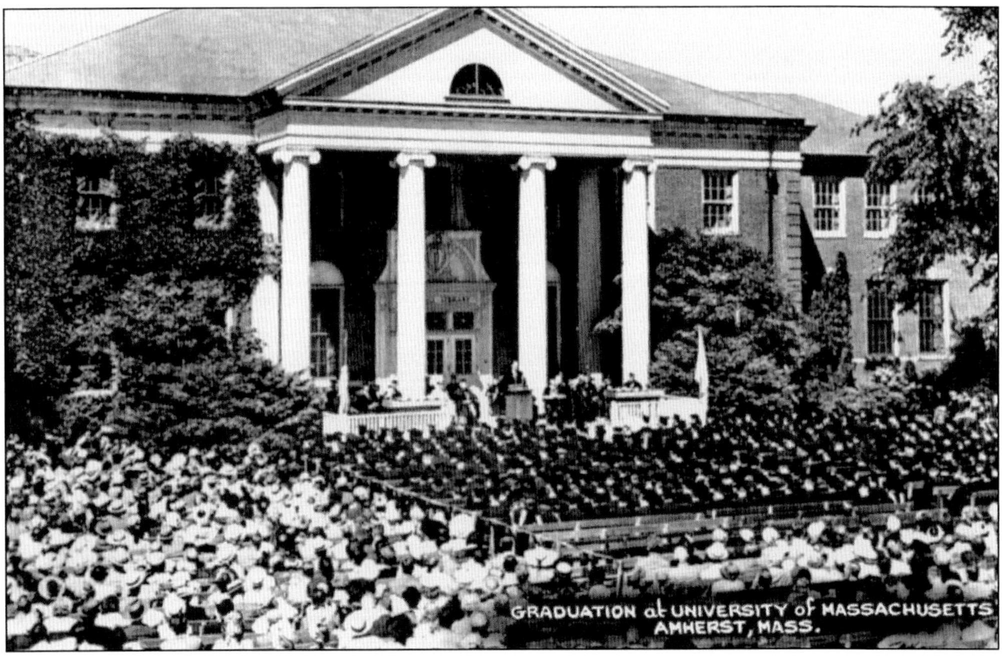

Before student enrollment expanded to more than 20,000 students, commencement exercises were held in the quad between the Old Chapel and Goodell Library.

Ellsworth Barnhard '28 and Mary Taylor Barnhard '34 were married in 1937. Many students have found the love of their lives on the campus in Amherst. (Photograph courtesy of Mary Taylor Barnhard '34.)

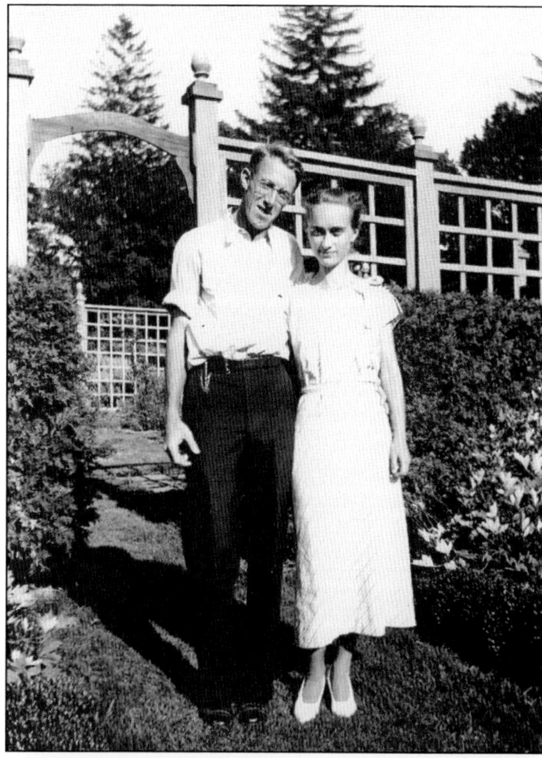

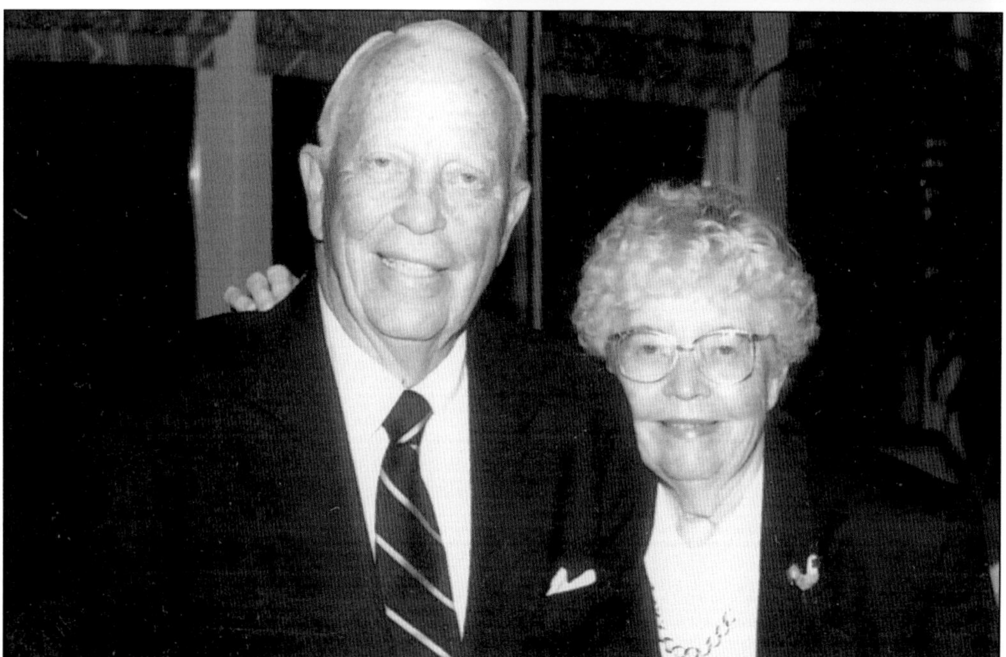

Robert C. Gunness '32 and his sister Marion Gunness Snuggs '39 pose for a photograph in 1992. Bob and Marion are the children of Christian I. Gunness, Massachusetts Agricultural College professor of rural engineering. Many families have graduated multiple children from the University of Massachusetts Amherst.

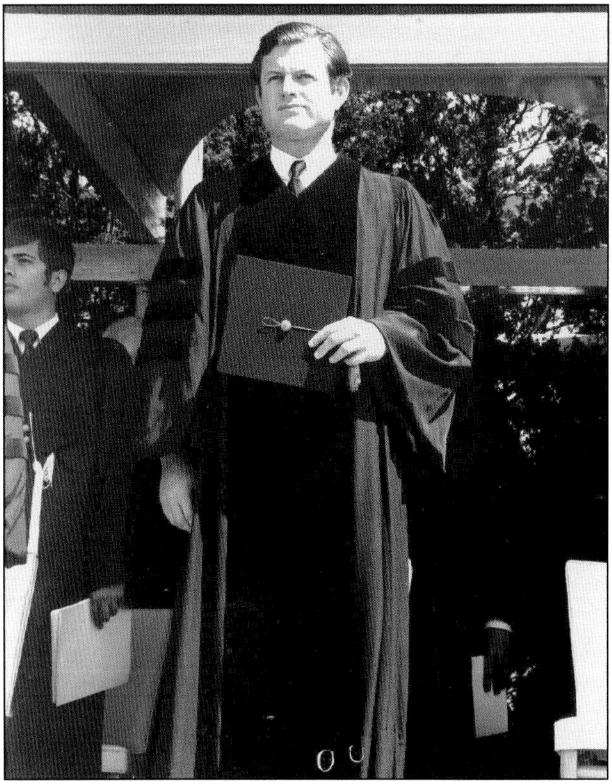

Sen. Edward M. Kennedy was the guest speaker at the 1969 commencement ceremonies on campus. Kennedy has always been a great friend of the University of Massachusetts Amherst. (Photograph courtesy of the Special Collections and Archives, W.E.B. Du Bois Library, University of Massachusetts Amherst.)

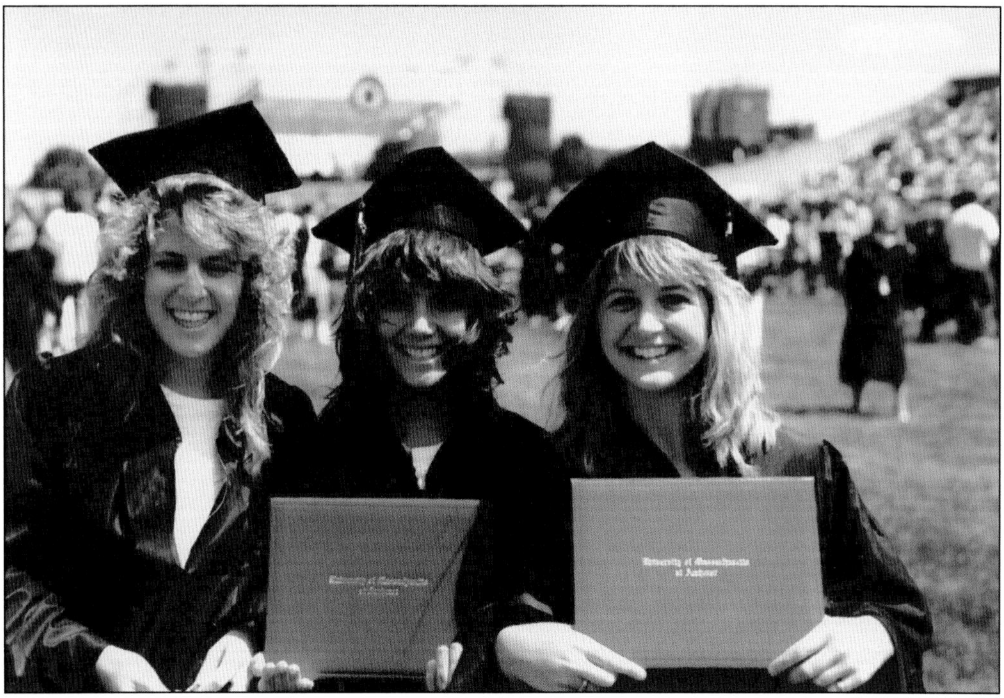

Shown here enjoying commencement in 1986 are, from left to right, Lauren Kaufman, Julie Gold, and Beth Salvador.

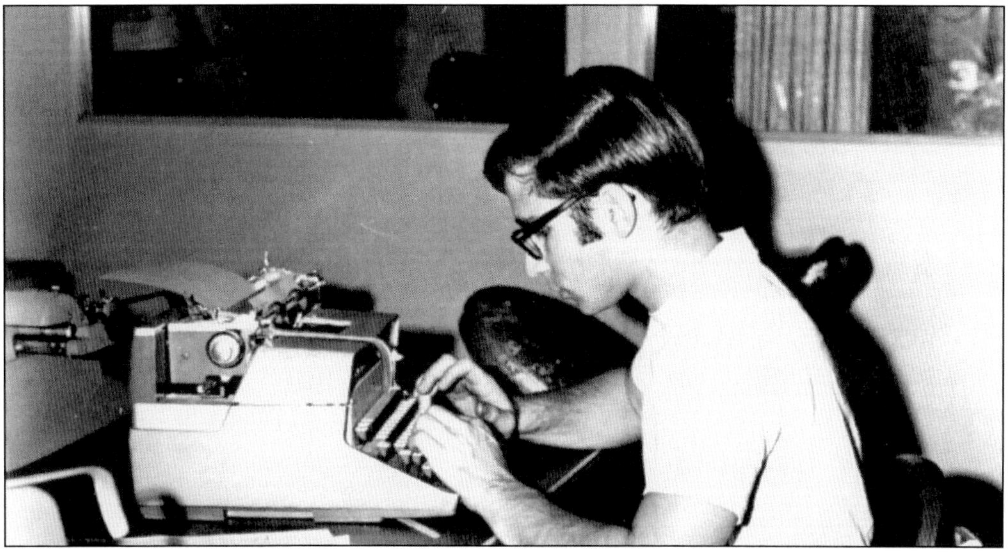

Collegian sports columnist Steve Shamban types away to make his deadline in 1970.

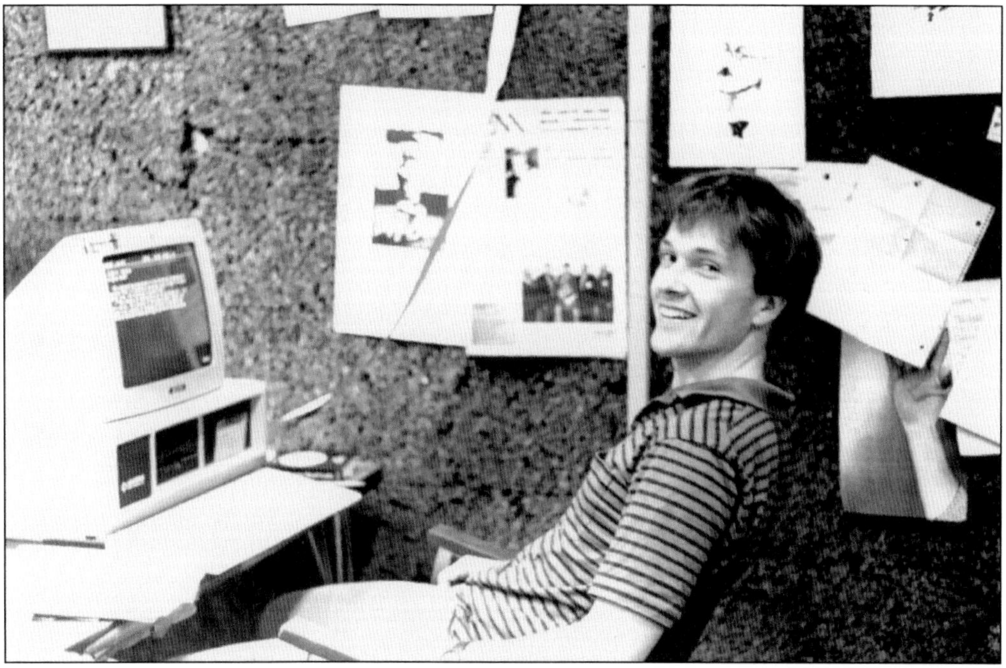

Joel Coffidis, news editor of the *Collegian* in 1985 and 1986, works on the newspaper's computer system, which debuted during that school year. In the mid-1990s, www.dailycollegian.com was launched. For generations, students, faculty, and staff at the university have received their news each school day from the *Massachusetts Daily Collegian*. Founded in 1890, the *Collegian* was also called *Aggie Life* (at the Massachusetts Agricultural College) and the *Signal* before taking its present name. The newspaper is published daily, and it has been financially independent from the university since 1967. Some of the nation's best reporters will always remember that they got their start at the *Collegian*, which is still the largest college daily newspaper in New England and has a circulation today of 14,000.

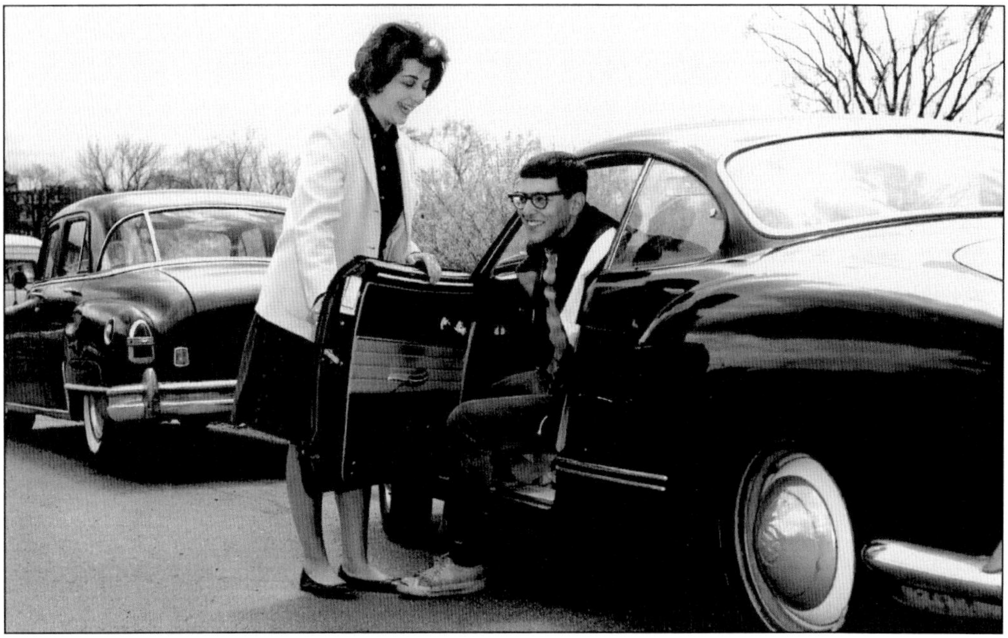

UMass freshman Diane LaFrance opens the door for freshman Arnold Wolfson. In 1966, the university's annual HER (His Economic Relief) Weekend was held May 3–5. Women were required to pay their dates' way and conform to masculine etiquette. (Photograph courtesy of the Special Collections and Archives, W.E.B. Du Bois Library, University of Massachusetts Amherst.)

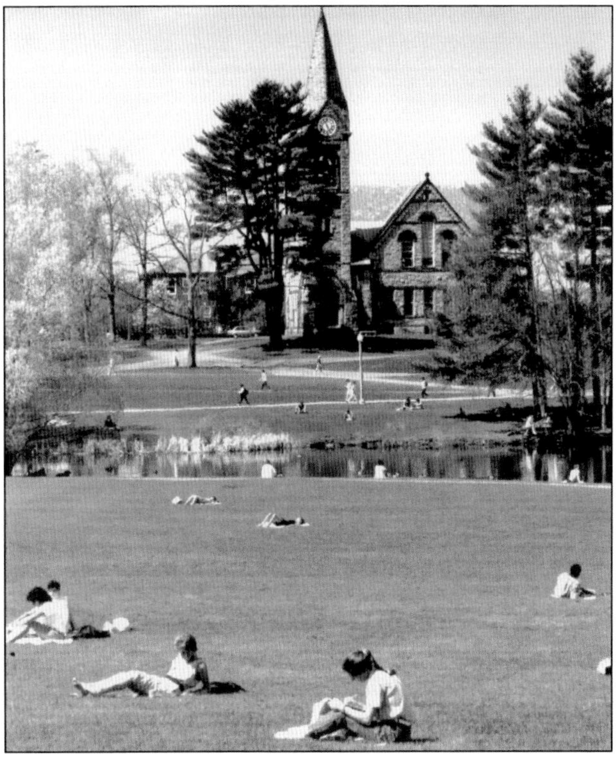

On a sunny day, there is no place for studying quite like the campus pond, as is shown in this 1975 photograph. (Photograph courtesy of the Special Collections and Archives, W.E.B. Du Bois Library, University of Massachusetts Amherst.)

This photograph depicts a student dorm in 1970. Take a closer look and you will find one of the old close-and-play record players. The campus dorm rooms have evolved since the days of kerosene lamps and potbelly stoves in South Dormitory.

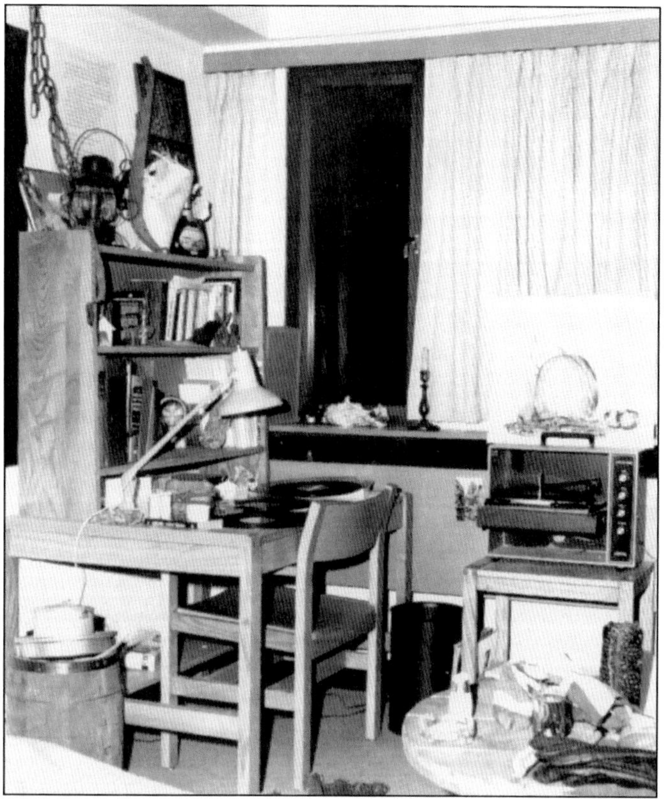

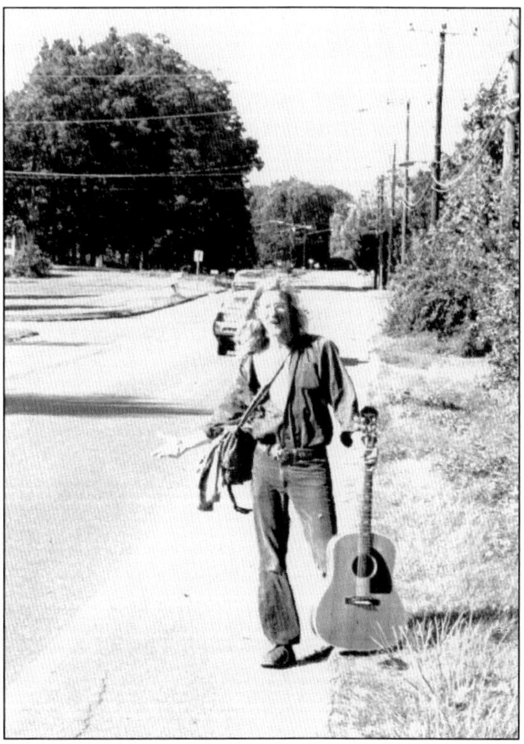

This unidentified man is hitchhiking his way to campus. Hitchhiking has been a longstanding student tradition at UMass. (Photograph courtesy of the Special Collections and Archives, W.E.B. Du Bois Library, University of Massachusetts Amherst.)

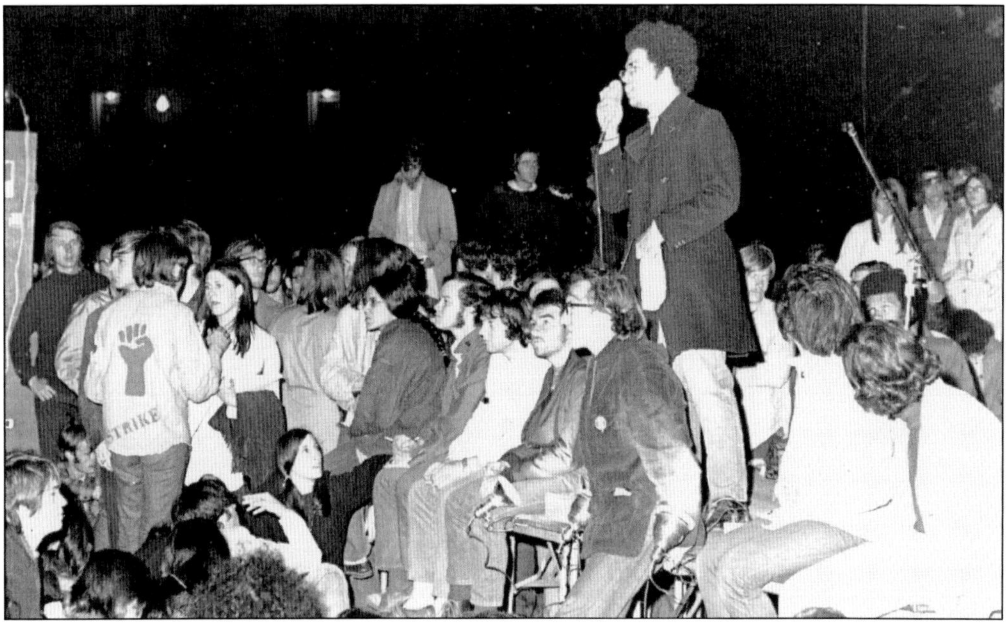

This was a very frequent scene on campus during the Vietnam conflict. There was much student unrest during the 1970–1971 school year. (Photograph courtesy of the Special Collections and Archives, W.E.B. Du Bois Library, University of Massachusetts Amherst.)

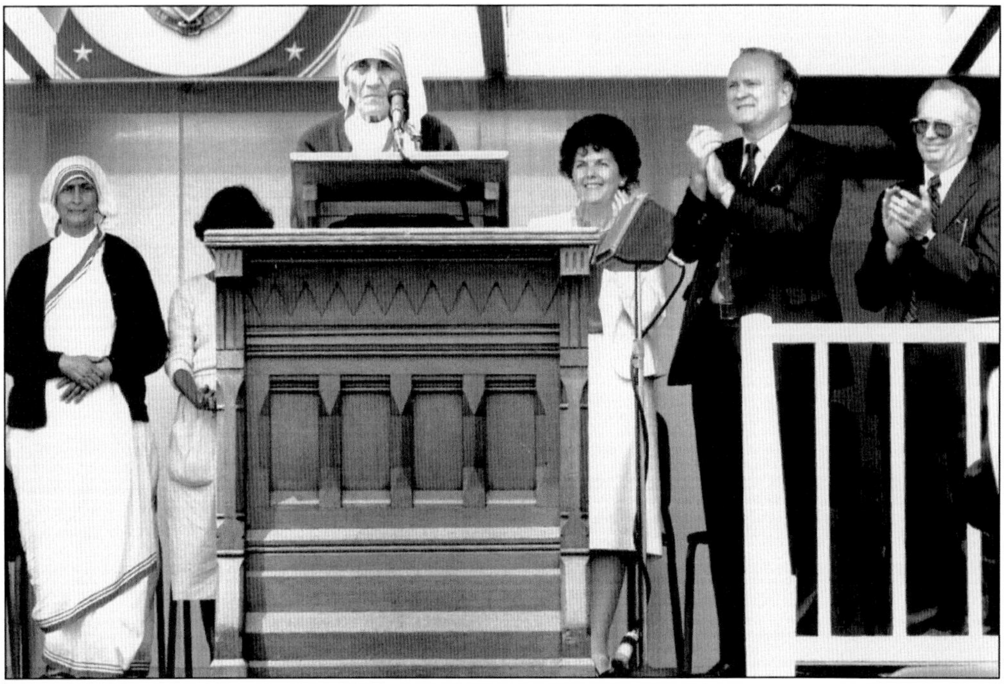

The Distinguished Visitors Program has brought many dignitaries to the UMass campus over the years. In this photograph, the passionate Mother Theresa of India addresses the campus as trustee Robert Quinn and Chancellor Joseph Duffey look on. (Photograph courtesy of the Special Collections and Archives, W.E.B. Du Bois Library, University of Massachusetts Amherst.)

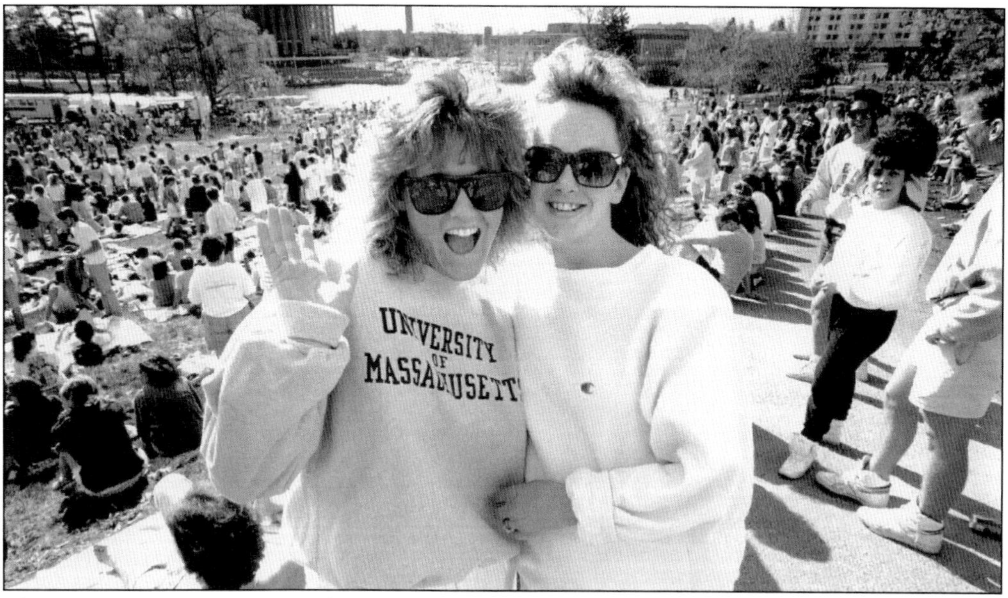

These two women seem to be enjoying Spring Day in 1986. An annual rite of passage at UMass, Spring Day is a huge gathering organized primarily for the soon-to-graduate seniors but attended by all the classes. Spring Day is comprised of a concert next to the pond and a barbeque. Some of the most cherished contemporary musical acts are hired to belt out music for the students. (Photograph courtesy of the Special Collections and Archives, W.E.B. Du Bois Library, University of Massachusetts Amherst.)

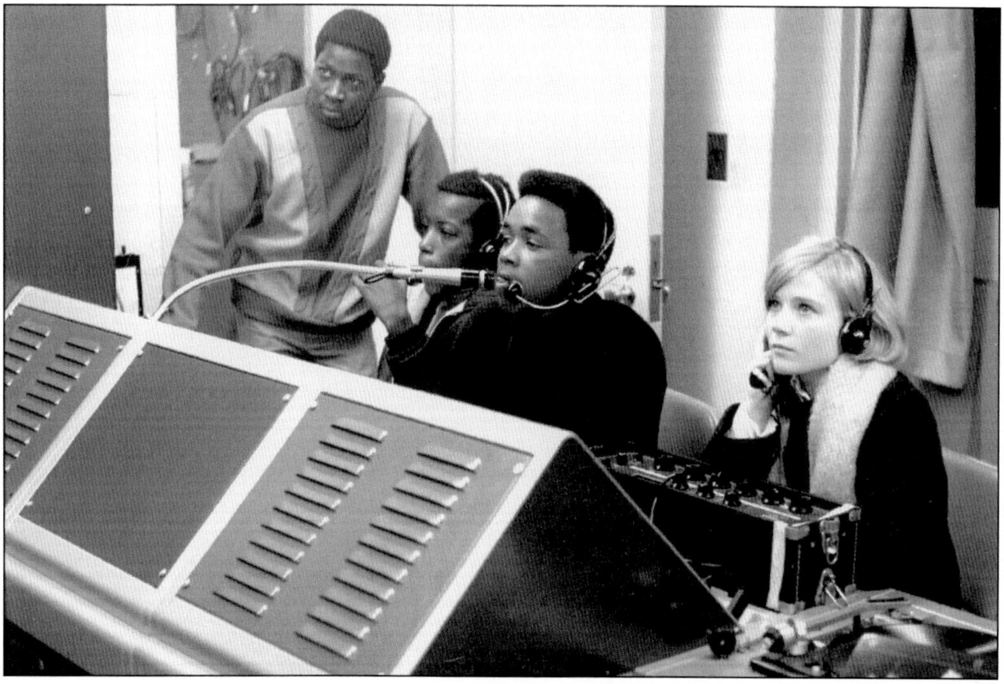

These students are testing radio equipment in the School of Education in 1966. (Photograph courtesy of the Special Collections and Archives, W.E.B. Du Bois Library, University of Massachusetts Amherst.)

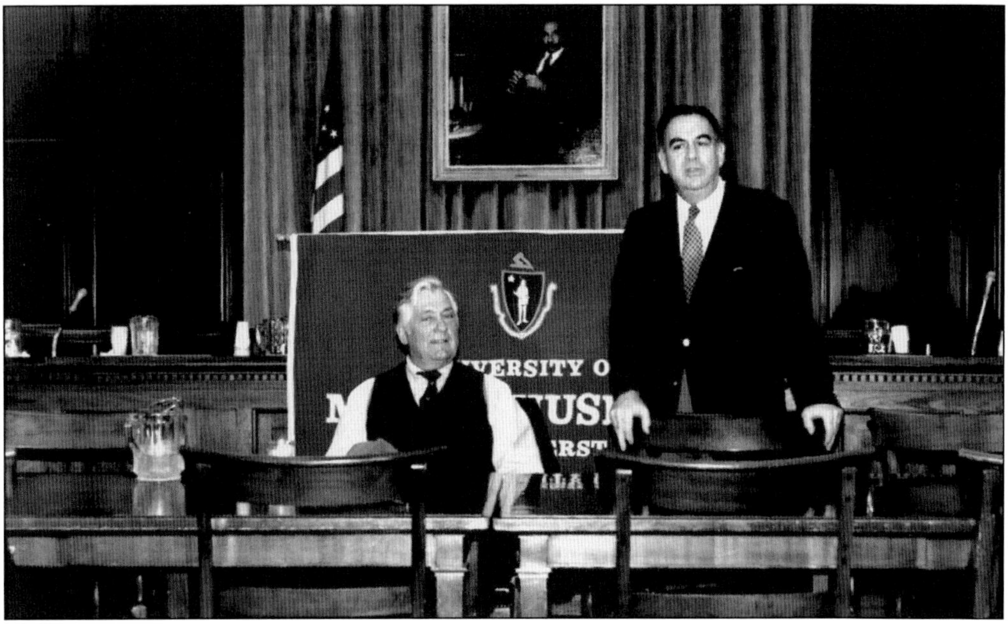

Prof. Gerald Grady introduces Congressman Silvio Conte (R-Mass) to a group of UMass students from SAFA (Students Advocating Financial Aid) in this 1985 photograph. SAFA was formed in 1982 to combat the student financial aid cuts proposed by the Ronald Reagan administration. UMass students boarded a bus and traveled to Washington, D.C., to lobby the U.S. Congress for more financial aid for college students. Conte was the chair of the small business committee and allowed the students to gather and make appointments from the small business conference room.

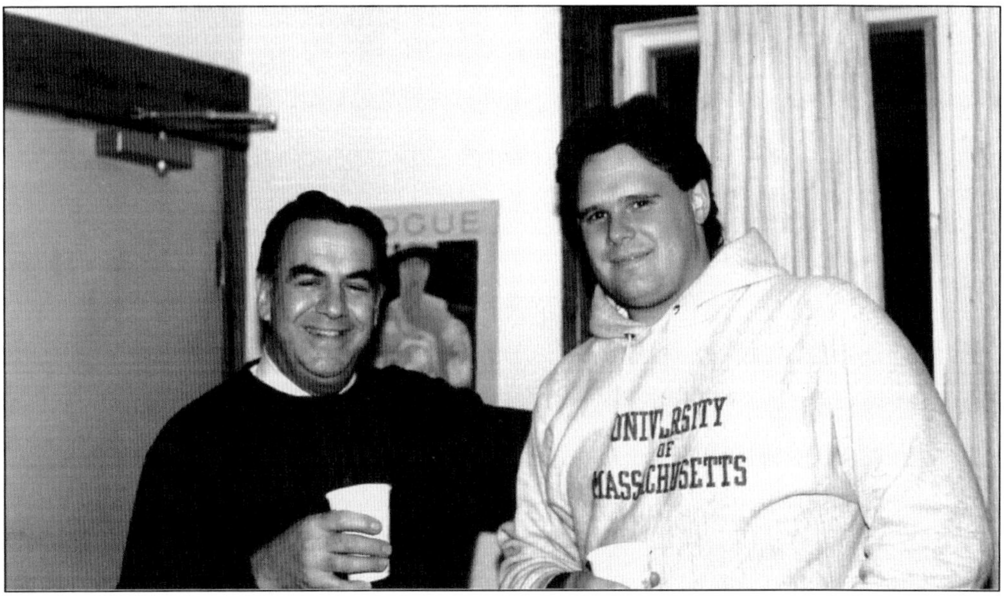

After a long hard day of lobbying on Capital Hill, Prof. Gerald Grady and SAFA vice president Steve Sullivan unwind and discuss the day's lobbying success in this 1985 photograph. Grady started working with the university in 1960 as President Lederle's business manager. Grady ran unsuccessfully for Congress from Maine in 1958.

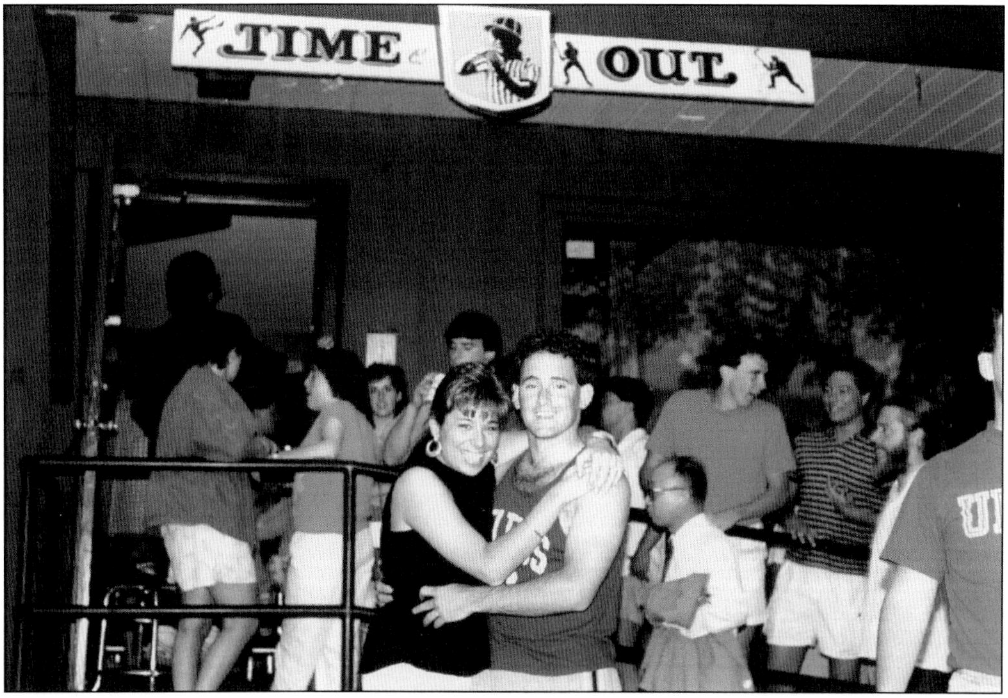

The sign inside read "Don't let college get in the way of your education." The very rustic Time-Out bar in Amherst Center was a favorite of many students for over 20 years. Shown here in 1987, it was owned and operated by the Fusia family; Vic Fusia was the UMass football coach from 1961 to 1970. Currently, the old Time-Out is named McMurphys.

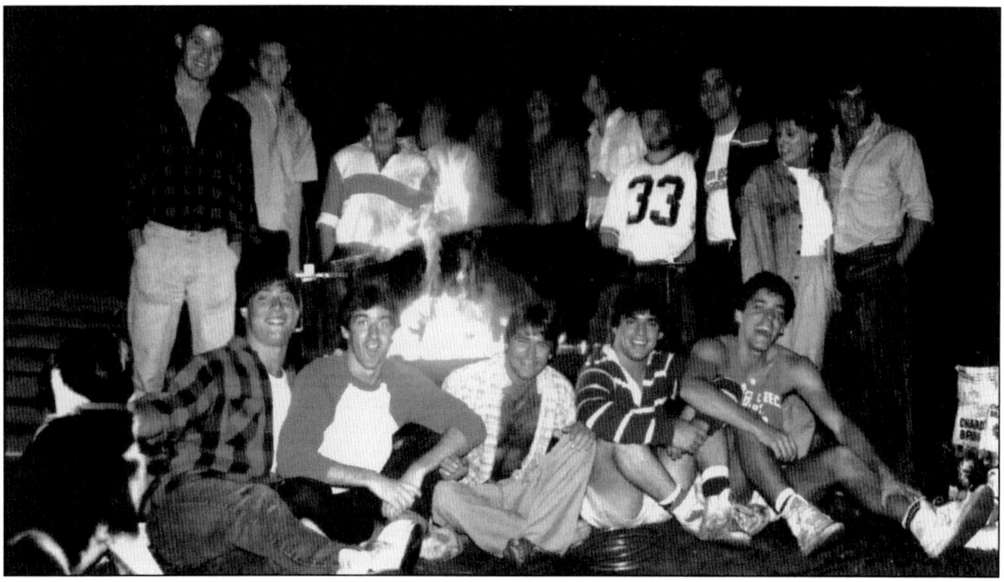

Off-campus extracurricular activities were frequent, but they were not as organized and extravagant as the gatherings at the house at 872 North Pleasant Street. This 1986 photograph depicts the annual pig roast held there. Hundreds of students used to attend these all-day into-the-night extravaganzas. Clyde, the dog on the left, used to attend daily classes with his owner, Steve Cavanaugh '86.

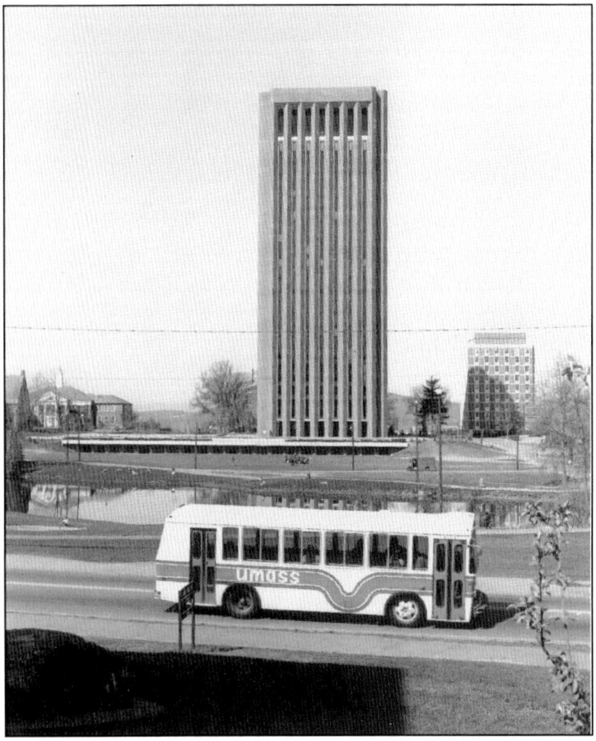

This 1974 photograph shows the Pioneer Valley Transit Authority (PVTA) shuttling students around the five-college area of the Pioneer Valley. Affectionately called the Happy Valley, the area is home to 25,000 students who attend college in the pioneer valley at five different colleges. (Photograph courtesy of the Special Collections and Archives, W.E.B. Du Bois Library, University of Massachusetts Amherst.)

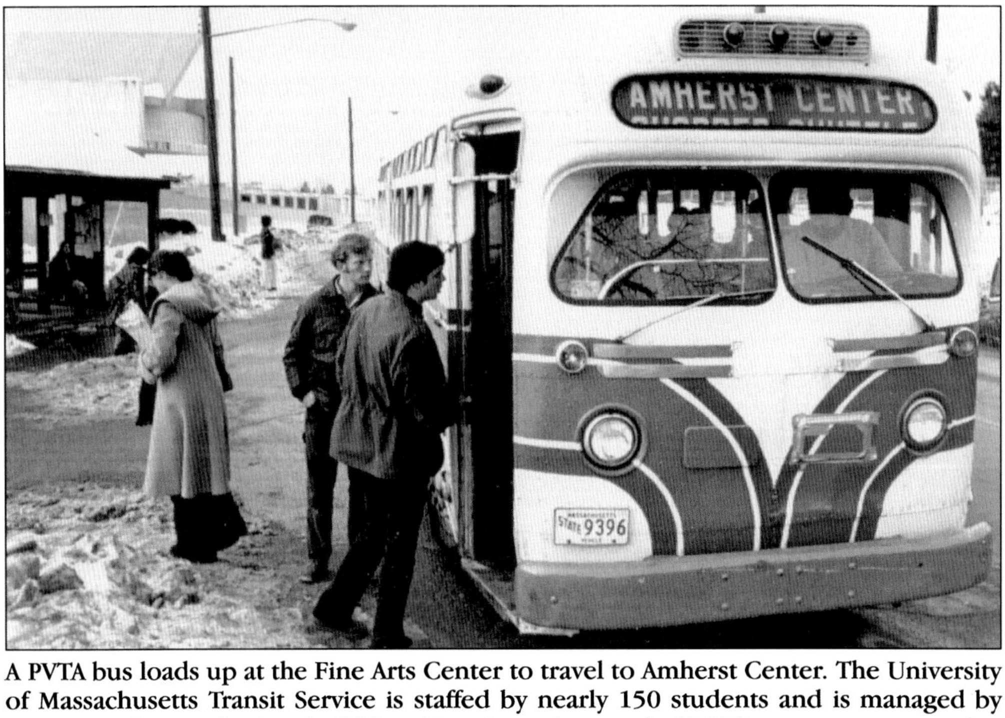

A PVTA bus loads up at the Fine Arts Center to travel to Amherst Center. The University of Massachusetts Transit Service is staffed by nearly 150 students and is managed by transportation professionals. UMass Transit carries nearly 19,000 passengers every day. (Photograph courtesy of the Special Collections and Archives, W.E.B. Du Bois Library, University of Massachusetts Amherst.)

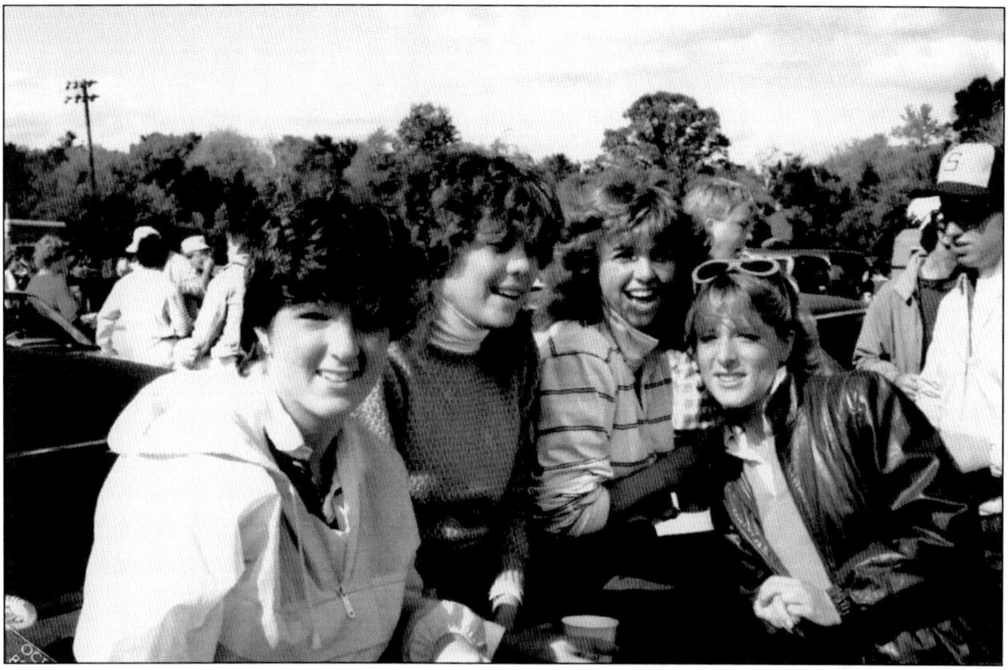

Certainly a part of the fall tradition at UMass, tailgating before the football games at McGuirk Stadium was a routine on game day for many students and alumni. Enjoying the pre-game festivities in this 1983 photograph are, from left to right, Sarah Flagg '84, Ruth Kelly, Robin Girouard '84, and Julie Paige '86.

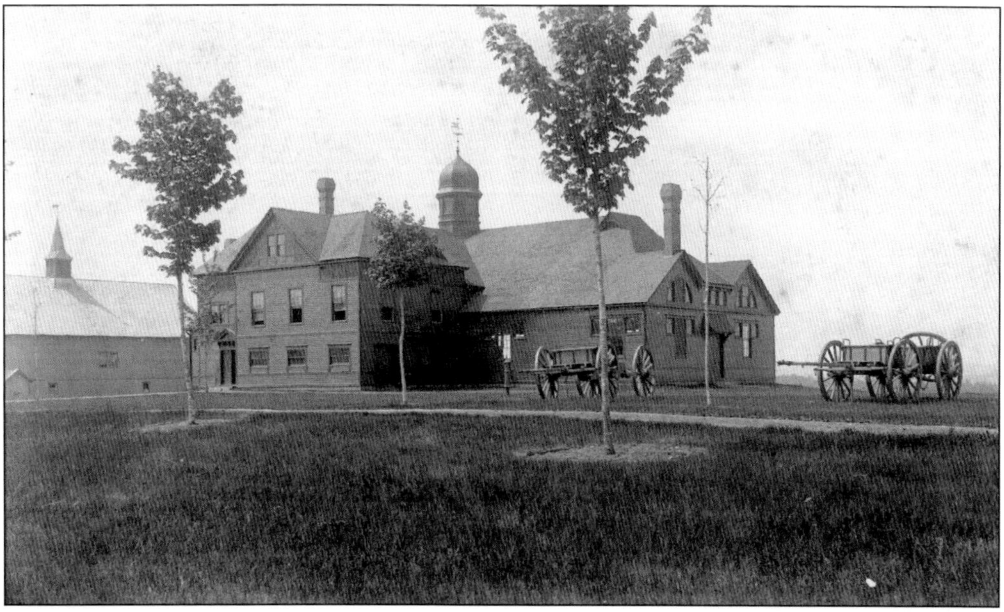

Drill Hall is shown here in 1883. The main hall of this large building was 123 feet long and 48 feet wide and had an asphalt floor. Drill Hall housed the guns and ammunition furnished by the U.S. Army to the college corps of cadets. The second floor of the building contained the commandant's office and a classroom for military tactics science. The old Drill Hall was torn down in 1958 to make room for Bartlett Hall.

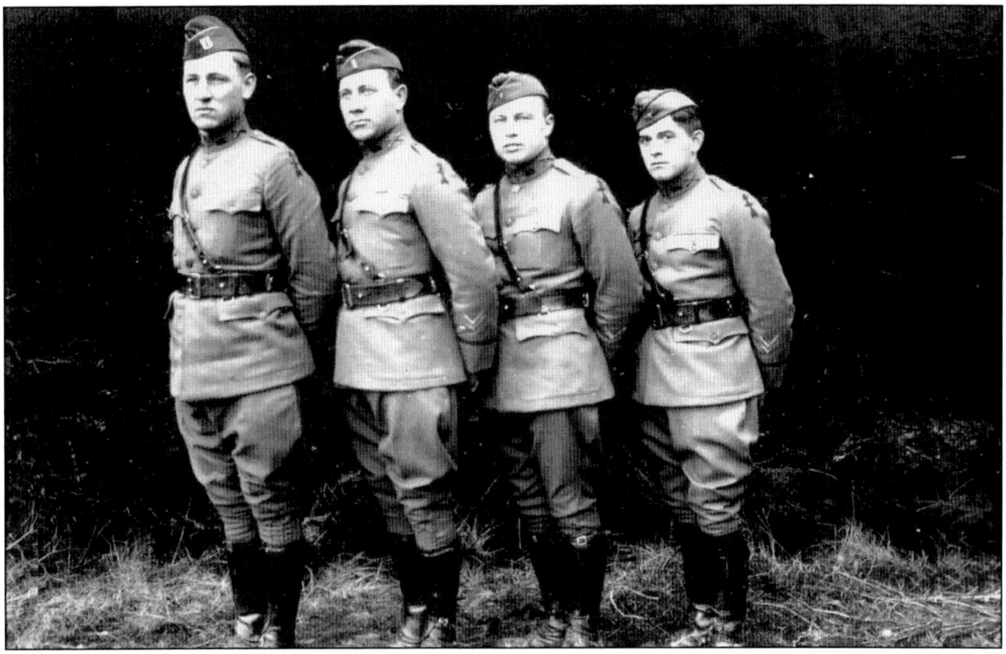

Capt. Herman Crites, 1st Lt. William Brittain, 2nd Lt. William Goodwin, and 2nd Lt. Wayland Miller, seen here from left to right, are shown standing in uniform in this class of 1916 photograph. (Photograph courtesy of the Special Collections and Archives, W.E.B. Du Bois Library, University of Massachusetts Amherst.)

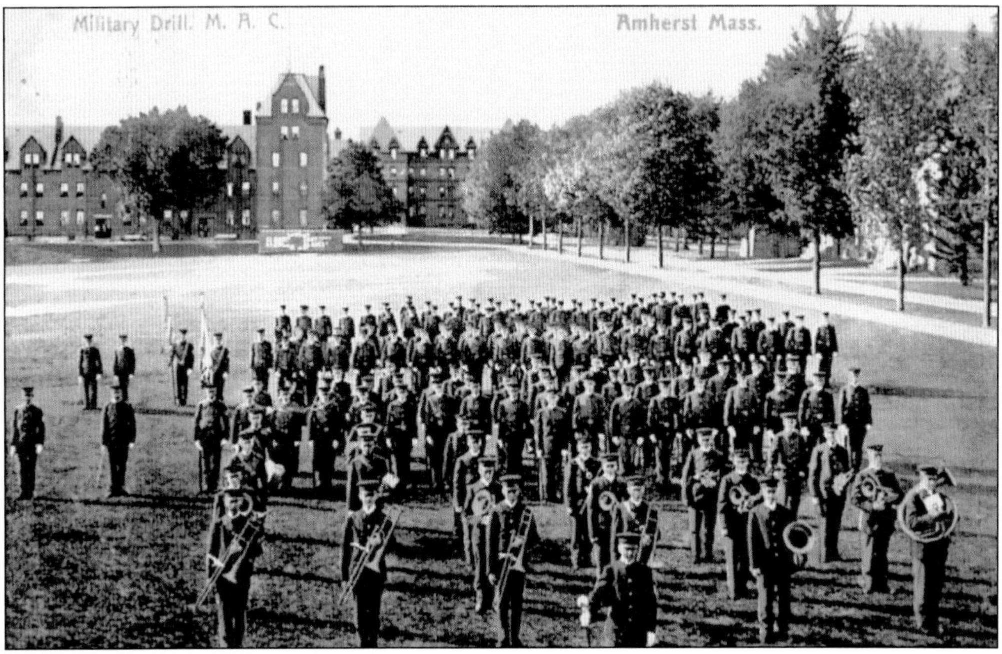

Due to the declaration of war in 1917 by the United States, students mobilized to prepare for World War I. Although war made military activities more serious, drills had been conducted since the opening of the college for physical conditioning reasons. Students are shown participating in a military drill at MAC *c.* 1917.

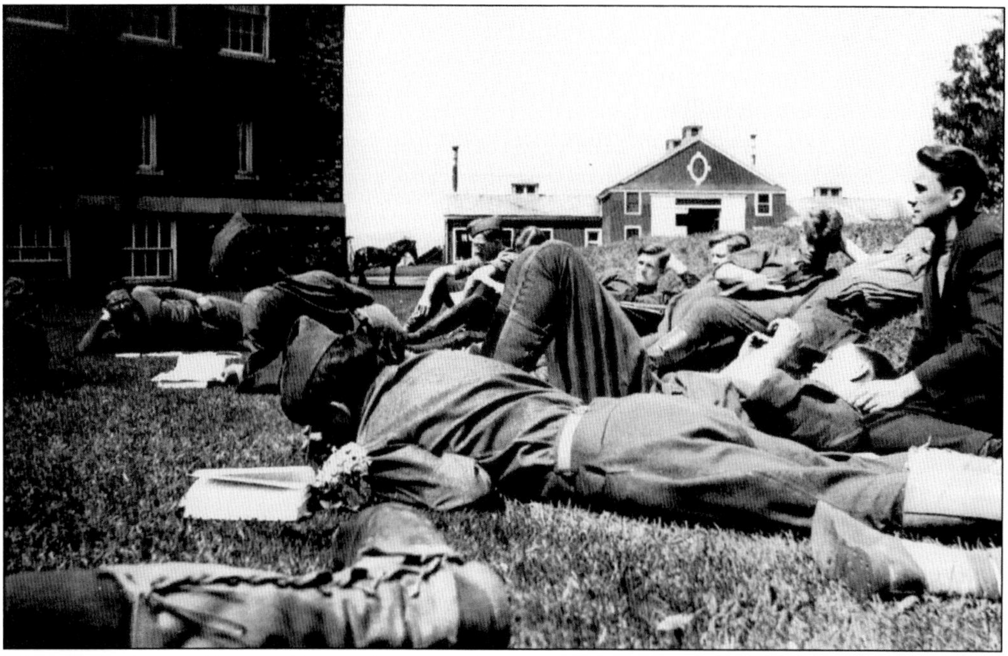

These students from Ellsworth "Dutchy" Barnhard's English class relax outside Stockbridge Hall in 1933. They are dressed for ROTC. (Photograph courtesy of Mary Taylor Barnhard '34.)

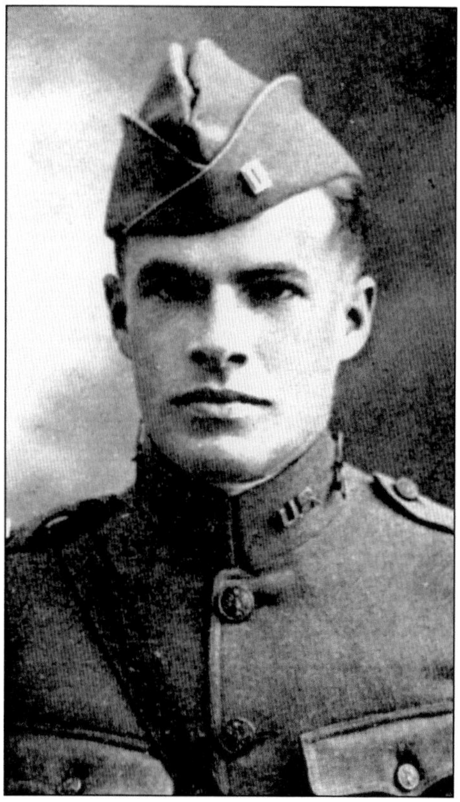

Hamilton Knight Foster of New Rochelle, New York—one of the MAC casualties of World War I—sacrificed his life for our country. Massachusetts Agricultural College had a total of 1,304 students, graduates, former students, and faculty in war service, including 446 commissioned officers and 454 personnel overseas; 51 died. Foster enlisted August 21, 1916. He was first lieutenant in Company A, 26th Infantry, 1st Division. He fought at Cantigny, Soissons, and in the second battle of the Argonne. He was wounded at Soissons and was killed in the battle of the Argonne on October 4, 1918. For his bravery in action he was awarded the following American citation: "Showing utter disregard of his personal safety he led his company over the top. Being held up by a strong machine gun nest, he displayed excellent judgment, making it possible for the nest to be cleared out. He was wounded during the action." The citation is signed by Brig. Gen. B. B. Buck. Foster also received, posthumously, the Italian War Cross of Merit from the King of Italy, Victor Emmanuel III.

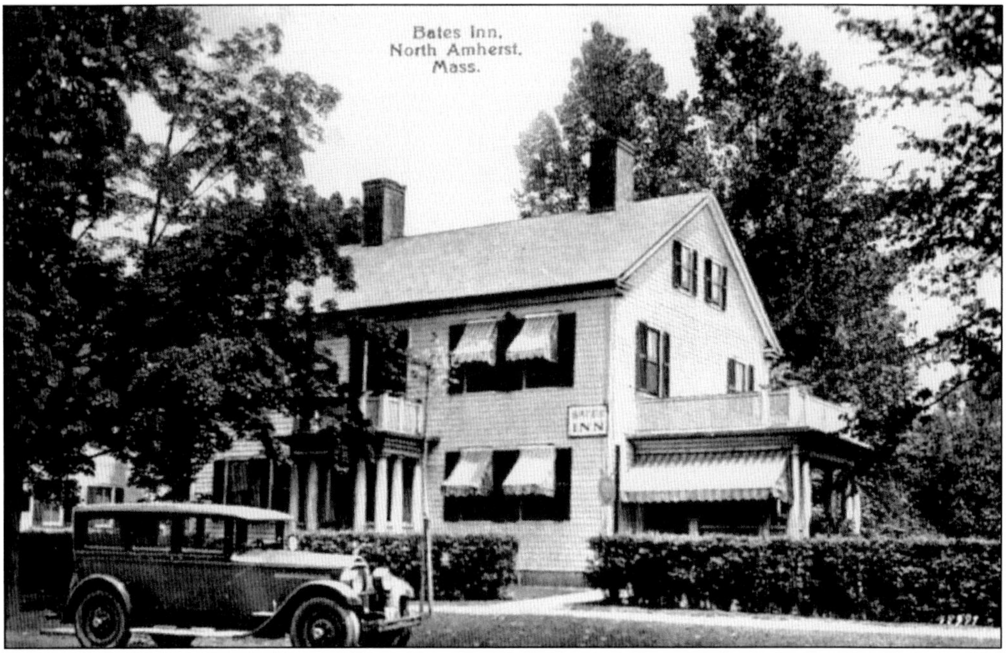

Formerly known as the Bates Inn in North Amherst, this beautiful old building has hosted many UMass students and faculty for breakfast and lunch for the past 20 years as Daisy's Restaurant. Sue Peterson '03 and partners Erin Reffsin and Megan Boreman became the new owners in 2003.

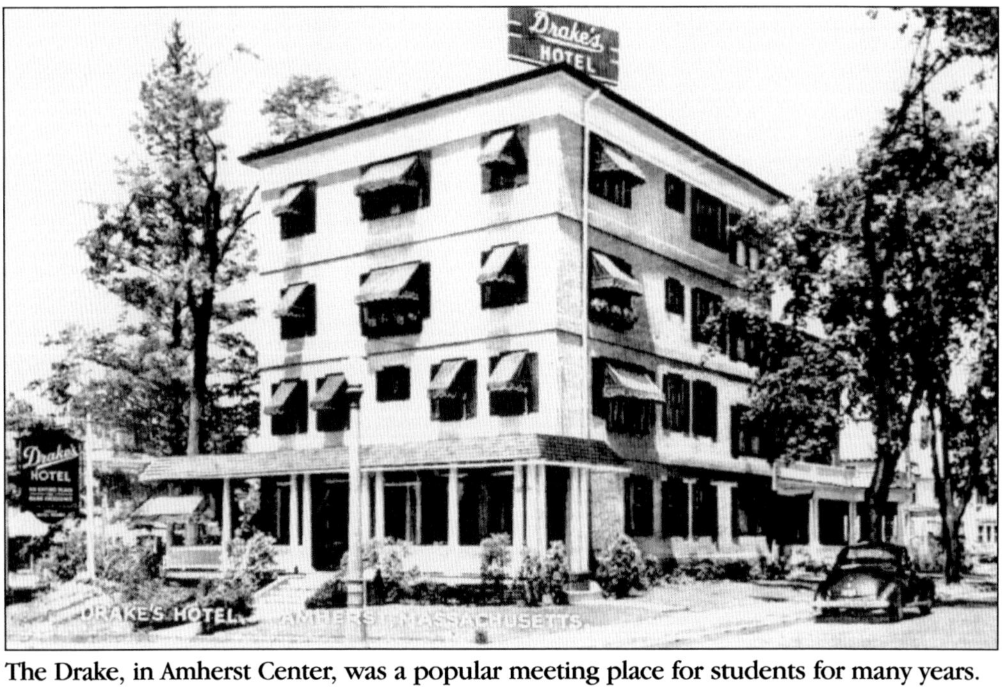

The Drake, in Amherst Center, was a popular meeting place for students for many years.

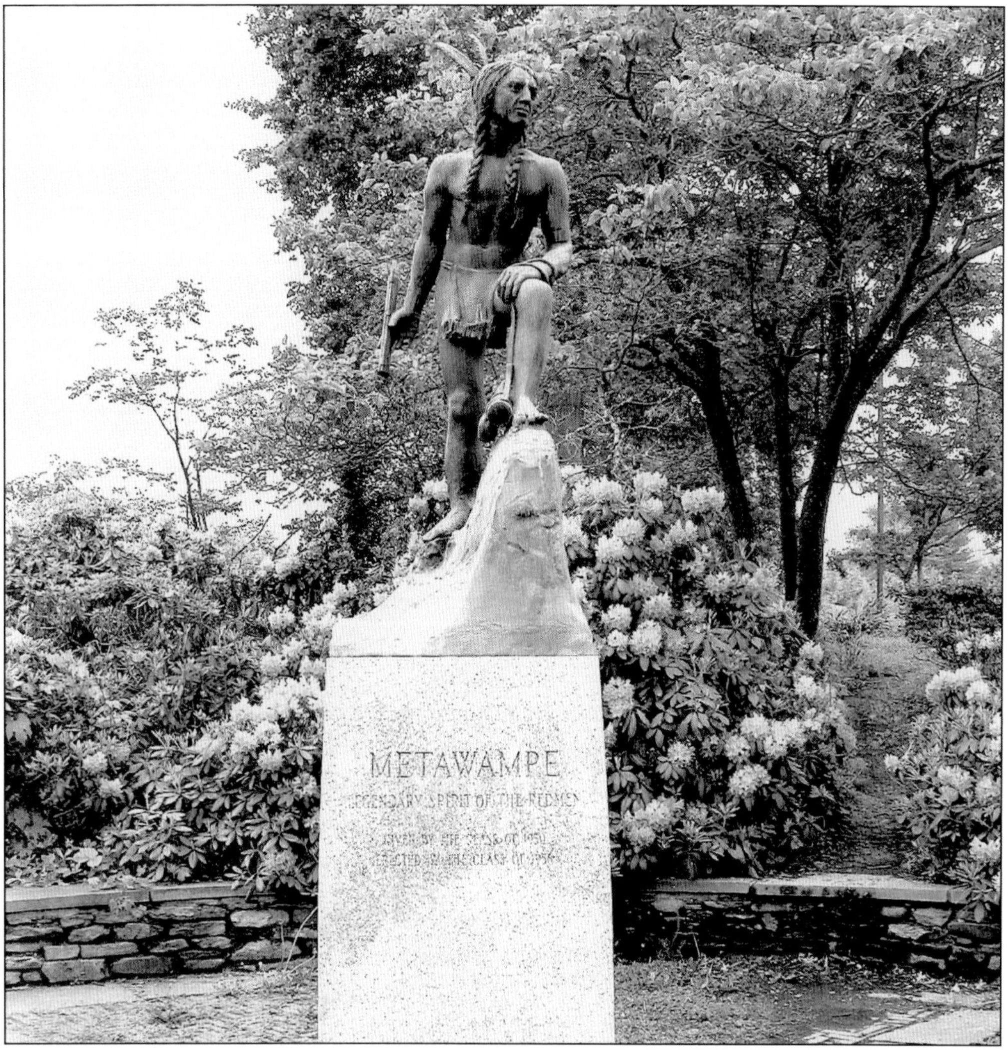

The UMass Amherst athletic teams were called the Redmen until the early 1970s. In the spring of 1972, a group of American Indians from New York wrote a letter to the campus administration asking if it was aware of the defamatory connotations of the word Redmen and if its use could be curtailed. The student senate, through a poll of the student body, came up with several options for a new nickname, including the Minutemen. Women's athletic teams became known as the Minutewomen. One portion of the letter referred to the "undesirable racial connotations of the Redmen nickname." The administration responded to this letter by asking all campus personnel and media to refrain from the use of the word Redmen as much as possible. The Student Senate resolved that the nickname connoted a stereotype of violence and savagery and created a "false picture of American history." When choosing the new name, the student senate, through a poll of the student body, came up with several options, the result of which was the Minutemen. This designation is a fitting and proper name for the athletic teams of the University of Massachusetts. The nickname, which was being used by the Amherst campus during the 1972–1973 academic year, has a historical and patriotic relationship with Massachusetts. It is a name that is uniquely linked with the commonwealth.

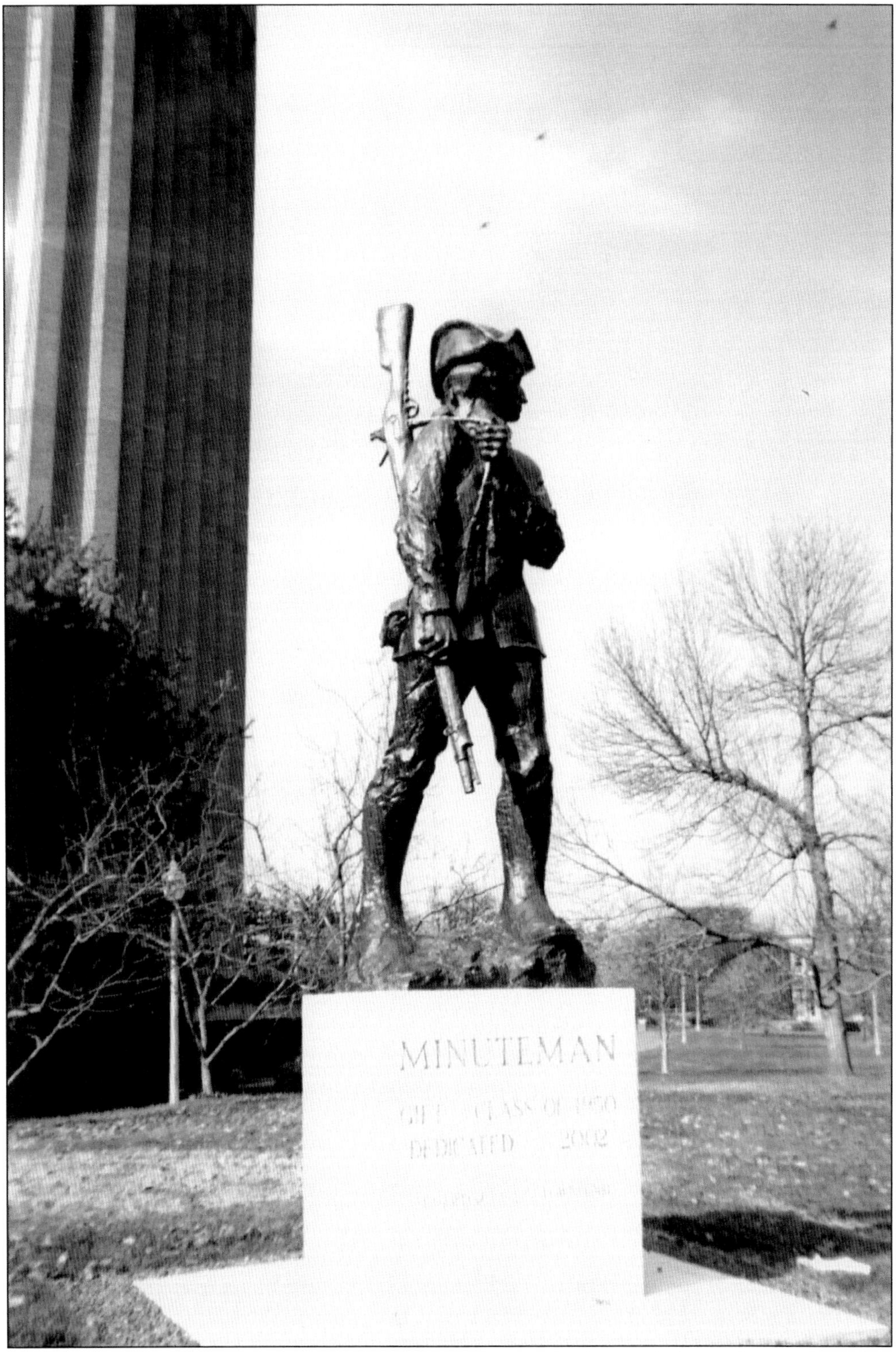

The Minuteman statue was a gift of the class of 1950 and was dedicated in 2002.

Seven

NOTABLE ALUMNI

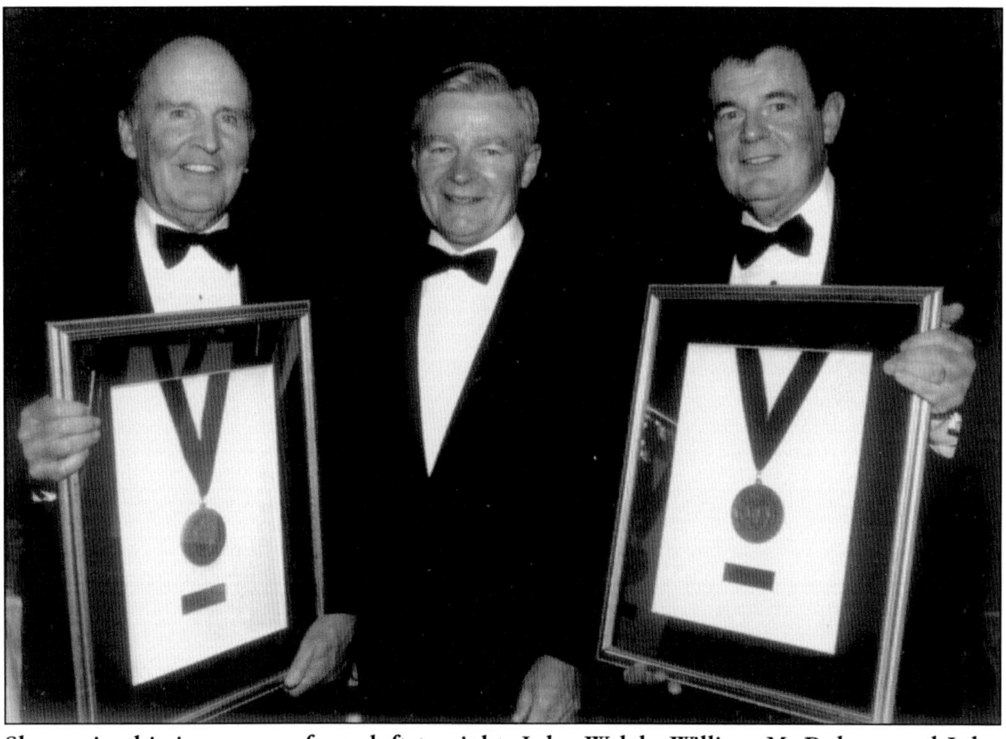

Shown in this image are, from left to right, John Welch, William M. Bulger, and John F. Smith Jr. John Welch was born in Salem in 1935 and is the retired chief executive officer of General Electric. Welch is a 1957 University of Massachusetts graduate and acquired a bachelor's degree in chemical engineering. William M. Bulger is the former UMass system president. John F. "Jack" Smith Jr. became chairman of the General Motors board of directors in January 1996. He received his bachelor's degree in business administration from the University of Massachusetts in 1960.

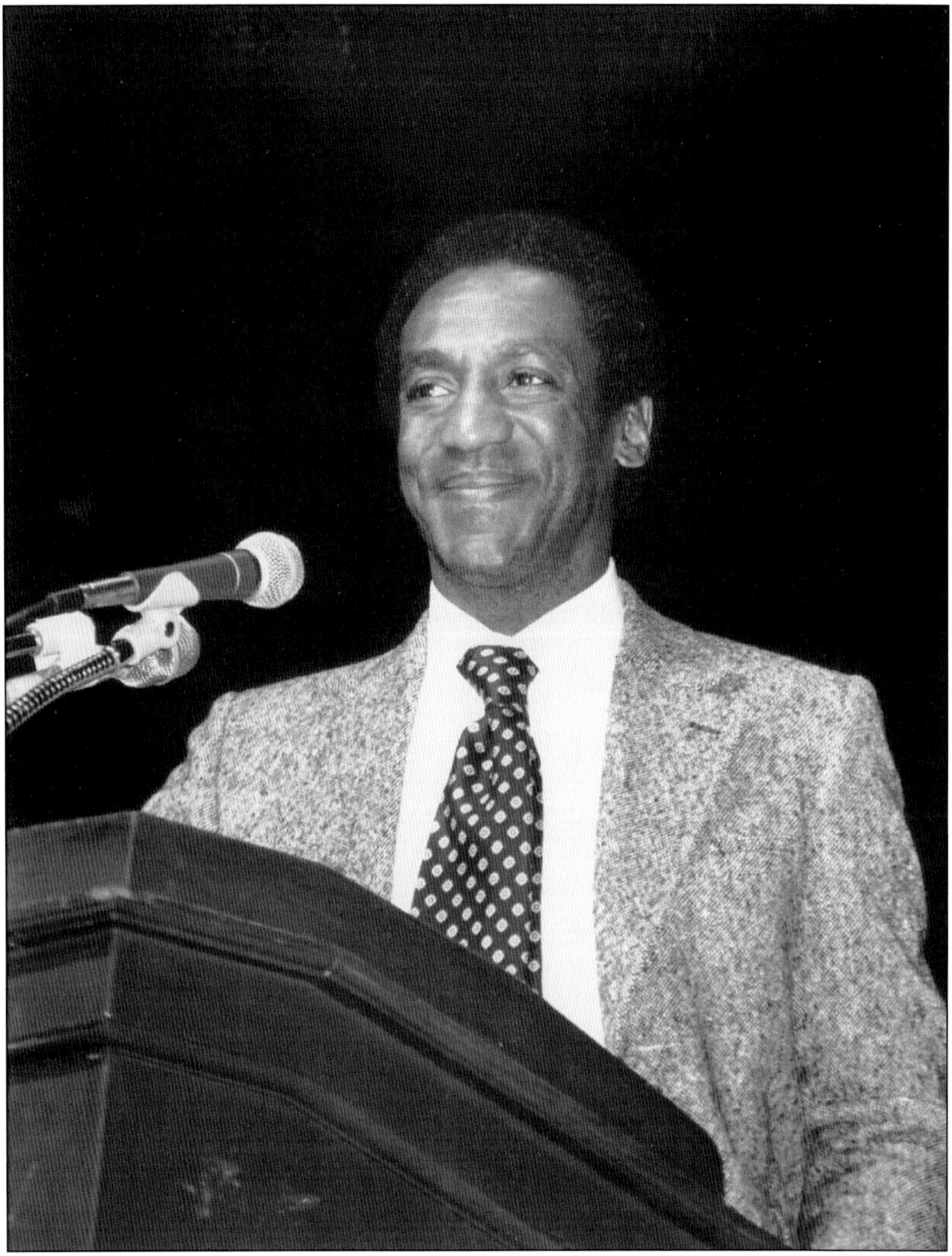

William H. Cosby Jr. '72 G and '76, Ph.D., was born on July 12, 1937, in Philadelphia and for more than 30 years has been one of the world's most respected and well-known entertainers and comedians. He studied for many years during his career in the 1960s and 1970s and received a doctorate in education from the University of Massachusetts. (Photograph courtesy of the Special Collections and Archives, W.E.B. Du Bois Library, University of Massachusetts Amherst.)

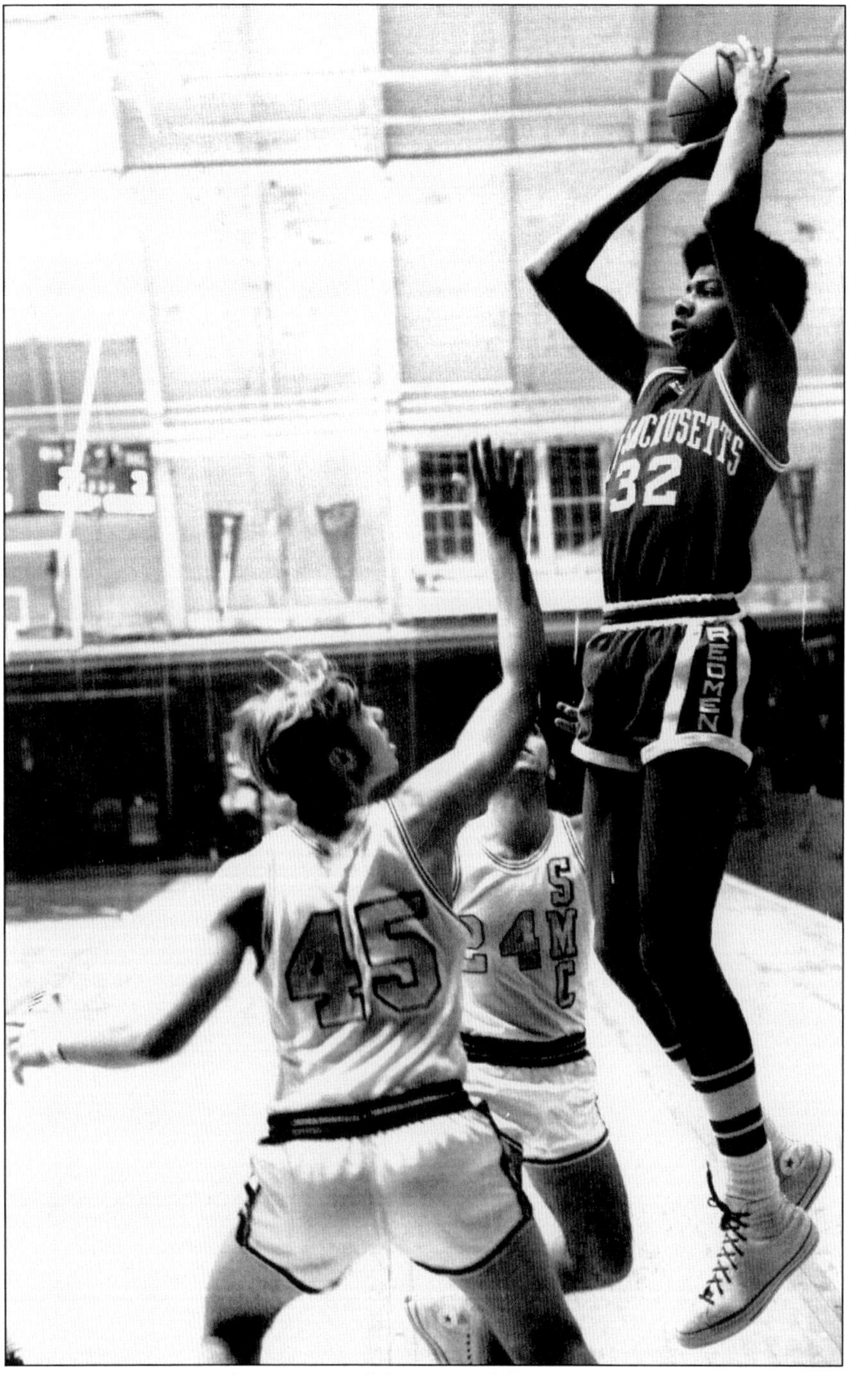

Without question, Dr. J is the most well-known athlete in UMass Amherst history. Julius Erving played two seasons for the UMass basketball team from 1969 to 1971. During those two short seasons, he averaged an astonishing 26.3 points and 20.2 rebounds per game. In 1983, Dr. J led the Philadelphia 76ers to the NBA Championship. He was inducted into the UMass Hall of Fame in 1980. (Photograph courtesy of the Special Collections and Archives, W.E.B. Du Bois Library, University of Massachusetts Amherst.)

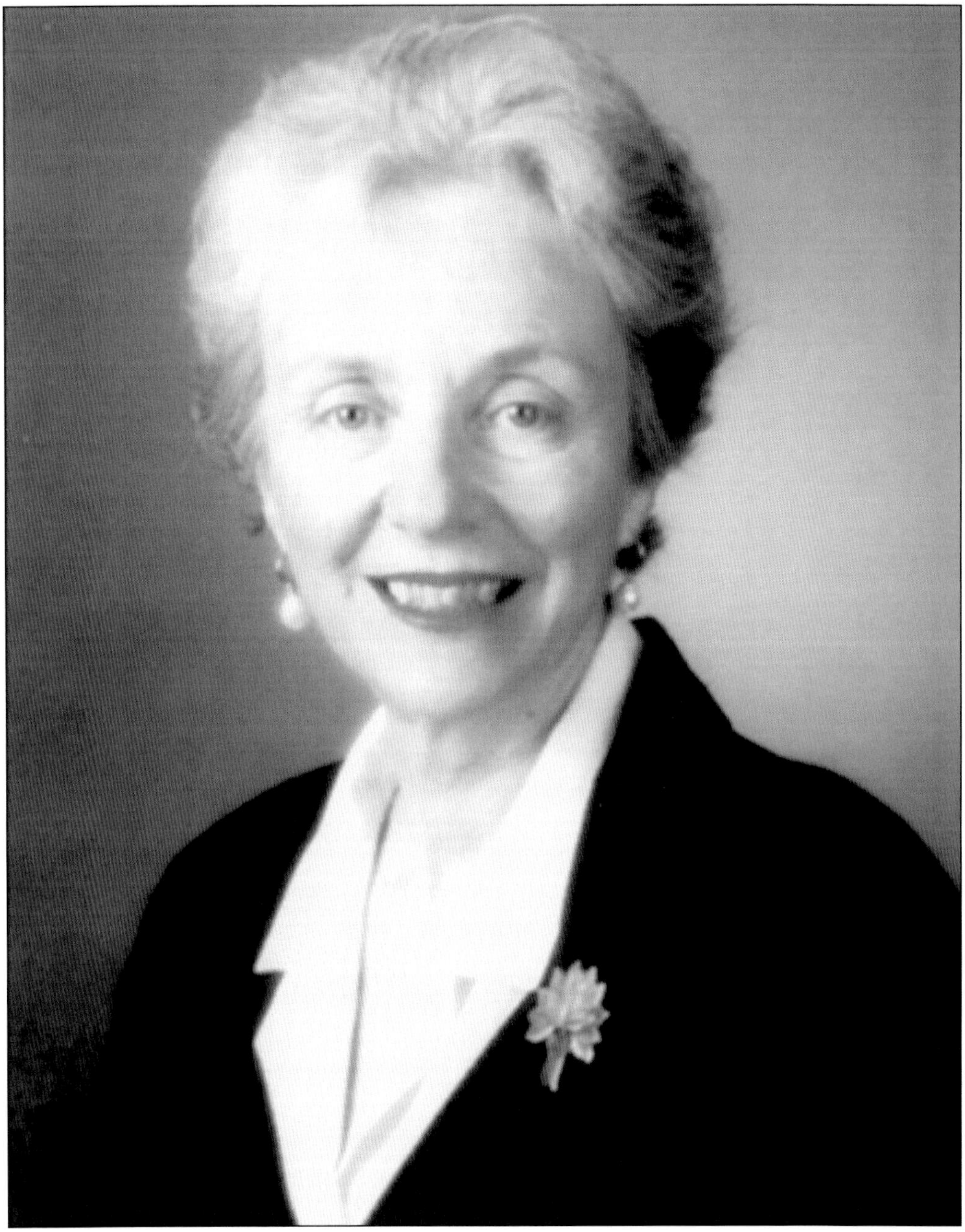

Madeleine May Kunin '56 served as governor of Vermont from 1985 to 1991 and was the U.S. deputy of education during the William Jefferson Clinton administration. Kunin's efforts in education, the environment, and women's issues played a large role in her rise through the political ranks in Vermont. She is the only woman to have served three terms as governor of a state. During her tenure in office, teacher salaries in Vermont rose from a rank of 49th to 26th, access to kindergarten was guaranteed, and early childhood programs were expanded. After leaving office, she founded the non-profit Institute for Sustainable Communities, an international organization that is active in environmental education and management.

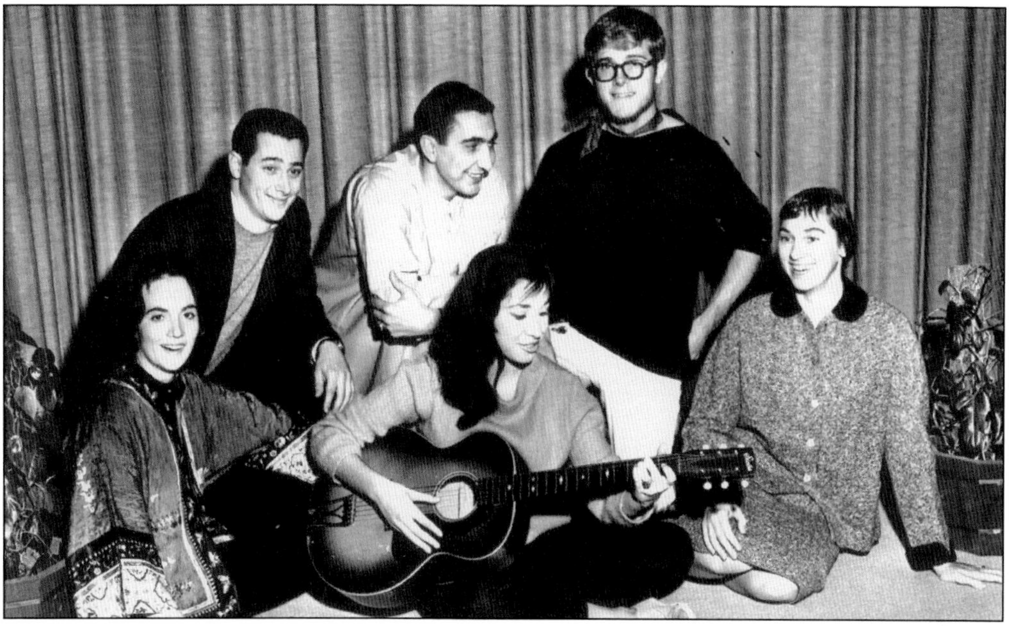

Born on a Cree reservation in Qu'Appelle Valley, Saskatchewan, Buffy Sainte-Marie '70 was adopted and raised in Maine and Massachusetts. She received a doctorate in fine art from the Amherst campus. She also holds degrees in oriental philosophy and in teaching, influences that form the backbone of her music, visual art, and social activism. As a college student in the early 1960s, Buffy Sainte-Marie became known as a writer of protest songs and love songs. Many of these became huge hits and classics of the era, performed by hundreds of other artists, including Barbra Streisand, Elvis Presley, Chet Atkins, Janis Joplin, Roberta Flack, Neil Diamond, Tracy Chapman, and the Boston Pops Orchestra. (Photograph courtesy of the Special Collections and Archives, W.E.B. Du Bois Library, University of Massachusetts Amherst.)

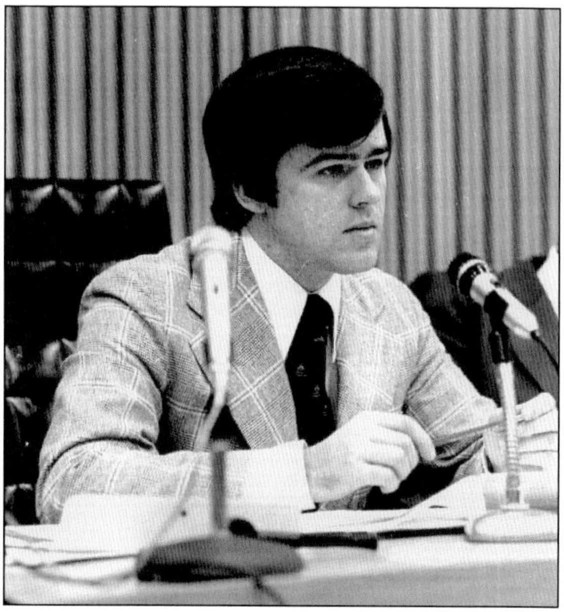

Jim Collins '68 (D-Amherst) is seen here at the statehouse listening to testimony. Collins was a tremendous advocate for UMass while he served in the legislature. (Photograph courtesy of the Special Collections and Archives, W.E.B. Du Bois Library, University of Massachusetts Amherst.)

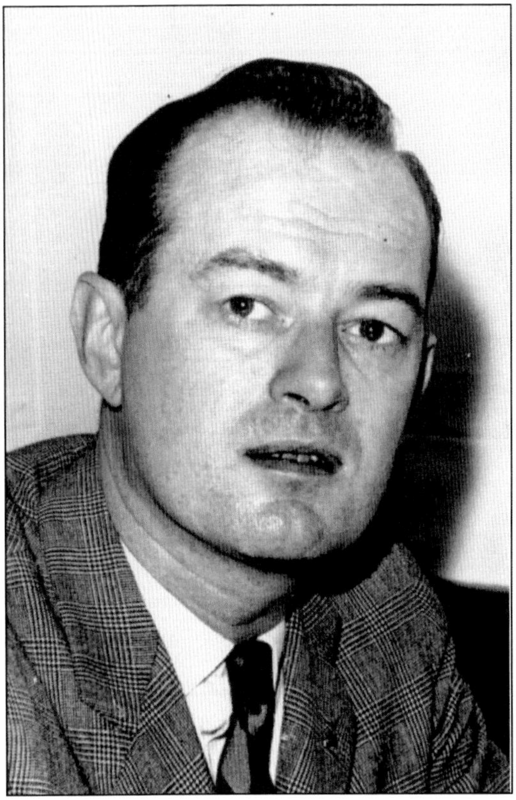

William Manchester '46, a prolific writer and the son of a soldier, was born on April 1, 1922. During the Second World War, Manchester served in the U.S. Marines and fought in Guadalcanal, where he was wounded in combat. Manchester and Pres. John F. Kennedy became friends in 1946 while both were recovering from debilitating war wounds. During the 1950s and the Camelot years, Manchester was a confidant and companion to Kennedy and a frequent visitor to the family's compound in Hyannisport. After the war, Manchester became adjunct professor of history and writer-in-residence at Wesleyan University. He has written several books. William Manchester died on June 1, 2004. (Photograph courtesy of the Special Collections and Archives, W.E.B. Du Bois Library, University of Massachusetts Amherst.)

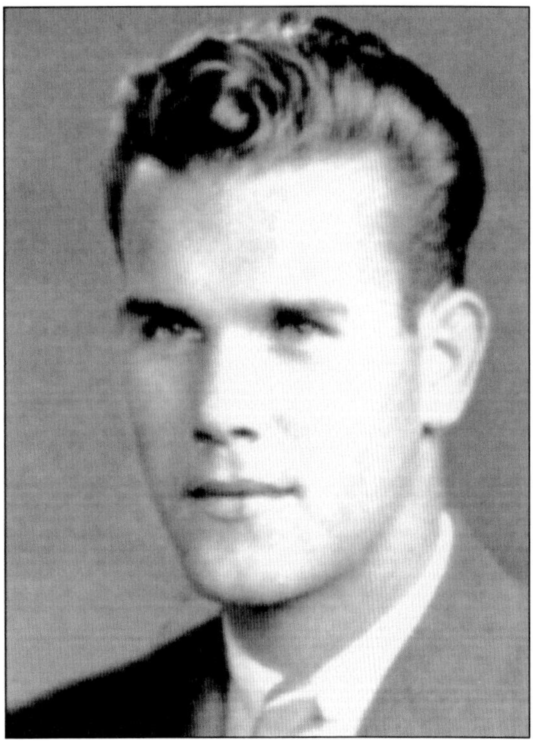

Leroy Fletcher Prouty '41 was born in Massachusetts on January 24, 1917. During the Second World War he served as an army tank commander. He later joined the U.S. Air Force and became involved in work for the Office of Strategic Services (OSS). Colonel Prouty retired from the U.S. Air Force and served as the chief of special operations with the joint chiefs of staff and as head of military support for the secret operations division of the CIA. Prouty's views on the assassination of President Kennedy inspired Oliver Stone's epic and controversial film *JFK* and led to Stone's portrayal of "Man X," played by Donald Sutherland. Prouty was also a banker, a Yale professor of military history, and a top railroad and aircraft firm executive.

James Kallstrom '66 was born May 6, 1943, in Worcester. He received his bachelor's degree in management from UMass Amherst in 1966. After graduation, he served in the U.S. Marine Corps during the Vietnam War, attaining the rank of captain. On October 10, 2001, Kallstrom took a leave of absence from MBNA America to become the director of public security for the state of New York. In this capacity, he was responsible for counter-terrorism planning and operations for the state of New York. He also was New York state's point of contact with Gov. Tom Ridge at the White House Office of Homeland Security. In June 2002, Kallstrom was elevated to the position of senior advisor to the governor for counter-terrorism.

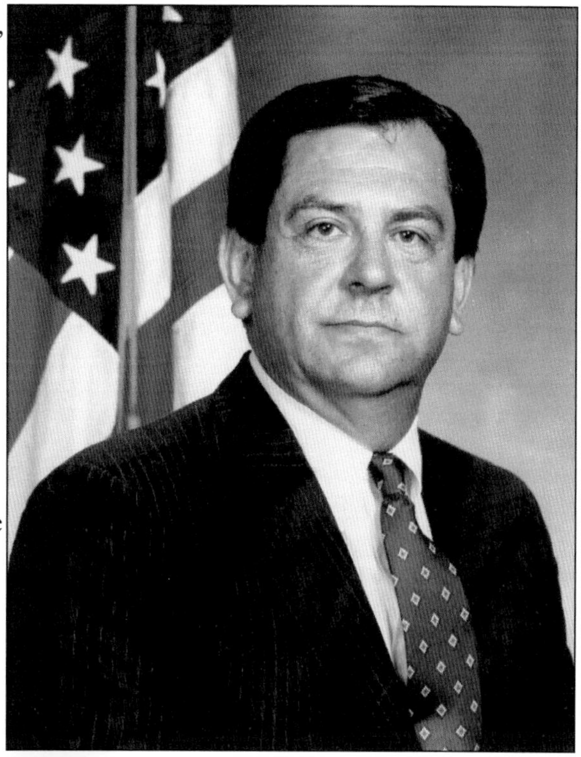

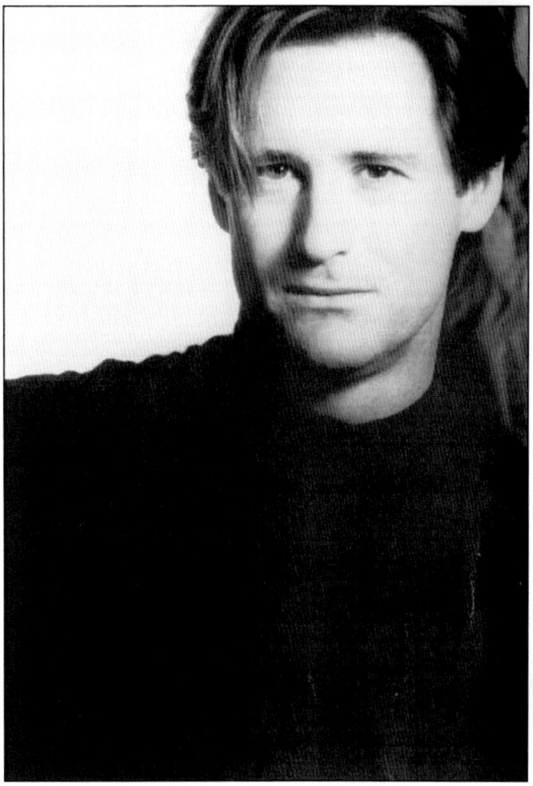

Bill Pullman '80 earned a master of fine arts degree with a major in directing. Pullman planned to concentrate on directing, but his adviser urged him to continue acting. While studying in Amherst, he met his wife, Tamara Hurwitz '81, when both were performing in a university production.

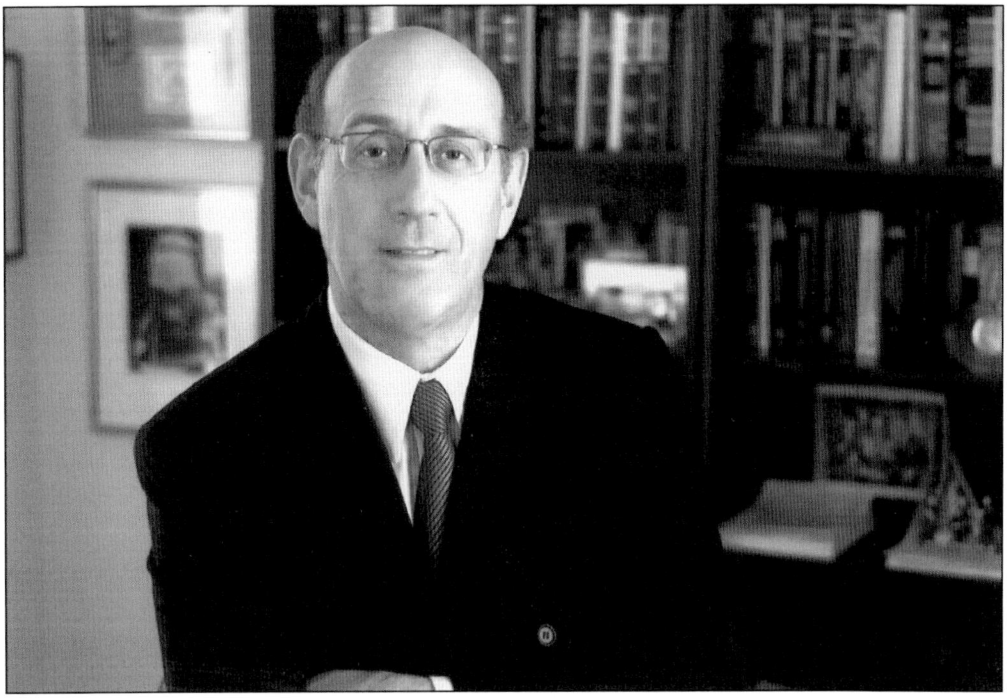

Ken Feinberg '67 was appointed the special master of the September 11th Victim Compensation Fund of 2001 by the attorney general of the United States. In this capacity, he developed and promulgated the regulations governing the administration of the fund. He is presently administering all aspects of the program, including evaluating applications, determining appropriate compensation, and disseminating awards. He is one of the nation's leading experts in mediation and alternative dispute resolution and is the founder and managing partner of the Feinberg Group.

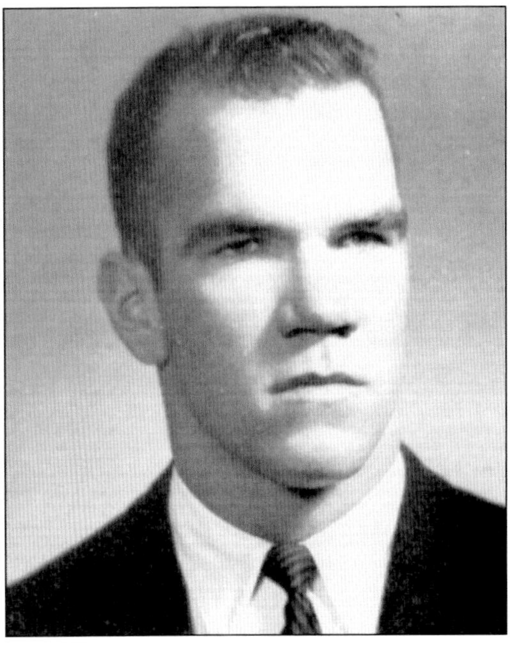

George "Trigger" Burke '56 was a marquee basketball player for UMass in the mid-1950s. He was the first player to ever lead UMass in both scoring and assists in the same season. Burke is one of only four Minutemen basketball players to have his number retired to the rafters. The UMass Athletic Hall of Fame is named after Burke. A successful lawyer by trade, Burke is a great friend of UMass.

ACKNOWLEDGMENTS

I would like to thank the following people and organizations for their assistance in the completion of this project: Jennifer Arsenault, UMass Alumni Association, Mary Taylor Barnhard '34, Alice Bishko, Linda Cahillane, Carol Cambo, Harold Whiting Cary, Joel Coffidis '86, Dave Curley, Elizabeth Dale '86G, '98 Ed.D., Chris Forman, Seth Gerard, Christina Geso, Robert Goodhue '70, John Hoey, Jess Kane '70, Teamsters Local 25, Chancellor John Lombardi, Daniel Lombardo, Deb Masloski, C. J. Masse '80, Mike Milewski '77, Mike Morris '63, Dr. James Ralph, Frank Prentice Rand, Marion Gunness Snuggs '39, Suzanne Miller-Sullivan, Roberta Sullivan, and William Thompson.

Bibliography

Barnhard, Ellsworth. *An Academic Apprenticeship.* Amherst, Massachusetts: The Dinosaur Press, 1985.

Cary, Harold Whiting. *The University of Massachusetts: A History of One Hundred Years.* Springfield, Massachusetts: Walter Whittum, Inc., 1962.

Caswell, L. B. *Brief History of the Massachusetts Agricultural College Semicentennial.* Springfield, Massachusetts: The F. A. Bassette Company Printers, 1917.

Goodell, Henry Hill. "The Massachusetts Agricultural College." *New England Magazine.* October 1890.

Hitchcock, Frederick H. *The Handbook of Amherst, Massachusetts.* Amherst, Massachusetts: Prepared and published by Frederick H. Hitchcock, 1891.

Keith, Vicky. "Mass Aggie Women 1910–1923" (term paper, University of Massachusetts Amherst, 1983).

Libby, E. H. "Massachusetts Agricultural College." *Scribner's Monthly.* October 1876.

Norton, Paul F. *Amherst: A Guide to its Architecture.* Amherst, Massachusetts: Hamilton I. Newell Company, 1975.

Rand, Frank Prentice. *Yesterdays at Massachusetts State College.* Amherst, Massachusetts: E.L. Hildreth & Company, Inc., 1933.